D0039007

MALI BLUES

TRAVELING TO AN AFRICAN BEAT

LIEVE JORIS

TRANSLATED BY SAM GARRETT

LONELY PLANET PUBLICATIONS
Melbourne • Oakland • London • Paris

Mali Blues: Traveling to an African Beat

Published by Lonely Planet Publications

Head Office:	PO Box 617, Hawthorn, Vic 3122, Australia
Branches:	150 Linden Street, Oakland, CA 94607, USA
	10a Spring Place, London NW5 3BH, UK
	71 bis rue du Cardinal Lemoine, 75005 Paris, France

First published as *Mali Blues: en andere verhalen* (J.M. Meulenhoff bv, Amsterdam, 1996)
This edition was produced with the support of the Administration of Culture of the Flemish Community.

Published by Lonely Planet Publications 1998

Printed by SNP Printing Pte Ltd, Singapore

Author photograph by Chris van Houts

Maps by Jenny Jones

Designed by Margaret Jung

Edited by Janet Austin

National Library of Australia Cataloguing in Publication Data

Joris, Lieve, 1953–
[Mali blues en andere verhalen. English]
Mali blues: traveling to an African beat.

ISBN 0 86442 532 5.

1. Joris, Lieve, 1953- – Journeys – Africa, French-speaking
West. 2. Africa, French-speaking West – Description and
travel. I. Title. II. Title: Mali blues en andere verhalen.
English. (Series: Lonely Planet journeys)

966

Text © Lieve Joris and J.M. Meulenhoff bv Amsterdam 1996
English-language translation © Sam Garrett 1998
Maps © Lonely Planet 1998

All rights reserved. No part of this publication may be reproduced, stored
in a retrieval system or transmitted in any form by any means, electronic,
mechanical, photocopying, recording or otherwise, except brief extracts
for the purpose of review, without the written permission of the publisher
and copyright owner.

CONTENTS

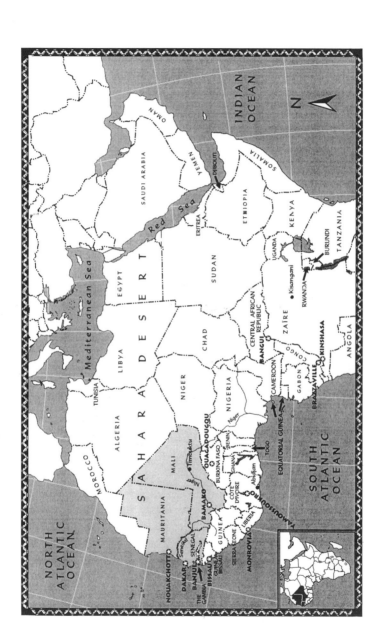

AMADOU

AN AFRICAN NOTEBOOK

DAKAR, 16 June 1993 – As soon as I feel Dakar's warm evening air, I know that I was right to come here. The tarmac, still steaming from the heat, is soft beneath my shoes. François is waiting for me. Am I imagining things, or is he shy? That's not how I remember him. The last time we saw each other was in Zaïre. We count off the dates in the car: that was seven years ago. Both of us are nostalgic for those days.

Arriving in a town at night – an immediate feeling of intimacy. Keba, the watchman at François's flat, takes my bags sleepily. The hallway smells of rust and damp – like stepping back into my cabin on the Zaïre steamer.

François's apartment is possibly even barer than the one he had in Kinshasa. Naive paintings by the Zaïrian Chéri Samba everywhere. None of them framed, some curled and flaking from the humidity. I like François's nonchalance when it comes to worldly things, but I catch myself feeling slightly irritated: Chéri Samba has had shows in New York. These pictures are worth money! I don't say anything to François, he'd only laugh at me – a museum in New York, he couldn't care less. He was born in Africa, and has lived here most of his life. It's interesting to see how that's shaped him. How long would it take for New York to stop being a reference point for me?

17 June – My room faces Avenue Georges Pompidou, the busiest street in Dakar. The kebab stand across the street is open all night. Sometimes it seems like the customers are talking right in my ear, that's how loud they are. Laughing, shouting, fighting too, so intensely that I almost feel like I'm in the middle of it all. How can people sleep through that kind of noise, for God's sake? I don't, and stay awake. Amid all those voices is the constant,

9

blissful awareness that I'm not back home: I'm in Africa. Just before sunup there is the singsong call of the *muezzin*.

When cars start moving through the street, I decide to get up. The Lebanese kebab man cuts a final strip of meat from his inverted pyramid and wipes the knife on his apron. Then the steel shutters rattle down and the sky-blue door drops into the lock. François says the Lebanese man has lived here for thirty-five years, but knows only the side of the Avenue Pompidou he walks home on every morning. There's nothing on this side of the street that could possibly interest him. He saves his money and watches porno films in his spare time.

There are a lot of Lebanese people here. They own restaurants, department stores, ice-cream parlors – they are to West Africa what the Indians are to the East: an indispensable, yet frequently threatened, minority. They attract jealousy.

From somewhere in the depths of the house I hear whispering, "*M'sieur, m'sieur,*" answered by a loud "*Oui!*" That must be Mamadou, the houseboy, waking François. He never used to have household staff, but now that he's director of the CCF – the Centre Culturel Français – he can't avoid it any longer. His position has done little to change him otherwise. He still has the same mussy, sun-bleached hair; his BMW motorcycle is parked in front of the door, and he only wears a tie when he has to. After he was appointed, he invited all the CCF's Senegalese employees to his house for dinner. They'd never even been inside the director's house before! The CCF used to be a place for the *petits blancs* to bask safely in the glow of French culture, and I can imagine that some of the French expats dislike him: François feels he's here for the Africans first, not for the French.

We're having breakfast on the patio when the cordless phone rings. François sighs, picks it up, barks: "*Allô! Oui!*" The CCF is organizing a music festival in Dakar's soccer stadium, the day after tomorrow. All the major Senegalese groups will be there. François is expecting forty thousand people.

Back home my friends were surprised to hear that I was going to a music festival: after all the stories about starvation, AIDS and civil wars, it's the last thing Westerners associate with Africa. But now that I'm here, the idea is quite plausible. Local music is very popular here, especially among young people, who make up more than fifty percent of the Senegalese population. Everyone worries about their country's youth: they grew up thinking the sky was the limit, but their future looks grim. Organizing concerts is François's way of keeping in touch with them.

In the shower my eye is caught by a naive painting of an African man and woman bathing in a river, surrounded by lush vegetation. The picture's just hanging there, getting wet, but a feeling of lightness and happiness runs through me when I look at it. How long has it been since I was in Africa? Five years? The last few years I'd been caught up with Syria, and it's only now that I realize just how difficult life was there. That's hard to explain back home too: things are much more cheerful here.

The clothes François wore yesterday are lying in a pile by his bedroom door. Mamadou puts them in the hamper, then N'Deye, the housekeeper, tosses them in the washing machine. Keba, Mamadou, N'Deye – that's three. What a life! Back in Amsterdam, my cleaning lady only comes twice a month. The whites here claim it's their way of creating employment; they say they pay their servants more and treat them better than the Senegalese elite do. I don't know – I have mixed feelings about it.

Around noon, I go down to meet François at his office. The CCF is a hive of activity. I was here once before, in 1987. That was before François came to Dakar; the place was dead then. François has a way of breathing new life into things. I find him in his office, strung taut as a bow. He ruffles one hand furiously through the clutter on his desk while screaming into the phone. People walk in and out. I wait for him on the balcony, leaning over the balustrade. The open-air café below me is a meeting place for film makers, musicians, groupies, students, layabouts. Leaning against a pillar, baseball cap on his head, is Youssou N'Dour; Baaba Maal will be meeting his fans here later this afternoon. The last place I'd seen these Senegalese stars was back in Amsterdam, on stage.

11

François and I have a drink at the bar. Everyone's watching Canal France International, the French African service, which broadcasts all day long. You have to go to Africa these days to find out that France still means something in the world. Or to hear the latest Parisian argot. There's lots of English loanwords, to the horror of French purists. They talk about *blacks* rather than *noirs*. I even hear someone say: "*C'est nice.*"

During the Gulf War, the CCF was the only place in town with a satellite dish. About two thousand people came by every evening to watch the news. François was worried there would be an outburst of anti-Western sentiment; after all, most Third World countries were rooting for Saddam Hussein. But, to his surprise, everyone was for the Americans, because Mauritania, Senegal's northern rival, had sided with Saddam.

Senegal is more preoccupied with its former colonizer than Zaïre is, François says. It was the first French colony on the west coast of Africa, and that's left a deep impression. "The Senegalese hold up a mirror to us," he says, "a distorted one, like in a funhouse." The streets of Dakar are full of wooden stands where bookmakers sell tickets for the daily double: everyone's betting on horses that are running in Europe!

'Mimicry', V. S. Naipaul called it. François is milder, more inclined to point a finger at himself. A man like Bokassa, emperor of the Central African Empire until 1979 – didn't the French create him in their own image? He was an officer in the French army for years. He used their symbols for his own purposes, started identifying with Napoleon; and the French played along with him. After all, who helped finance Bokassa's imperial coronation? France! Dignitaries from all over the world came to congratulate him. They only dropped him later, when they'd had enough of him.

The colonials wanted to make something of Africa, François says, but the Africans turned it into something quite different. He likes the chaos that produces. To François, Europe is a model landscape where everything is finished. What he loves about this place is the creativity that comes from chaos.

It's good to see François in his new surroundings. As usual, he's working on dozens of projects at the same time. Africans have a way of rambling on, he complains. When they come into his office, he warns them: you've got five minutes, what do you want? His work is zapping: he zaps from documentaries to video clips, from music to money. And through it all the phone rings constantly and fax after fax rolls in. At night he's dead tired, and sometimes not quite sure what he's been doing all day.

He zaps in the longer term as well: he stays in one place for four years, then moves on. It breaks his heart every time, but he has to leave, otherwise he'd become too attached to keep moving.

François introduces me to his friends. I don't say much, I still feel like a square peg in a round hole – everything is taking place right in front of me, but at the same time it's all very far away. I still have to learn how to decode this landscape, to find a tone in which to talk to people, discover what moves them. But in the city I never succeed; I need to go into the countryside where things are clearer, simpler.

François is a city boy. We often argued about it in Zaïre – he thought I should take a greater interest in city life. But I'd never been in Africa before; I couldn't understand what was going on in Kinshasa, and all I wanted was to go into the interior. That difference between us has remained; if anything, it's become stronger.

On our way home, people greet François from all sides. He stops to buy cigarettes from a little boy on the corner, waves to someone walking by, pokes someone else in the back: "Hey boy, ça va?"

"Compared to the average Parisian, you've got quite a life," I comment.

"You said it." François stops in front of a woman selling cashews and slices of green mango, five to a plastic bag. Her baby is lying behind her, asleep in a cardboard box.

"But you're better off not being an African." I've blurted it out before I know it.

François laughs. "You know what a Zaïrian said to me before

13

I left? 'You'd better make the most of being white, because after you people die you'll come back as blacks. Then you'll find out what we're going through. And we will come back as whites, so you'd better brace yourself.' Ever since, I've done my best to be good to blacks, so I don't come back as one of them. But I pray that all racists will come back as blacks, so they can find out how it feels!"

We pass his motorcycle, which he'd had decorated with dancing figures in Zaïre. François gives it a smack. "So let's both pray we never come back as blacks. And especially not as Zaïrians!" He says it laughingly, but I can tell he's moved. We'd both like to go back to Zaïre, but everyone warns us against it. Mobutu has lost his grip on the country: it's not safe anymore, and people are fleeing like rats. Not long ago, a totally destitute Zaïrian barged into François's office – he'd come all the way from Zaïre on foot!

It's unnerving to think that only seven years ago I was able to travel freely in a country I can no longer visit. It's as though parts of the continent are silting up, becoming *terra incognita* again. And what about me, do I only go where it's safe? If so, who will testify to what happens in dangerous places? Ever since I decided to return to Africa, these are the questions that have been on my mind.

Things are still fairly quiet here in Senegal. Then again . . . This morning I was walking down Avenue Pompidou with Suska, François's ex. She pointed out a shop that used to be owned by a Mauritanian. One morning she bought a pack of cigarettes from him; that same afternoon, his head was paraded through the streets on a pole. That was in 1989, when the conflict between Senegal and Mauritania led to frenzied killings on both sides.

For a moment, I was struck dumb. I hadn't realized that the clash between the two neighboring countries had reached such a pitch. We walked past little stalls hung with sandals and hand-bags, rusty racks of postcards, stands selling batik trousers – it was hard to believe that this same street had served as backdrop to such violence.

Back at the house I meet François's six-year-old daughter Lea, who's lived with him part-time since the divorce. A little blonde angel with light blue eyes. Here she plays with Penda, N'Deye's daughter, but in France she spends her vacations with her cousins. She's come back from France with a song:

> *My name is Mustapha*
> *and I live in the Sahara*
> *and I play the tom-tom*
> *on my good wife's bottom.*

She sings it at the table with all her might. I suddenly remember a different song, one we sang as children, the meaning of which only became clear to me years later:

> *Between two dromedaries, out there in the Sahara,*
> *Two little boys were playing, Kasavubu and Lumumba.*
> *While they were playing, the two boys traded knocks,*
> *and Kasavubu locked Lumumba in a little box.*

It's a highly simplified version of the power struggle that took place in Zaïre just after the former Belgian Congo became independent. Kasavubu was president when his opponent Lumumba was murdered. How that song ever made its way to our village in Belgium is a mystery to me. Or did I learn it during summer camp at the seaside, where there were children from all over the country?

After her bath, Lea simply tosses her clothes and the soaking-wet towel on the floor, the way François did this morning. Bad habits! When I was fifteen I spent a few months taking care of two little boys from Zaïre. They too were used to having a nanny, and they left their things lying everywhere.

18 June – Despite the hectic atmosphere, François and I talk more than ever. He was born in Madagascar, where his father worked as a veterinarian. They lived in the bush. When his father was off traveling, his mother stayed home with the children and taught

15

them herself. It was a solid, middle-class family, with strict rules that François was soon doing his best to evade. His parents thought he would never amount to anything. In the pictures taken at the time, François's mother is always trying to neaten his hair.

After studying philosophy in Paris, he found a job at a gas station where he made a pretty penny by sabotaging the meters on the pumps. He was saving money to go to Kathmandu but had only got as far as Greece when a letter came from his father, who was then head of the department of development cooperation at the French embassy in Chad. In his letter, François's father wrote that he'd found a job for him teaching philosophy. François decided to meet his father face-to-face and tell him he wasn't interested. When he finally showed up in Chad, he looked so disheveled that the embassy personnel refused to let him in. He had to wait on the street until his father came outside to see this young man who claimed to be his son.

He never did make it to Kathmandu. By way of Sudan he traveled to Yemen, where he took a dhow – an Arab sailing ship – to Djibouti. After seeing how the farmers in Ethiopia were repressed by their Marxist-Leninist regime, he jettisoned all his academic ideas about Communism. He drank cow's blood with the Maasai in Kenya, was thrown into prison in Idi Amin's Uganda.

He earned a little money along the way by giving readings about his travels at the Centre Culturel Français. When he heard they were looking for someone to head the CCF in St-Louis, Senegal, he applied for the job and got it right away. Four years later, they transferred him to Zaïre.

François was the first white person to show me that there was a new way for whites to relate to blacks after the paternalism of the colonial period. I'm grateful to him for what he taught me – it forged a bond that even after seven years is immediately restored.

In the meantime, I've learned more about Africa, and François has matured. He has mixed feelings about his work in Dakar; he misses the old way of doing things on a shoestring. In St-Louis he would head into the interior in a Land Rover to show films; in Lubumbashi, in southern Zaïre, he was the initiator of a *train cul-*

turel that called at every stop along the route from Lubumbashi to Kalemie.

François is particularly nostalgic about that *train culturel*. A theater troupe and an orchestra traveled with them, and on board there was a library and a compartment where they told people about AIDS and handed out condoms. When François asked the provincial governor at Lubumbashi for financial support for his condom campaign, the man had looked at him mockingly. "You whites are strange people," he said. "Am I to believe that you eat candy, paper wrapper and all?" The actors and musicians led such dissolute lives along the way that François sometimes wondered whether the *train culturel* did more to spread AIDS than to prevent it.

But even after Lubumbashi, Dakar is still a challenge for him: this is an important post for the French, so he can organize big events. In Paris he would never be able to put together a music festival with such limited means. Everything would have to be organized down to the smallest detail, insured and contractualized. But in Africa, connections are what count. François does it all by word of mouth – nothing is put down on paper – and he exchanges services on the barter system. To obtain protection from the police, the army and the fire department during the festival, he pays for their gasoline, feeds them and hands out hundreds of free tickets. "In Africa there are no problems," he says, "only solutions."

But he's still worried: what if the kids up front start pushing and a fence collapses?

20 June – The concert is supposed to begin at six, but when we arrive the stadium is still empty. François spends the first few hours nervously pacing back and forth, afraid the evening will be a flop. Flashy sunglasses, white shirt, orange blazer – he looks like a real impresario. But before long he's walking around in shirtsleeves again, like the François I know.

Lying on the grass, I see the bleachers filling with people as the supporting acts from Mali, Guinea and Cape Verde warm up the crowd. François comes by before nine to say the queues outside are so long that the police have to keep them under control. The concert is being broadcast live on television. When the spotlights are aimed at the crowd, people stand up and start howling and dancing. Most of them are underage. It's quite a sight, all those teenagers moving as one.

I go outside to see how the people queuing in line are getting along. It's almost as busy outside the stadium as it is inside. All the shops are open: the vendors are selling cola nuts, *beignets* and soft drinks by the light of kerosene lanterns.

I think I hear my name being called from the shadows. I stop and look around in amazement. It must have been my imagination, for who knows me around here, besides François and Suska? But then I hear it again. Someone's waving to me from across the street. "Lieve! C'est Jacques!" It's an actor I met a few days ago at the CCF. I walk on, at peace with the world, no longer anonymous – I'm part of the masses that have come together here.

Back home people sometimes ask me if I'm lonely when I'm traveling, or afraid. How can you be lonely or fearful in a country where, after only three days, you're picked out of the crowd by someone who's gone to the trouble of remembering your name? Africans must feel wretched when they come to Europe – to have no identity anymore, to be deprived of all signs of recognition. Maybe it's not so strange, the way they band together, looking for shelter against the anonymity that suddenly surrounds them.

A boy is walking beside me. He's holding one of those little plastic bags of chilled lemonade. They cost twenty-five CFA, around eight cents; children can usually afford that. I've shaken off quite a few young panhandlers already.

"What do you want?"

The boy keeps walking beside me with a determined step, and says: "I want to go inside."

I take a good look at him. Ragged trousers, baggy T-shirt, just a kid really.

"How old are you, anyway?"

"Fourteen." He's lying – he can't be any older than ten. Who knows how far he had to walk to get here. Does his mother know where he is? Not likely.

"Who do you want to go and see?"

He looks up at me, eyes shining. "Youssou N'Dour."

I'm sold. "How much does a ticket cost?"

"Five hundred francs."

He has two hundred and fifty. When I give him the rest, he's off like a shot. I feel a bit ridiculous, like a boy scout who's done his good deed for the day, but satisfied too.

The police inside the stadium have done their best to eject gate-crashers and keep fans from crowding the stage, but as their attention starts to flag, more and more kids succeed in clambering up onto the podium to show off their moves. Some of them are astounding. One boy, his legs bent by polio, uses his crutches to spin in circles like an acrobat. There's a dance they call 'the pissing dog': raise a leg, tilt to one side and shake – quite hilarious.

A group of soldiers have settled on the grass just in front of me. They sit there in their uniforms, straight as ramrods, as if they couldn't care less about the music. But when a girl gets up and dances in front of them, swaying her hips, one of them tosses her his cap, jumps to his feet and starts dancing. Soon dozens of caps are flying through the air. I can't take my eyes off them: a moment ago they were seated, captives to the discipline that goes with their uniform, but in a matter of seconds they've dropped their disguise. They're just as nimble as everyone else – their stiff uniforms don't seem to hinder them in the slightest.

I try to imagine a platoon of Dutch soldiers suddenly joining in with the crowd at a concert. It wouldn't occur to them, and the audience probably wouldn't stand for it either. Here, no one is surprised – I'm the only one watching them. Their eyes sparkle as they fling their legs in the air and fall into each other's arms, laughing.

It's heartwarming, but at the same time disturbing. How easily they forget that they're soldiers. With one sweeping gesture, they've cast off their role. It reminds me of something, but what? Where have I seen this before? Images of Zaïre's mutinous soldiers suddenly flash through my mind. The same ecstasy, the same bright eyes. What here leads to merriment, leads elsewhere to bloodshed.

The lights go down. Youssou N'Dour comes on, a torch burning in each hand, and launches into his song about Steve Biko. The atmosphere is electric. During the past few days, François has often talked about the power exerted by Senegal's young people, about the pressure their sheer numbers bring to bear on politicians. Tonight, in this stadium, under the darkened sky, it's suddenly tangible. I can feel the energy of tens of thousands of people around me.

It's impressive to see Senegalese musicians performing in their own surroundings. Baaba Maal in particular moves me. A slender Toucouleur from the Fouta Toro, the area along the Senegal River, he has a crystal-clear voice and radiates something angelic, almost prophetic, in his wide, bright yellow *boubou*. I don't understand a word of what he sings, but his ballad-like songs clearly draw on old traditions.

François, of course, is a fan of city boy Youssou N'Dour, whose inspiration comes from across the globe. François recently sponsored him on a pan-African tour – Banjul, Bangui, Ouagadougou, all those capitals without skyscrapers. N'Dour was glad to be back in Dakar. He's admitted that he feels more at ease in Paris than in the hinterlands of Africa.

I strike up a conversation with a Tunisian film maker, probably the only Arab in the stadium. The Lebanese people living in Senegal aren't interested in African culture – some swear it doesn't even exist. But the Tunisian is a real aficionado of African music, which he admits is generally more modern than Arab music. "The Arabs are living in the wrong century," he says. "They listen to the Egyptian singer Oum Kalthoum. They're still crying over their past."

Omar Pene, the last act of the night, sounds much rawer and harder than the rest. He is the voice of a desperate generation, of the street corner kids in the slums of Pikine. He's still singing when the first rays of dawn appear on the horizon.

20

And no one drinks a drop of alcohol all night. According to François, even the musicians are completely 'clean'.

21 June – Adama is in Dakar! I found out this morning when I tried to call him at home in the Casamance region of southern Senegal. I was planning to look him up, because yesterday François suddenly announced that he was leaving for France on Saturday. And I'm here for three more weeks! It's typical of François not to mention this earlier.

Adama has just come out of hospital. There's not much evidence of the energetic man who was my guide in the Casamance in 1987. His room in his brother's house has a clinical smell to it. There's just a bed, a table covered with old newspapers and a plastic bag full of medicines. Lots of antibiotics, I see. They're crazy about them around here – some people even use them for preventive cures.

Adama lifts his shirt and shows me an incredible gouge in his back. Last year he slipped a disc. The specialists in Dakar claimed it would be a routine operation and at first everything seemed to go well, but during the post-operative massage the wound came open and began to fester. The surgeon said he'd have to operate again. This time they gave him only a local anesthetic, and while they were sewing the wound shut, a terrible stab of pain shot through Adama's body: the anesthetic had worn off. The pain didn't stop after the second operation. It took a while before the doctors discovered why: they'd left a bandage sewn up in his back.

Adama's been feeling pretty weak ever since the third operation. Every time they worked on him the wound got bigger, the incision deeper. He's terrified that it will start festering again. He lies on the bed as he tells me this, for he can't sit up or stand for very long. His illness seems to rule his life. He wants me to look at X-rays, shows me the hospital bills and gives me a running inventory of the medicine bag.

The room's sourish smell almost makes me choke, but I steel myself: Adama has been leading this life for the past year, can't I share it with him for a couple of hours? Seeing him like this gets me down. Back in the Casamance, surrounded by his two wives and twenty-two children, he ruled the roost. He belongs to the Diola people, who were long able to ward off French influence and who still uphold a great many animist traditions. Diola males are initiated in the sacred wood. "But this year the operating room was my sacred wood," Adama says bitterly. "I've entered it three times, and every time I came out I felt worse."

He seems broken in body and spirit, and haunted by dark thoughts. As a young man he was paralyzed after a bad accident, and he spent a year in hospital. That was in 1956, four years before independence. How comfortable hospitals were in those days! Friends brought him grapes and chocolate; a hefty Russian nurse carried him in her arms from one room to the next and taught him to walk again, step by step. When he came out of hospital he was as good as new. But during this last year he had to ply the hospital staff with money, and if his family hadn't cooked for him, he would have had nothing to eat.

Adama used to be very anti-French. When General de Gaulle made a speech in 1958 asking the Senegalese to maintain their ties with France, Adama and his friends were in the front row holding placards that screamed 'Non!' De Gaulle addressed them personally: "You there, with your signs, you can all become independent tomorrow as far as I'm concerned!"

"You know, I sometimes lie awake thinking about that," Adama says. "I wish we'd shown de Gaulle a little more respect, let him have his say." In 1980, President Senghor came to the Casamance. An old man asked him: how much longer is this independence going to last? Senghor didn't laugh, Adama remembers; he just looked worried.

All kinds of visitors come in while we're sitting on the bed. A nephew talks about an explosion that happened earlier this year at the factory where he works. Four hundred people were killed by toxic ammonia fumes. "Workers?" I ask him. Not only workers, he tells me; the people who had come to see what was happening dropped like flies as well, as did the women and children who were selling food at the factory gates.

Once his nephew has left, Adama starts complaining: some visitors think they can boost his spirits by talking about disasters they've been through. Some even come to report illnesses that make his pale by comparison.

I don't say anything about the music festival – he doesn't seem in much of a mood for it. In fact, I wonder whether he's even heard of musicians like Youssou N'Dour; he's from another generation, and probably prefers traditional music.

In the taxi on the way home, I feel confused. How can I reconcile François's upbeat world with Adama's tale of woe? This kind of confusion used to make me feel desperate; now I know that one day I'll see the connection. If I only stay long enough.

22 June – To the beach with François on the motorcycle. On the way there, a policeman pulls us over. "*Merde!*" François swears, for neither of us is wearing a helmet. François shows his diplomatic pass. The policeman glances at it indifferently, pulls out his ticket book and demands six thousand francs. How is François going to get out of this one? He speaks Wolof pretty well, and starts saying things that make the policeman laugh. After a while the man sticks his ticket book back in his pocket, slaps François on the back and lets us go.

"How did you do that?"

"Oh, it wasn't too hard. If you know a few expressions in Wolof, people are so impressed that you can get away with anything."

Later he translates a few of them for me. Life isn't easy. We're all in the same canoe. The monkey doesn't plant his crops so the gorilla can harvest them.

23 June – Went to the opening of a new club, the Waw. Sort of a grand café, sparsely furnished with iron tables and chairs, a long bar and high-tech lighting. It had a varied clientele; lots of vests with African motifs in evidence, made by local designers. I pick up plenty of new slang, but *boy* and *nice* are the clear favorites. *Comment ça va? En forme? Nice, boy.*

23

All night I have the feeling that something's not right. The people here act as though they were in France! The word 'mimicry' pops up again. I miss the recalcitrance of the Zaïrians – at least the Belgians weren't able to steal their souls. But I don't trust my own skepticism either. Why shouldn't they have cafés here like in Europe? What do I want? It's not as though the Zaïrians, for all their recalcitrance, aren't a lot worse off. But still – the falseness of the evening gnaws at me.

One of the waiters is the son of Mamadou, François's houseboy. He launches into a long, complicated conversation and wants to know if it's true that there is so much racism in France. Everyone in Senegal automatically assumes that if you're white you come from France. When I tell him that I live in Amsterdam, he asks whether things are better there, and starts hinting that I might be able to find him a job. I soon put an end to his pipe dream. I'm surprised to realize that I have no patience with people who don't know how things have changed back in Europe.

Maybe I've just had enough of Dakar. I need to see what's going on behind the French façade.

St-Louis, 25 June – Left at five-thirty this morning, traveling by motorcycle along the beach to St-Louis. How far would that be, as the crow flies? Two hundred kilometers? It takes us about three hours. The air is chilly; we're wearing helmets and windbreakers, and our bags are strapped to the back of the bike. When François returns to Dakar, I'm traveling on to Podor, a village on the River Senegal.

In the beam of our headlight we see hundreds of crabs running for their lives. A creepy sight. It reminds me of the opening scene of Werner Herzog's film about Bokassa: a legion of pink crabs crossing the railroad tracks are caught in the misty light of a train that's about to run over them. We crush quite a few ourselves.

We pass the washed-up carcasses of dolphins and giant sea turtles. François says they're victims of Korean and Japanese fishing off the coast of Senegal: they get tangled in the trawlers' nets and are tossed overboard. Every time he sees one, he stops to inspect it. I think it's disgusting; at first I don't want to look, but François makes fun of me for being a sissy.

The dolphins have razor-sharp teeth and are bloated from the heat. Crabs are crawling all around the cadavers, digging tunnels to get at their undersides. Whenever a giant sea turtle washes up on the shore, the villagers hurry out to claim its shell. "You see," François says, "even on the beach there's life. Not like in France, where they pick up the dead fish right away and rake the sand."

We have to be careful whenever we get close to the fishing villages, because the fisherman have strung invisible lines at eye-level. Sometimes they lower them to the sand when they see us coming; sometimes we have to duck and ride under them.

It's impressive to see how everyone in these villages joins in the struggle with the sea. By the light of the rising sun, long rows of young men are pulling heavy nets out of the water; they're barefooted, their clothes torn. Horses and wagons stand ready to load the fish, and women walk around with baskets under their arms. The old men of the village pace up and down, keeping an eye on things while they listen to their transistor radios.

Whenever we stop, a curious crowd surrounds us. Two whites on a motorcycle! François trots out his Wolof again and makes everyone laugh. As we near the end of our ride, we see the tip of the Langue de Barbarie peninsula, a tongue of land dotted with pink flamingos.

At the hotel I discover that my jeans and tennis shoes are spattered with oil. "You'll never get that out," François teases. But nothing can spoil my mood.

I've been in St-Louis before. Built on an island, it was the first French settlement in Africa. Ocher-colored warehouses rise up along the waterfront on the mainland side of the Faidherbe Bridge. Parts of *Coup de Torchon* (aka *Clean Slate*), one of my favorite films, were shot here. It stars Philippe Noiret as a colonial policeman who comes unhinged and takes the law into his own hands – the old theme of the white man on the Dark Continent. François was working at the CCF in St-Louis during the shooting, and had a bit part as a French policeman.

Something of the old colonial atmosphere still lingers in the air-conditioned bar of the Hôtel de la Poste, but the city outside breathes a deep post-colonial sadness: many of the houses are decrepit, and the streets are almost deserted.

François finds it all wonderful. Just think, there used to be a Renault dealer here, and now Senegalese families are camping on the floor of the old showroom. The irony of it! He's fond of St-Louis, he even dreams of buying a house here one day to retire to – no twilight years in France for him.

St-Louis is also home to his good friend Cheikh, who used to work at the garage where François parked his Land Rover, his motorcycle and his plastic Mehari jeep. After a while, François offered to let him use his own garage so he could go into business for himself. Every afternoon after work, François spent hours with Cheikh and his helpers. They became friends for life. Years later, François rode his motorcycle from Zaïre to St-Louis. When he arrived he heard that Cheikh was working in a factory. As he drove onto the grounds, Cheikh came running out to meet him. To the amazement of the other factory workers, the two of them fell into each other's arms and wept.

Now that François is working in Senegal again, he leaves his bike with Cheikh whenever he goes to France on vacation. If he ever buys a house here, he tells me, he'd like Cheikh and his family to move in downstairs.

Two hundred kilometers east along the Senegal, in Podor, there lives another person who's important to François: old Demba, the man he calls his 'spiritual father'. Demba spent much of his life working for white people. At the age of eight he already had a job as a *panca*, fanning the whites by pulling the cord that moved a canopy up and down above their heads. Later he became cook to the French district administrator, driver for the health service and captain of a motorboat that carried patients across the Senegal. By the time François met him he was a retired prominent citizen.

That afternoon we go for a swim. The sea is wild, the current so strong that I drift further and further away from the beach.

Whenever I try to swim to shore, high waves pull me back. I panic for a moment, and have great difficulty getting out of the water. In the distance, François is swimming away from me with powerful strokes.

Half an hour later he's standing in front of me, dripping wet. "You were worried there for a minute, weren't you?" He loves to swim when the sea is like this. In France you never get the chance because they run up the red no-swimming flags right away. Europe is one big rest home; it makes him feel coddled when they try to eliminate every risk. He'll decide for himself whether the sea is too rough for swimming.

"Here you go." He reaches into the pockets of his swimming trunks and tosses me a handful of shells. "Here's your lunch." He breaks one open and hands it to me. The animal inside shrinks convulsively, and I make a disgusted face. "Not on your life."

"Don't be such a baby. If they were served to you on a plate of ice with a glass of white wine, I bet you'd eat them."

He's right of course. I'm not about to be caught out, so I carefully pry open one of the shells. Uggh . . . it's salty, and sand grinds between my teeth.

"Where did you find them?"

"Dug them up out of the sand." He reaches into his pockets again. "I've got a whole bunch of them." He points out to sea. "And there are a lot more out there!" But I'd rather have François laugh at me than eat another one of those sandy creatures alive.

26 June – By way of farewell, François takes me to the fishermen's quarter in St-Louis, tucked in between a branch of the Senegal and the sea on the Langue de Barbarie. On my own, I'd never even think of showing my face in these narrow streets. A white person stands out, and everyone knows you have no business being here. But François doesn't worry about that: he approaches things head on.

The neighborhood smells of dried fish, and everything moves to the rhythm of the catch. Men sit in their doorways mending nets, and behind wooden partitions people are building boats. We try to peek through the cracks in a fence, but a watchman chases us away. The dugouts are being constructed for a contest; the size and model of each competitor's boat is top secret.

Down on the beach, dozens of young men are pushing colorful dugouts into the surf. It's hard work, but a bit later they are dancing high on the waves. The fishermen standing upright in them radiate enormous strength.

Men lie resting under wooden awnings along the waterfront, playing checkers, drinking tea or napping. Children blow bubbles through a split piece of wood. Someone throws a stone and hits François on the neck. "Hey!" He turns around, startled, but the culprit has disappeared.

When he worked in St-Louis, he came to this neighborhood once to show a movie about life underwater. "The fishermen are highly superstitious. They think it's full of evil spirits down there. You should have seen them, they couldn't believe their eyes!"

The public showings continued for a while after he left St-Louis, until the projector broke down. No one bothered to get it fixed. That's how it often goes, he sighs.

"And what about Zaïre? Do you think you left anything of yourself behind?" That question has been on my mind for days. Four years in Kinshasa, four years in Lubumbashi: so much enthusiasm, so many projects, so many friendships – and what's left? All the CCFs in Zaïre have been closed. The railroad the *train culturel* traveled down became the route along which thousands of terrified Baluba fled from the ethnic rioting in Shaba province. The heart of this continent is on fire, and we've been driven to the edge.

"I don't know. It's not the kind of thing you worry about when you're busy." But to think of all the personal possessions François left behind in Lubumbashi. Traditional works of art he'd been given during his travels with the *train culturel*, books, a collection of video-taped documentaries his father had sent him over the years. He wanted all these things to remain there, he wanted the people he'd worked with to use them. All he took with him was one souvenir: a little wooden *train culturel* that a Zaïrian had carved for him, a brightly painted toy train with little black dolls looking expectantly out the windows.

A few months after he left, rebel soldiers looted the CCF in Lubumbashi. They took all the books and equipment, and went on to pick the building clean, right down to the doors, toilets and light switches. The *train culturel* was wrecked. "Still, if I could go back tomorrow, I'd do it." He looks at me. "Shall we go together?" We shake on it.

François leaves in his usual cloud of haste and chaos. Cheikh takes him to the station to catch the *taxi-brousse* to Dakar. It's so late that François has to hire a whole taxi for himself. His plane leaves for Paris tonight, and he still has to pack.

Once he's gone, it suddenly dawns on me: I'm on my own now. But I don't have much time to think about it – I have to find a car to take me to Podor. I'm in luck. At the Hôtel de la Poste I meet Dr Diack, who works at the Podor Medical Center. He's leaving tomorrow morning at six.

Podor, 27 June – Dr Diack has a Renault 12 that talks! We drive into the African interior, accompanied by a metallic voice: "Lights on. Please fasten your seat belts." He bought the car from a European. That's the way to do it, he says; Europeans take better care of their cars than Africans.

Dr Diack grew up in Dakar. At first he was afraid he'd never get used to Podor, but to his amazement it happened faster than he expected. His friends can't understand how he tolerates it, how he finds anyone to talk to. But he just laughs at them: life in Dakar isn't that much more interesting than it is in Podor.

This part of the country was once green and lush, as the Senegal used to flood its banks each year. But in the last few decades, the desert has begun to move in from the north. It's now part of the Sahel savannah; the rainy season has started, but not a drop of rain has fallen. Masses of people have left for France since the drought began. To stop the emigration, development agencies from all over the world have focused their attention on the Fouta Toro region.

The road to Podor is paved and in much better condition than I'm used to seeing in Africa. I see fields of rice and sorghum along the road, but the most striking elements in the landscape are the abandoned tractors and pieces of farm machinery. Sometimes there are wrecking yards full of abandoned equipment. Haven't we learned our lesson yet?

The development specialist at the Dutch embassy in Dakar told me about a project on the Kaskas peninsula, just upriver from Podor. When the Dutch suggested building a ferry that the passengers could pull back and forth across the river on a fixed cable, the Senegalese were indignant: who did these people think they were, slaves? But the Dutch were persistent. It takes twenty minutes when the river's high, but anything is better than the motor launches at other crossings, which are always breaking down or running out of fuel.

The few paved roads running into Podor peter out into a labyrinth of dusty streets. One of them leads to Demba's compound: a house of clay, built around a courtyard full of oxen, goats and chickens. Parked in the middle of the yard, like a trophy, is an old Citroën Deux Chevaux.

We find Demba in his parlor – a tall, thin man wearing a light blue *boubou* and an embroidered skullcap. He has a white goatee and lively, gentle eyes. He's been expecting me – François called to say I was coming. Demba's wife is having an asthma attack in the bedroom, so Dr Diack has work on his hands right away.

I sneak a look around. Behind Demba hangs an impressive array of framed family photographs and portraits of Muslim marabouts. Against the backdrop of stately figures on the wall, the furnishings seem measly. There's a large refrigerator in one corner, and a dusty assortment of pots and pans, plastic bags and old Nescafé cans under the bed.

François warned me that Demba would try to treat me like a visiting dignitary. Of course, François always refuses to allow it; he sleeps under the reed awning in the yard and eats from the communal platter. But when Demba says I can spend the night at the Belgian mission, I don't object. François would laugh at me, but let him!

Demba sends his grandson Kao along with me. It's eleven o'clock in the evening and a hard wind is blowing through the streets. The mission is in a former merchant house on the quay. It's a beautiful building, with blue doors in a yellow façade and a courtyard with trees.

My room looks out over the river. The Toucouleur once cultivated the land on both sides of the Senegal, and the nomadic Peul let their animals graze there as well. But now that the river forms the border between Senegal and Mauritania, it lies like an open wound in the landscape.

Suska's Mauritanian shopkeeper, whose head was paraded through the streets of Dakar – how abstract that story had sounded back in the capital. Here it suddenly takes on meaning. The conflict between Senegal and Mauritania escalated four years ago, in 1989, after an incident at Diawara, a village upriver. Two Senegalese farmers working on the Mauritanian side of the river were murdered by Moorish nomads who wanted to graze their animals on the same piece of land.

The Belgian missionary is getting ready to leave for Dakar. He shows me around the kitchen. Beer in the fridge; Nescafé, powdered milk and sugar in the blue cabinet. All mission posts in Africa look the same: clean sheets on the bed, a sink, a table and chair – the austerity of my boarding-school years seems luxurious in these surroundings.

I look out the window and think about Kisangani, that city on the river. When will I stop comparing everything with Zaïre? It's a sickness, François says – he suffers from it too. But he at least seems to have reconciled himself to Senegal. How many African countries will I have to visit before Zaïre begins to pale?

On the way back to Demba's house next morning, I pass a group of children swimming in the river. The splashing, the peals of laughter – Dakar is already far behind me. The benevolent effect of the interior is taking hold.

Demba is waiting with lunch. A girl spreads a plastic tablecloth on the ground and sets places for two, a basket of French bread, paper napkins. "Make sure he doesn't try to feed you French food!" I hear François's voice in my ear. A mixture of cowardice and curiosity keeps me from saying anything. We eat salad vinaigrette and steak with french fries. When the girl takes the Coca-Cola out of the refrigerator I almost object, but keep my mouth shut – they probably bought it especially for me.

While we're eating, Demba rattles on about the Podor of his youth, a prosperous, bustling city. During the rainy season, the current was so strong it uprooted trees on the river bank. People paddled their canoes in places where cars now tear by at a hundred kilometers an hour. When the waters receded they sowed sorghum, which grew by itself. Podor was a training center for *tirailleurs*, African infantrymen in the service of the colonial army. Along with the French civil servants and traders, they gave the town an international cachet.

Demba looks back on the colonial period with reservations, but he admits that things were better organized back then. "At least you could build up a career. If you worked somewhere for a couple of years and did your best, you got promoted, but these days . . . The only way to move up the ladder is to have a cabinet minister in the family. That's why everyone in this country wants to go into politics: it's the surest way to fill your pockets."

After he retired he became a Red Cross volunteer; the Deux Chevaux in his yard was the ambulance. The Red Cross used to serve the poor, he says. But the last time a plane with medicine arrived in St-Louis, a female Red Cross worker diverted the cargo to a nearby village, where her husband was a politician.

In another room, a group of girls is listening to music. Occasionally one of them gets up to dance. I see that 'the pissing dog' has made its way to Podor as well. Demba follows my gaze. "Those are my grandchildren," he says. "My daughter in Dakar left them here to torment me." He turns up his nose in disapproval. "Young people these days – all they think about is music. The entire generation born after independence has sawdust between its ears."

Once the dishes from the main course have been cleared, he looks at me expectantly. *"Fromage?"*

Cheese! Where in the world did he find that? Sometimes the missionary gives him a piece, Demba explains, and he bakes the occasional pie in return.

For someone who began working at the age of eight, I can imagine that having your grandchildren loafing around like this must be a thorn in the flesh. But his grandchildren probably get just as tired of his stories of the glorious past, in which all the leading roles are reserved for merchants from Grenoble and Marseille.

After lunch Demba leads me to a room where I fall asleep amid the music and noise from the street. When I wake up, my whole body is covered with beads of sweat. It's dark outside, and a crowd has gathered in the courtyard. They're watching the television that's been placed on a table in the open air. Demba is sitting on his reed mat with his back to them, praying.

Suddenly the audience raises a cry of protest. The picture's gone. Demba's son Amadou stands up and twists the antenna that's planted in the ground next to the set, but the snow on the screen won't go away. The group remains seated for a while, but they eventually drift off in disappointment, one by one. Amadou looks at me. "That was a typical evening of television in Podor."

Once again, Kao accompanies me back to the mission post. He's about sixteen, and I can't always understand what he's saying; the post-colonial French in vogue here has rules of its own. I have to pick my way through the darkness, but Kao marches along, greeting people who are only shadows to me. The street is busier now than it was during the day. In the light of a streetlamp, children are playing in the sand. They yell *"Toubab!* Whitey!" and run up to shake my hand. I feel a whole crowd of sandy little palms in mine.

"Good thing the wind has died down," I say with relief.

"Actually, we have nothing against the wind," Kao says, "especially when it comes from the west. The west wind blows television pictures our way."

I laugh, thinking this is a joke, but he's serious. When the wind is right, there's a chance of good reception all evening.

The mission is deathly quiet, the beer in the refrigerator luke-warm. I open the window to hear the trees rustling on the quay and then, behind the trees, across the river, a woman singing. She sounds sad, or is it just me?

28 June – Yesterday, just before the missionary left, a girl had wiped down the table on the roofed-in patio. This morning it was covered in a thick layer of dust. The table and chair in my room are also powdered with a sandy film. Nasty stuff. There's no way to keep things clean.

But the sky is bright blue and the air is clear of the sand that hid the stars last night. I take a walk along the quay. Above the main entrance to the mission hangs a sign saying 'Friendship House'; on the right is a smaller door leading to the library, to the left is the lecture room. Most Senegalese are Muslims – mission posts are probably only tolerated if they play a cultural or human-itarian role. The nuns' quarters a bit further along are boarded up; the two Dutch nuns who live there are on vacation.

The merchant houses along the quay are fronted by old cail-cedra trees, their branches like outstretched arms and knotted trunks covered with scars; the bark of the cailcedra is used as a medicine. With a bit of imagination, I can conjure up what it was like when little Demba still worked as a *panca* and merchants parked their camels and donkeys in the shade of the cailcedras while the boats at quayside were loaded high with cargo.

But the trading houses have seen better days; the stucco has fallen from the façades in great, uneven chunks, and fire-blackened courtyards filled with roaming animals gape at me through the open doorways. A boat lies rusting at the quay; children play hide and seek in its hold, diving from the railing into the water. François, of course, would relish all of this.

I turn the corner and pass a poster erected by the fan club of Baaba Maal, who was born here. My instinctive fondness for the musician was confirmed yesterday by a little incident at Demba's house. Demba had been grumbling about the music pouring out of his grandchildren's room when suddenly his eyes lit up. He smiled: this was a song from his childhood, he said with obvious emotion. It was Baaba Maal singing.

At the pharmacy, Dr Diack is leaning on the counter, talking to the pharmacist's assistant. He offers to drive me to Demba's house. His car is parked outside, but I prefer to walk. Men saunter down the street, their *boubous* flapping, black umbrellas held up against the sun. A group of children are sitting under a tree bleating like goats, supervised by a bearded man holding a stick, with which he deals out well-aimed blows – the marabout and his dreaded Koran school.

A woman passes by, enveloped in a cloud of perfume. Where have I smelled that before? In the Casamance. It's sticky stuff, made from musk and the roots of plants that grow beside the river. *Thiouraye*. You burn it in a censer full of hot ashes.

Demba has just come home from the mosque. If I'd seen him on the street I wouldn't have recognized him: in his pointy reed hat and sunglasses, he looks like a Chinese. He's saved me some milk from a cow that just calved, and laid out two photo albums that we end up flipping through all morning.

His employers were fond of him, they all wanted to take him to Europe when they went home on vacation. He was hesitant at first, afraid he'd like it so much he'd never come back; he didn't want to hurt his elderly mother's feelings. In 1961, he finally let himself be convinced: he had nine children by then, so there was no longer any danger of him staying for ever.

He took the boat to Marseille with the last of his employers, a Frenchman. Leaning over the railing, he saw flying fish jump out of the water. If the boat sinks, he thought, they'll eat me. He'd rather have gone by plane – at least then he wouldn't have had to see what was going to eat him if he crashed.

From Paris, he traveled to Vienna to visit a former employer, a Czech physician. In the train he came across only one other black person. The man winked at him. In Vienna everyone thought he was a refugee from the Congo, where a civil war was raging.

People stopped on the street when he walked by. I can imagine why: in his dark blue *boubou*, with meters of white cloth wrapped in a turban around his head, he does look impressive. Here he is dangling in a cable car in the Austrian Alps; there he is beside a swimming pool, next to a woman in a bikini.

When he went back to Europe ten years later, he noticed that things had changed. In 1961 everyone had treated him with the greatest respect. Now, for the first time, he encountered racism. "I couldn't really blame the French," he says. "At first it was only the Peul, the Toucouleur and the Soninké who went to France. But when the Wolof started going, the problems began. All they care about is making money, it doesn't matter how." I laugh. He belongs to the Toucouleur, who are traditionally a farming people. They have an affinity with the Peul, who are herders, but their animosity towards the more citified Wolof is common knowledge: the Wolof form the majority in this country, and Dakar is the base from which they try to force their language and laws on everyone else.

Many of the photos were taken in Demba's yard. Here's a much younger François on his motorcycle, the wind in his hair. And there we have Philippe Noiret, lying on his back under the awning, surrounded by the whole crew of *Coup de Torchon*. François must have had a hand in that.

In the photo album, the old giant tortoise that's been lying motionless in a hollow next to the dovecote ever since I arrived is still at the height of its glory. I recognize little Kao, a yellow cap on his head, sitting on the animal's back. Demba found the tortoise in 1962, during a medical mission in the desert. The tortoise has been through a lot since then: it once fell into a six-meter hole and came out with a huge crack in its underside, which healed by itself. And one of its legs had to be amputated after it had been tied to a tree so long that the rope grew into its flesh.

While we're leafing through the albums, people wander in and out of the yard. Demba can be delightfully disrespectful at times. When an old woman shakes my hand enthusiastically and launches into a long monologue in Pulaar, Demba taps his forehead. "Don't mind her, she's crazy." He refers to a white nun who recently visited Podor as *une grosse patapouf*, a fat lump.

This afternoon we eat squabs and spaghetti. Demba's granddaughter clears away the remains of our meal and takes them to the verandah, where his wife is seeing to the family's dinner. I'm starting to recognize faces, remember names, connect life stories. Kao, Mammie and Marie-Thérèse belong to Demba's daughter in Dakar. They all have different fathers; their mother is married to a fourth man, which is probably why she left them here.

Aminata is the only one of Demba's daughters who lives in Podor. She's married to a man who was divorced when he met her, but has since re-married his first wife. He lives with Aminata most of the time. For some reason, her daughter Rams has also moved in with Demba.

Viewing these complex family relations, I can see what's so special about Demba having always lived with one woman and raising his nine children himself.

Demba's son Amadou still lives at home. He's thirty-four. I don't see a wife or any children in his vicinity, and except for a few chores at the mission he doesn't seem to have much to do. Demba says he's smart, even though he left school when he was only fifteen.

Amadou's friends are the ones who come and watch television every night. Just before dark the little table in the courtyard is put upright and dusted off, then Amadou and a helper carry the television set outside. By that time the chairs have all been arranged in formation. Latecomers go looking for a wooden stool, or settle down on the concrete floor of the lean-to. The youngest children simply sit in the sand.

This evening everything goes well for half an hour, but then, in the middle of an episode of a television series, the power goes out. Amadou remains seated, but some of the audience jump up and run out into the street.

"Where are they going?" I ask in amazement.

"To a different neighborhood, where the electricity is still on." The power plant in Podor doesn't have enough capacity, so they turn off the electricity in one neighborhood for a while, then the next, and so on. "Just wait, they'll be back," Amadou predicts, "they just charge around after the charge." And indeed, a few minutes after the television blips on again, they're back.

Amadou tells me that the snow on the television screen later that evening is the fault of the relay station in Podor. Owners of televisions who have their antennas on the roof, and whose reception fails when the signal breaks down, come and watch television at his place. They know that Amadou's bag of tricks isn't nearly exhausted, and after twisting and turning the antenna a bit, he succeeds – thanks to the favorable westerly winds – in receiving programs from Louga, to the west of Podor. When Louga goes down as well, he homes in on the even more distant Thiès, where the main transmitter is located.

"What we're getting here aren't technological images, but images from nature!" he says. Experience has taught him that the west wind brings pictures from Mauritania, Cape Verde, even from Morocco and Guinea, but the east wind blocks reception. The other people in Podor don't stop to think about things like that, they just turn on their sets and wait. There are farmers who save for years to buy a television, then use it as a piece of furniture. Some people claim that Amadou has a special machine to attract images. There are days when he's the only person in Podor who receives them, so what other explanation is there?

Amadou has been keeping statistics on television reception in Podor since 1987. He divides them into three categories: good, weak and none, and he also notes whether the pictures come from Senegal or Mauritania. "Sometimes I wonder why they call it RTS, Radio Télévision Sénégalaise. Judging from how often the pictures come from Mauritania, you'd think we were Mauritanians!"

When asked where he finds time to keep track of his statistics, he says: "As long as there's no reception, I have all the time in the world!" He has asthma, just like his parents: the television helps him to forget about it.

His latest dream is to buy a signal decoder, so he can receive

Canal Plus. He's already started a fund-raising drive among his friends: their monthly dues are noted next to their names. At the top of the list, Amadou has written in elegant lettering: *CPRP Cotise Pas, Regarde Pas* – No Payment, No Viewing.

I'm reminded of what I've been told in the last few months about the new African resolve. Is this what they were talking about? Demba still believes that God put the politicians in power, so you can't act against them. But Amadou belongs to the opposition, he knows that people have to organize, that no one will do anything for them unless they fight for it.

The Senegalese, he says, have a beggar's mentality. He sees it at the mission all the time. Sometimes people will be standing happily talking to him, but as soon as they see the priest they put on a tearful expression and start complaining about their harvest, their health and their children, hoping the priest will feel sorry for them and give them something. Amadou himself never asks anyone for anything, no matter how badly off he might be.

Kao isn't around to take me back to the mission, so Amadou walks with me. After his busy talk in the courtyard, he's fallen silent. I'm not sure what to say either. I'd like to ask him why he still lives at home, why there's no woman in his life. But how to broach the subject?

When we pass a group of women who greet Amadou, I casually ask whether young people from Podor usually marry each other.

"It depends," Amadou says, "my wife, for example, was from here."

"Where is she now?"

"She's dead."

I'm startled. So young, and already a widower.

I'm reluctant to ask any more questions, but Amadou tells me the story unbidden. They were still newlyweds, and his wife was six months pregnant, when one morning she began bleeding. They took her to the maternity clinic in Podor, then to the hospital in Ndioum, forty kilometers down the road. The doctors there decided to perform a cesarean.

She'd lost a lot of blood by then, but they couldn't give her a transfusion because the medical director had taken the refrigerator that was used to store blood and installed it in his home. He was also driving around in the car that served as an ambulance, so one of the nursing staff had to take a taxi to St-Louis to get the blood. But instead of coming back that same evening, he spent the night there. When he finally returned to Ndioum, Amadou's wife was already in a coma. She died the next day.

"I wanted to file a complaint against the director," Amadou says, "but everyone warned me not to. 'What do you think this is,' they said, 'a democracy? Do you think a little man can win against a medical director?' "

It's late, and we're the only ones out on the street. As we walk along in silence, I think of the clientele at Café Waw, and suddenly realize why everything there seemed so unreal to me: step down a rung in this country and you fall into a dizzying abyss. How can they pretend they're in France when, four hundred kilometers down the road, a young woman dies for the lack of a blood transfusion? Things were still fairly unclear until this evening, but now the first pieces start to fall into place. "When did this happen?"

"In 1989." He laughs, short and hard. "My parents wanted me to marry her younger sister, but I refused. I was married to *her*, what did her sister have to do with it?!" A lot of young people from around here move away, he says. The ones who stay behind are often ridiculed, but she never laughed at him. That's why he loved her.

"Everyone wonders why I don't get married again. They say, 'You work at the mission, but that doesn't mean you have to live like a priest!' Or: 'What's wrong, have you lost your nerve, aren't you a man anymore?' " He recently told his father that he wanted a video recorder. Demba was dead-set against it: if he brought one of those things home, he'd never go looking for a wife.

We've arrived at the mission. How do you say goodnight to someone who's just told you a story like that? We linger on a bit, then Amadou says cheerfully: "But listen, the night she died I still kept my television statistics!"

29 June – Having cautiously taken stock of the situation, I've moved to Demba's house. The room where I took my siesta was fine, the shower in the yard was working, the toilet was clean – no reason, in other words, to stay on at the mission.

When I arrive I find all kinds of attentive touches: Demba has brought in a table and chair for me, a burner of smoldering *thiouraye* is standing in one corner, there's a clean sheet on the bed. The youngest granddaughter, Marie-Thérèse, a bouncy little thing of about eleven, brings me a *pagne* – a colored length of cloth – to wrap around myself when I come out of the shower.

Amadou is his usual deadpan self. He repairs the rattling shutters outside my room and scolds the asthmatic young neighbor who stands gasping for breath in front of the window. But a bit later he gives the boy a pill. "He knows my weakness," Amadou says. "An asthmatic can't stand to see someone else have an attack; he *has* to help out."

He's a jack of all trades in Podor. A clogged gas pipe, a broken light switch – the villagers always know where to find him. When the nuns got a television recently, they sent for him: they were standing in front of it, helpless, afraid to even touch the thing.

Amid all the bustle of moving, it takes a while before I realize that today is a holiday: *tamkharit*, the Islamic New Year. The girls are ironing clothes on a table on the patio. They're using an old-fashioned iron filled with hot coals – when was the last time I saw one of those? The enormous sky-blue *boubous* take a particularly long time.

Demba always wears a neatly pressed *boubou*, but Amadou and Kao usually walk around in jeans. They only change their clothes when it's time to go to the mosque. It's quite an operation, especially on a day like this when prayers are held any number of times.

Seven families in the neighborhood have gone in together and bought a black bull for tonight's feast. They slaughter it in the field behind Demba's house. When Kao takes me back there, the animal is already lying lifeless on the ground and Demba's daughter Aminata is cutting it into pieces. Nothing goes to waste: Amadou rinses out the stomach with a garden hose and the girls shovel the contents into trenches they've dug around the trees. The meat is carefully divided between seven platters.

I sit on a rusty, upended bathtub and watch in fascination: the casual expertise with which they perform this ritual amazes me. I thought these teenagers could only dance, play Scrabble and watch television.

Marie-Thérèse is the only one who breaks the spell, by demonstrating a dance they call 'the Cat': she scratches one foot over the ground, like she's piling dirt behind her. But watching her walk down to the river later, thin and graceful, a tub full of laundry on her head, I realize that there is more knowledge and skill beneath her playfulness than I could ever know.

Behind the field where the bull was slaughtered lies Podor's cemetery. There are no gravestones; Demba says the ground belongs to no one. Yet some family members have left tokens of recognition: a piece of wood, an old sewing machine, a dead car battery.

As evening falls, the streets of Podor vibrate with festivity. The sound of tom-toms is everywhere, and singing children come by with gourds, which Demba's wife fills with couscous. Demba sits in the perennially patched garden chair that his Czech employer gave him back in 1956, and shakes his head in disgruntlement: in his day, children sang Islamic songs at *tamkharit*. Now they sing whatever comes to mind – first Pulaar, then Wolof, and that blasted tom-tom music never stops!

At first the yard is full of 'television subscribers', as Amadou calls them, but suddenly all the seats are empty. Amadou is nowhere to be found either. "Where did everybody go?" I ask Kao.

"They're out taking the evening air," he smiles knowingly.

"All at the same time? Where are they headed?"

"To the prefecture, if I'm not mistaken."

"What for?"

"To protest, because there are no images on the television."

That Amadou! Kao and I walk outside and run into a group of friends sitting and talking under a streetlight. They pull up a chair for me right away. A few minutes later we're in the midst of a heated discussion about the Berlin Conference, where the groundwork was laid for the division of Africa between the Western nations; about colonial guilt; about the corrupt politicians in this country.

They seem well informed, and quote local writers like Senghor, Sembène Ousmane and Cheikh Hamidou Kane with ease – but what good are literary references in a landscape like theirs? I remember something Adama told me: "Senghor taught his people the importance of culture, but you can't eat culture."

"First we were an underdeveloped country, now we're a country on the road to development," one boy says.

"On the road to underdevelopment, you mean," another one snipes.

"It's all because of the French," someone sighs, "they exploited us. They always said: 'Belly full, happy Negro.' "

Kao, who's sitting next to me in the sand, jumps to his feet: "No, it's our own fault!" The discussion becomes so heated that someone calls for order. Great hilarity ensues when, in the heat of battle, Kao puts up his hand like a schoolboy and calls out: *"Monsieur, monsieur!"*

These are the young people François was talking about. They live beyond the city lights, but that only makes them more painfully aware of their predicament. There's no future for them in Podor, they fear; but at the same time they realize that going to France like earlier generations is no longer possible. They'll have to make do with what they have. "But not with the government we've got now," Kao says, "not with a government that talks about democracy but pays parliamentarians to applaud for it."

A group of silhouettes comes walking towards us in silence. It's Amadou and his television subscribers, back from their march on the prefecture. Amadou launches into a tirade against the stick-in-the-muds here on the corner: why didn't they come along? Don't they care about television images? The group walks away defiantly, full of the importance of their mission. As I watch them go, I have the feeling that although I might be far from where the world turns, at the same time I'm right in the midst of it.

30 June – Five minutes after I come out of the shower, Demba strolls into my room with his folding chair and installs himself pontifically. How can I make it clear to him that I need some time for myself in the morning? He was up at six, and has been waiting for my door to open ever since. As pleasant as I find my warm nest, this is a bit too much. I perch uneasily on the edge of the bed, wearing a wrinkled T-shirt, *pagne* tied around my waist. But Demba doesn't even notice my discomfort.

Mammie brings me breakfast. Ice water, fruit-juice, Nescafé – my wish is her command. This is how you get spoiled! Talking cheerfully the whole time, Demba watches to make sure I eat enough.

Once Demba has left – it's time for him to go to the mosque again, there's a lot of praying going on around here! – Amadou comes into the room and says with a mysterious smile: "Did you know I almost touched your hand last night?"

We sleep in adjacent rooms, so for a moment I'm confused. As it turns out, the wooden shutters in my room were banging away so loudly during the night that Amadou went outside to fasten them. Just as he was standing there with a hammer and nail, I suddenly stuck my hand out the window to close them!

"That must have made you jump," I say.

"Not too badly, at least I knew it was your hand. But imagine if *you'd* suddenly felt a hand, you would have jumped!"

I like his humor. He reminds me of the Zaïrians I know. "Zaïre or Senegal – when you get below the surface you find it's all Africa," François told me. I thought he was only saying it to console me, but maybe he was right.

A skinny Peul comes by to pick up the goats that had spent the night in one of the sheds. Demba begins a melodious conversation with him. "What were you talking about?" I ask him once the shepherd has left. Demba does his best to translate. "How are you? And how's the family? And the herds?" If he had been talking to a Toucouleur, he would probably have asked how the crops were doing. People are always asking me questions too: "How's it going? And how was your trip? Not too tiring, I hope? How are you holding out in the heat here in Podor? Don't you mind the dust?"

It is pretty damned hot and dusty, but I notice that the others are bothered by it just as much. During the day, everyone stays under the roofed-in part of the courtyard. Demba's wife tears cardboard boxes into strips and leaves them to soak in a bowl of water. It's feed for the goats. Kao claims there are vitamins in it: the animals in Mauritania eat nothing else, and they're nice and plump.

François obviously felt the most affinity with Demba, the *pater familias* trying to pass his values to his children. But my gaze is drawn irresistibly to the young people.

Marie-Thérèse is always coming into my room, nosing through my things, asking whether she can comb my hair. I think she's the only one of the girls who still goes to school; the other two take sewing lessons from the nuns. They knit old-fashioned baby smocks that seem better suited to a cold climate. These are international nun patterns – I saw them in Zaïre as well.

Amadou comes back from the post office with the latest issue of the satirical weekly *Le Cafard Libéré* ('The Liberated Cockroach'). He has a subscription to this Senegalese equivalent of the French *Le Canard Enchaîné*. Later I see him heading off on his bike, the magazine tucked under his carrier straps. He's taking it to the next reader. *Le Cafard Libéré* is his contact with the outside world, and his letters about television images in Podor have made the opinion page on a number of occasions.

He keeps records of his battle. When he offers to show me his archives, I follow him to his room. On the threshold, I hesitate for a moment. This is his private territory; something of the tragedy

45

he told me about a few nights ago may lie hidden here. But he calls me to come in. A bed under mosquito netting, a table piled high with papers, a picture of a young woman on the wall.

"Is that . . . ?"

He smiles, takes down the photo and hands it to me. A shy-looking girl, swaddled like a mummy – the picture was taken on their wedding day. "No one understands why I keep that picture on the wall," he says, "but I see no reason to take it down."

My eye is drawn to a poster of Thomas Sankara, the president of Burkina Faso who was murdered by rebel officers in 1987. Sankara is a big hero to young Africans: he preached frugality, made his cabinet ministers fly economy class, propagated the bicycle as means of transport.

"There's a politician after my own heart," Amadou says, "he set a good example. Not like the politicians here, who say we should buy Senegalese, but do their own shopping in Paris." So many Africans live in mud huts and dream of owning a car! In Podor they laugh at Amadou because he rides a bicycle, but he can't afford anything else.

His archives include more than just his letters to *Le Cafard Libéré*. Every year he sends a New Year's greeting to Radio Télévision Sénégalaise, in which he bombards them with questions like: Why is it that Podor enjoys the best television reception in the month of June? Why is there a second Senegalese channel when the first one isn't even nation-wide? He's even written to President Abdou Diouf. Years ago, when the president visited Podor, Amadou and his friends stood at the front of the crowd holding a banner that read: *RTS, Radio Télévision Sénégalaise, Rien Tous les Soirs!* – Nothing Every Night.

Amadou flips through his files. "I'm not in a position to travel like others do," he says; "the television is the only way I get to see something of the world."

This evening the winds are favorable, so I decide to sit down and watch for once. I don't tough it out for long, though. What a hodge-podge! First half an hour of Islamic wailing, then some second-rate American series with skyscrapers and screeching tires, followed by a Brazilian soap opera. I sneak a look at the little boys sitting with their bare feet in the sand: they're glued hungrily to the set, dreaming themselves away from this dusty yard.

"What would Sankara have to say about this?" I ask Amadou.

He grins. "As long as we get pictures, we don't complain. We make do with what we've got."

It strikes me that this crowd does a lot of coughing, sniffling and panting: the dust in Podor gets to everyone. Later on, when the sound goes out, Amadou comments: "An asthmatic can live with it, but imagine if you had a heart condition!"

3 July – Despite the incredible heat, I've succeeded in coming down with a bad cold. Now I walk around sniffling like everyone else. Aminata went to a marabout to have him cure her asthma. He gave her a prescription: she's to pound cola nuts to a paste and boil them with sorghum above a fire of leaves. Amadou turns up his nose when he hears about it. He has no faith in marabouts: they're all charlatans as far as he's concerned.

Tomorrow I'm going back to Dakar, and I spend my last day in Podor with Amadou. This afternoon he's working at the mission library, which is open three days a week. It's just a dusty hole in the wall, with books stacked every which way on the shelves, but Amadou sits there like a king. The books are in such miserable shape – so 'tired', as Amadou puts it – that he has to glue and tape up every one that's checked out, which he does conscientiously. There's lots of French classics, and some African literature too. The books are from the French embassy in Dakar, but nothing new has come in since 1989.

The doors are left wide open; a gentle breeze blows in off the river. Amadou is in his element. He chides a boy for failing to return two of his copies of *Le Cafard Libéré*, sits thumbing through back issues of *Jeune Afrique* and recruits passers-by for an upcoming demonstration on the square in front of the prefecture.

After work he fills the birdbaths in the mission courtyard, locks the doors behind him and walks over to the nuns' quarters;

he's keeping an eye on them while the nuns are away. He uses the garden hose to water the orange trees, feeds the cat, jots down the temperature on a calendar on the wall. I poke around inquisitively. The table in the living room is covered with packages – probably Dutch wool for knitting little vests. There are rinsed margarine tubs on the counter, dental hygiene posters on the wall.

By the time we get back outside, the sun is going down. A marvelous light radiates from the clay houses, blending with the yellow sand in the streets. Green and red lights blip on in the little shops around the market square. Advertisements are hanging everywhere: Coca-Cola's giving scholarships, Nescafé and Schweppes are offering free trips.

At one time most of the shopkeepers here were Mauritanian, Amadou says. They fled after the violence in 1989, and Senegalese merchants have taken their place. The transition hasn't always been smooth. The Mauritanians lived in their shops, they saved all their money and owned only one *boubou*. Many Senegalese shopkeepers went bankrupt; they spent their money so fast they hardly had time to count it.

Dakar, 4 July – On my way back to Dakar in the *taxi-brousse*, I notice that Marie-Thérèse has written in my notebook: *I know that you are going to come back, but until you come back I'm going to be sad.*

When I arrive, François's apartment is dark and empty; his staff have the month off. I nose around in his bookcase, watch a terrible series on television – a sort of Senegalese 'Dallas' with cardboard characters – and think of Amadou. Is he watching too?

Adama has taken the boat back to the Casamance. That means his back must be getting better.

François calls from Paris. He's at his parents' apartment, but they're not home. He slept for three whole days after he arrived: fatigue after the music festival, he claims, but I can imagine other reasons as well. After Dakar, stepping out onto the streets of Paris might not come so easily.

7 July – My last night in Dakar. I go to the kebab stand across the street with Frédérique, an acquaintance of François's. We sit drinking beer at a little Formica table under artificial lighting. I tell Frédérique about *Coup de Torchon*, and describe the opening scene in which Philippe Noiret is sitting under a tree from which black vultures rise ominously. A Senegalese with dreadlocks and a Malcolm X T-shirt overhears the word 'vultures', nudges his friend and says at the top of his voice that I'm claiming vultures walk around the streets of Senegal.

I refuse to take that lying down, and we get into a terrible row. "Don't tell me about Europeans," he sniffs. "Amsterdam, Paris, Milan, I've been everywhere, I know what goes on in your minds." I feel offended, powerless, angry: life in the courtyard in Podor is still so close – how dare he deny me any understanding of this world, just because he's black and I'm white!

I walk out in a huff. It's just the kind of thing you run into in a city like Dakar. Frédérique calms me down, takes me by the arm and grins: "What do you think he was doing in the West? I'll bet he was dealing drugs."

While I'm packing my suitcase I think back to the last moments in Podor. Demba, Aminata, Amadou, Marie-Thérèse – they were all sitting around me. It's such a fine way to say good-bye. They do the same thing with sick people: they sit with them. Aminata said everyone would be sad when I left.

Amadou was a bit subdued. As we were standing by the car, he said: "The best thing, of course, would be if the wind was strong enough for you to send us pictures from Holland." It was his way of saying goodbye. I wished I could have done it my way, by putting my arms around him, but they were all standing around us, so I didn't dare.

SIDI BOÎTE

ASS glances at my baggage. "Is that all?" The plastic jerry can I bought yesterday at a Lebanese shop receives a pitying look. "I don't think you'll be needing that. I have lots of water with me."

It's dark and quiet: the city is asleep, the morning still full of desert cold. Sass climbs noiselessly onto the roof of his Toyota jeep and lashes down my suitcase. He's wearing a *hawli*, the light blue shawl that nomads wrap around their faces, the kind tourists sometimes wear when they come out of the desert. For the rest, he's dressed in jeans, sandals and a jacket – no trace of the affected elegance Moors of his class usually exhibit in their sweeping *boubous*. With his dark brown eyes, wavy hair and beard, he looks more like an East Indian.

I threw all my plans overboard after our first meeting. My friends said I was crazy. What was I going to do in the east – wasn't I planning to head south? Hadn't I arranged a ride and letters of introduction; weren't people waiting for me there? Until they heard who I'd be traveling with.

Sass has crossed centuries in his lifetime. He was born in the tent of his nomadic parents, studied in Paris and returned as a sociologist to Nouakchott, the capital of Mauritania, a city that barely existed thirty years ago but has now grown to half a million. It's an odyssey that has left many intellectuals in this borderland between the Arab world and black Africa with complexes and contradictions. But Sass, I noticed right away, was full of irony and self-mockery; he didn't feel the need to defend anything.

All those nomads who build immense villas full of monstrous furniture to compensate for their former stray-dog existence, who lay claims to nobility and bloodlines running back to the Prophet,

53

who fervently believe their mongrel tongue, Hassaniyya, consists of eighty percent classical Arabic – he couldn't help laughing at them. "We still live in the Stone Age around here," he said, "the rest is all veneer, take it from me."

He could easily imagine living in a Western democracy, but the way things were . . . well, he was here. He lived with his French wife in a house with a wall around it. The world he came from began outside his gate, but he remained an outsider – it was often just as foreign to him as it was to me. He preferred to stay home with his books and his thoughts, but sometimes his work forced him to go out. Now he was going east, to visit village schools that had received funding from an international organization. His trip would take him far off the beaten track; he would be spending the night in places with few creature comforts. If I liked, he said, I could go along. That is, if I didn't mind roughing it. He didn't have to ask twice.

At a shantytown we pick up a man in a dirty *boubou* who will take over the driving when Sass gets tired, and be our guide once we've left the asphalt behind. I go to give him the passenger seat, but Sass stops me. "Abdallah sits in the back," he says. Abdallah smiles, exposing a clutter of teeth, then pushes his hunting rifle, blanket, pillow and torn bag into the car, before swinging up onto the backseat himself.

I've heard Mauritanians sing the praises of the Road of Hope, which runs east from Nouakchott and strings together all the cities that lie along it on the way. But no one had told me there were huge holes in it, or that the desert sands nibble at its edges, so that sometimes all you can see is a thin ribbon of asphalt winding off into the distance. Sass cuts back and forth, dodging tall piles of drifting sand, and tells me about a Dane who came up with the brilliant idea of building a wall of sand along the road. The wall itself, however, has grown so frighteningly high and precarious that it's become a cause for widespread concern.

"*Road* of Hope!" Sass laughs mockingly. "More like the *Rut* of Hope!"

We drive into Boutilimit, the first of the cities strung along this eastern cord. Mud houses lie every which way across the landscape, donkeys trot to and fro – in any other country, this would be called a village. But everything's changed since the days when Sass was born here. The old main street which once ran from the prefect's house on the hill to the camel market in the valley has been rudely chopped in two by the asphalt road, and has shifted Boutilimit's axis a full ninety degrees.

Sass's mother lives here. So does his older brother Ahmed, an outspoken atheist who's become a mystic. He's withdrawn from the world and lives in a tent. You often hear such stories in Mauritania: Moors who seemed totally adapted to city life go to live in a tent again, and become well respected. The nomads have a high regard for the wisdom accumulated during travel.

When I ask about his family, Sass shrugs. He hasn't visited his mother in years.

"Why not?"

"It's too complicated." He hesitates for a moment, then says: "I went there once with my wife and our oldest son. My father was still alive then. Everything went wrong. A son isn't supposed to introduce his wife to her father-in-law, someone else has to do that. What's more, she's supposed to wear a veil. My little boy went over to hug my father and was punished for it: in Moorish society, it's not customary for children to take the initiative." His son doesn't speak Hassaniyya and hasn't had a religious upbringing – his little cousins scared him, they said he would burn in hell along with his parents. Sass looks over at me. "And those were only a few of the misunderstandings."

His mother sends him messages saying she'd like to see him and the children, but if he gave in he'd have to renew contacts with other members of the family as well. That means they would come to visit him in return. He doesn't mind so much himself, but his wife won't have it. Right after they moved to Nouakchott, his sister and her husband came with their child and hung around for weeks. It made his wife nervous.

Sass's brothers have all studied abroad as well. "Ever since we cast off the old family rituals, we don't know how to act when we're together," he says. "So we never visit each other – that makes life a lot easier." He and his brothers went to different schools and never really associated with each other during their 'French period'. But he's stunned whenever he hears them speak French: they use the same syntax, have the same vocabulary as him. They're so much alike, it's uncanny.

From the backseat, Abdallah reminds us in rapid Hassaniyya that we mustn't forget to buy bread. We pull over at a rest-stop where buses and bush taxis pick up passengers, and where travelers spend the night in tents. Cigarettes, batteries, lotions and other odds and ends are lying on wooden tables in the hot sun. Little boys carrying trays full of fresh bread on their heads walk back and forth. Abdallah buys five loaves and places them next to him on his dirty blanket with a satisfied air.

There's a gas station a little further down the road. Sass has taken off his jacket and looks like a tourist in his blue batik shirt. The pump attendant, an old man in a dusty *boubou*, glances at him absentmindedly and mumbles: "*Bonjour, monsieur.*" But then he takes a better look and launches into a lively conversation. Sass disappears into the clay hut to pay for the gas, then comes out again, laughing secretively.

"You missed something!" There were slates in one corner of the room, the kind children use to do their dictation in Koran class. The gas station attendant, it seems, is a local marabout who runs a Koran school from his home. He had a visitor, a herdsman who had lost a young camel a few days ago. The gas station attendant-cum-marabout had apparently made a *gris-gris* – an amulet – for him; the shepherd had come by to thank him for helping him find the animal. "But he still haggled as hard as he could," Sass says knowingly. "Because he hurt himself while he was out searching."

The air shimmers above the asphalt. We've left the clay houses behind and tents begin popping up again. "Losing a baby camel is a real disaster," Sass says. "The mother kicks you when you try to milk her. She'll only let you get close when her calf is around."

I look at Sass and think of his study in Nouakchott with the books stacked to the ceiling, most of them in Arabic and, Sass told me, highly indigestible for the lay reader. A relative who died a while ago had written a huge biography of his great-grandfather, a famous marabout. Sass was wrestling his way through it. It was a meticulous and fairly pointless task, he'd said laughingly, and the paths it took him down led him further and further away from life around him.

But he's every bit as interested in modern-day marabouts. "Borges said that theology is a branch of the literature of the fantastic. I agree with him one hundred percent." A freelance marabout recently arose in the Adrar, a region in the center of the country; Sass would like to write about him someday. The man became famous after he discovered a natural well in the desert. He built a village around it, and the neighboring villages were given the names 'Mecca' and 'Medina'. "He created a world of his own, he even built a dam! It was a speculative dam, of course, an act of optimism, an abstraction."

Many of the men from that area worked in the northern industrial town of Zouérat, so there were a lot of unmarried women around. The marabout conjured up a saying by the Prophet to the effect that women need not be ashamed to marry their slaves. "These days, he's a respected senator," Sass grins. With a bit of luck, the gas station attendant in Boutilimit might move on to bigger things as well.

"He seemed to recognize you," I say.

"He thought I was Ahmed. My brother and I look a lot alike, even though he's twenty-five years older than I am." His brother was a cabinet minister before he became a holy man – that's why everyone knows him. "No matter how hard I try to slip the family ties," Sass says with a touch of anguish in his voice, "I can't. They follow me everywhere."

Sass comes from a noble family. His ancestors were scholars who wrote in classical Arabic; his generation was the first to learn French. At first, the Moors' stubbornness and pride kept them from sending their children to French schools. It was a tug-of-war for their memories: the parents were afraid their children would learn more about French history than about their own ancestors. But Sass's great-grandfather was smart; he realized that, in the end, the Moors would lose the struggle against the French.

The tenth of twelve children, Sass always felt he was one too many. In Moorish society, fathers don't bother about their children; that's a woman's job. But his mother had so many – she didn't seem very interested in him either. As soon as he started school, he more or less stopped coming home.

The first Moorish students made life miserable for their French teachers. They were an undisciplined, unruly lot. A pebble in the rice? Reason enough for them to go on strike. Sass still remembers what one of his teachers used to shout: "You're all a bunch of arrogant, emaciated nobodies."

After secondary school he went to the University of Dakar, where once again he became involved in student strikes. After he was expelled, he decided to take a trip around the world. In 1969, Sass caught a boat to Marseille. His original plan was to take off with the scholarship money his brother had arranged for him, but when he arrived in the provincial town of St Etienne, he liked it so much that his trip around the world ended right there.

Later he continued his studies in Paris, where he wore Clarks shoes and an ink-stained green anorak full of holes, became a Maoist and an Althusian like everyone else, and forgot that he came from a prominent nomadic family that had once owned slaves. But when he went camping with his wife in Norway and they entered the forests of the far north, he felt like he was being suffocated: he was a creature of the desert, he was used to broad horizons.

"For thirty years I've been struggling against my nomadic background," he says, "but the older I get, the more it beckons. I'm a nomad, in spite of myself.

"Nomads don't really want to be nomads. The best thing that can happen to them is to find an oasis with water and trees where their animals can graze, so they can stay there. Fear strikes every time they have to leave such a place."

Abdallah interrupts him. In a minute we'll be passing a place where we can drink tea and have breakfast. "These drivers are really set in their ways," Sass says resignedly. He'd rather keep moving, but instead he pulls over meekly in front of the half-open tent Abdallah is pointing to.

We take off our shoes, settle down on thin mats beneath the canvas, drink tea and watch Abdallah wash down his newly purchased bread with gulps of tea. Abdallah is a driver for the organization that's commissioned Sass to do this study. Sass was a bit put out when Abdallah showed up wearing a *boubou*, because long robes are hard to drive in. But he understands: if Abdallah had to sit in the back wearing trousers and a shirt, it would make him look like an apprentice.

Sass hires out his services as a sociologist, jeep and all. "It's a way to stay independent." The jocular smile I'm beginning to recognize appears at the corners of his mouth. "But in fact I hate traveling. And I hate asking questions even more. The sociology of the dunes would suit me much better. Give me a landscape with no people in it!"

Sass is reclining with his back to the others, resting on one elbow, his knees slightly bent. Abdallah and the man who runs the place are watching us from the corner of their eyes. A Moorish man and a Western woman talking and laughing together – it's a strange, perhaps even offensive, sight.

"In the long run, you can do one of two things when you come from a country like this," Sass says, "emigrate or withdraw completely. My wife is afraid I'll do the latter, and become a Saharan monk. That's something that appeals to me. My brother's already set a good example." It's an opposite that attracts him; a possibility, an extreme, even though his wife has sworn she'll never follow him down that road.

His brother's best friend lives in a tent as well, not far from

59

Ahmed. The two of them couldn't care less about the rest of the world, and they don't own a thing. Ahmed's friend is said to be a great writer and sage, a reputation he owes to the one article he's had published, which no one seems to have read, plus the rumor that he's working on a book. He's credited with making the statement that most Moorish nomads are monogamous because their women are too fat for more than one to be taken along with them when they move. Ahmed's friend doesn't have a very high opinion of intellectuals in this part of the world: having learned to read and write, they seem to think they have the right to put forth the fuzziest of opinions. He calls them 'casualties of literacy'.

"I dream of becoming like him," Sass says, "and I'm already making excellent headway: my thesis is every bit as notorious as it is unread. I even suspect my mentor in France of having put it through the washing machine to make it look well thumbed!" His thesis shares all the defects of the old Moorish books he loves to get lost in: it summons up a world of knowledge that serves as its own focal point and leads nowhere. "I was still working on the foreword when, to my horror, I discovered that I'd already written a thousand pages! So I stopped right there."

At the beginning of his trip around the world in 1969, when he crossed the river between Mauritania and Senegal, he was picked up by a Senegalese border patrol. They were used to merchants in dirty *boubous* shuttling back and forth, but who was this long-haired freak? During the night he spent in custody, they became friends. As soon as the *gendarmes* realized he wasn't a smuggler, they started asking him about popular music. After all, anyone with hair as long as his should know all about it. "That's where the misunderstanding concerning my person began," Sass says, "and since then it's only gotten worse."

We must be enervating company for talkative Abdallah, who doesn't understand a word of French. Sometimes he just breaks into our conversation from the backseat. The desert landscape passing by seems a bit monotonous to me, but to Abdallah it's teeming with life. He mentions the old names the nomads gave to the places we pass, recalls a battle between rival tribes fought here in the distant past, quotes a poet who praised the beauty of a particular palm oasis and the quality of its water.

This kind of knowledge has been handed down from generation to generation in the oral nomadic tradition, but it has rapidly lost its significance during the last few decades. When the big drought of 1968 killed all the cattle belonging to Sass's parents, they stopped being nomads. Twenty-five percent of all Mauritanians live in town these days.

Every now and then we stop at a military roadblock, where armed soldiers come sauntering up to the car. Sass hands them a letter from the Ministry of Education; they glance at it, then at us. What are they looking for: guns, contraband? It never becomes clear. Not far south of this road lies the enemy territory of Senegal. To the east, close to the border with Mali, is an area no one ventures into these days; travelers have been robbed or have disappeared. Tuareg rebels or just plain bandits have been blamed, but no one knows who's really responsible.

The sun is high in the sky. Sass would like to drive on to Kiffa, but Abdallah has started talking about a village where we can eat lunch and Sass gives in to his wishes once more. We stop in front of another tent; pieces of sheep and goat are hanging above the entrance, still dripping blood. Through a cloud of flies, people are staring at us from behind the meat.

Hesitantly, I stoop to go in, but Sass stops me. "Wait a minute, Abdallah will find somewhere else for us." A carpet is being rolled out in a cool room – a deserted shop from the looks of it. Abdallah finds pillows for us to lean against, brings me a reed fan to wave away the flies and goes looking for a suitable piece of goat to roast.

"Abdallah seems determined to make us lose a lot of time," Sass sighs.

"Do you think there's a toilet here?"

"Oh, I'm sure there is, but I'm afraid of what you'll find."

Abdallah leads me to a walled-in hole with a rusty car door for an entrance.

"No problem," I say when I come back and find Sass looking apprehensive.

But he doesn't seem convinced. "Don't tell me about Mauritanian toilets!"

≈≈≈

After lunch, Sass lies down on the backseat of the jeep and Abdallah climbs in front. He's folded up his blanket into a cushion and he sits on it, gripping the wheel, his forehead almost touching the windshield. When I say something about this to Sass and get no reply, I turn around and see him lying there like a mummy, his head wrapped in his *hawli* – a larva in a cocoon. How can he breathe through all that cloth? I turn back to the front again, feeling self-conscious and alone for the first time that day.

We pass a *taxi-brousse* parked along the road. Its passengers have all climbed out. The men in their flapping *boubous* kneel in the sand, facing Mecca; at a safe distance, the women too are praying.

By the time we reach Kiffa, Sass has taken the wheel again; Abdallah drives too slowly for his liking. Kiffa has paved roads and brick houses, and a weathered billboard advertising the Hôtel de l'Amitié's spacious rooms and beautiful view. We take Abdallah to the part of town where he'll spend the night. Hunting rifle in hand, he disappears through a gate with a tent behind it – the same kind of wayfarer's pavilion we saw along the highway.

"What's the rifle for?"

Pensively, Sass watches him go. "He says he's going hunting. He hopes to shoot a gazelle."

The Hôtel de l'Amitié is a prefab barrack built around a courtyard with scrawny trees. The rooms are windowless cells with gray iron doors. Sass looks around angrily. "Didn't that billboard downtown say something about a view?"

Two young men were catching the last rays of sun on the steps across from the hotel when we drove up; now they have come into the yard and are watching our every move with undisguised curiosity. Are they guests, or do they work here? After we've taken a shower, they're still there. Their eyes have the dull look of men worn down by loneliness and boredom. "Like prisoners," Sass whispers. While he goes to the kitchen to arrange dinner, I walk over to them.

They're Tunisians, teachers at the technical school here. They get a discount on their rooms at the hotel, and do a few odd jobs in return. One teaches electrical maintenance, the other plumbing. "But Kiffa doesn't have electricity or running water!" they moan. The hotel has a generator that runs for a few hours every evening.

Their story echoes with despair. The schools in Mauritania have been closed for the last few weeks because of the municipal elections. Classes should have started again by now but the students haven't shown up, and so the two men hang around, with nowhere to go. Have I had a good look at Kiffa? The only buildings here worth mentioning date from the French period. "So why don't they take care of them?" the two complain. "They're the only nice things they've got." I think about Tunisia – it's not as though they take such wonderful care of their colonial architecture either! But, seen from here, I can imagine their native country seems like paradise. At first, they weren't able to understand a word of Hassaniyya. They preferred Tunisian – at least it's eighty percent classical Arabic!

In the kitchen, the cook is plucking a chicken for us. To bide time till dinner, Sass asks the Tunisians where we can find Kiffa's bright lights. They point listlessly to the neighborhood behind the hotel.

We head off into the night. "Didn't they say they do odd jobs around the hotel?" Sass asks. "Wouldn't you think they'd repair the leaky faucets and cover up the bare pipes?"

The market's sandy streets are almost deserted. A little boy is sitting on a corner, trying to sell his last loaves of French bread. "The Champs Elysées of Kiffa," Sass says. Being city people who still haven't sloughed off their pace, we walk around quickly.

63

When he's alone, Sass almost never sleeps in a hotel; at nightfall, he usually drives into the desert, parks his car at the bottom of a dune, eats some muesli and crawls into his sleeping bag. That sounds much more appealing to me, but how can I make that clear to him?

≈≈≈

When we pick up Abdallah the next morning, he's in excellent spirits. He hasn't shot a gazelle, but he did run into a fellow tribesman. They spent the evening together. The world has exploded, he says, tribes live scattered all across the country.

"Does he regret that?"

Sass smiles. "No, I don't think so; in fact, his genealogy is his calling card. On the road, it's like a secret password." Moorish society is one of castes: Abdallah belongs to the class which traditionally serves the nobility. He's from around Boutilimit, but his own family has moved to the area where we're headed. Sass suspects that Abdallah's father was ostracized by his tribe for some reason and had to seek his fortune elsewhere – that happens pretty often.

We turn off the Road of Hope and drive north along a faint track through the desert. Not far from here, close to the town of Tamchekket, is where Sass is going to do his fieldwork. Abdallah knows the area well, and begins coloring in the landscape: there's the *wadi* where a lovely little stream runs in winter; that village over there is the home of one of the instigators of the 1978 coup.

Out of nowhere, a man suddenly dashes out onto the road, waving his arms. His baggage, a bundle of lashed-together odds and ends, is lying beneath a bush. Sass pretends not to see him, and keeps driving; he reacted the same way yesterday when drivers with car trouble tried to attract our attention. He never pulls over, unless there's been an accident; but when we meet a jeep coming from the opposite direction, he stops it to ask about the road up ahead. Abdallah peers into the other vehicle, searching for a familiar face.

"Do you smell the acacias?" We've stopped under a tree with yellow blossoms. I stick my nose out the window, then shake my head. Sass climbs out, pulls down a branch and hands me a couple of flowers. They have a faint, sweet aroma. Now I can pinpoint the smell that's been in the air for a while. "Sorry," Sass says, "I forgot – you're used to stronger odors. The desert is more sparing." His boyhood, he recalls, was marked by the smell of acacias.

Abdallah hands me a fistful of orange jujube berries he's gathered from under a tree. The peel is hard, the fruit tangy. "It grows on you," Sass says, "we always chewed on them when we were kids."

Abdallah's wife and children live close to here. It's hard for me to imagine people living in these surroundings. Sass tries to avoid paying a visit, but Abdallah insists, and guides us expertly to a point where we suddenly see a tent in the distance.

"They're going to be shocked," Sass warns.

"Because I'm with you?"

"No, because of me!" We wait until Abdallah has greeted his family and an old man walks over to us, beckoning in welcome. Moors greet each other at length, but Sass makes do with a few token courtesies.

Women and children are lying on reed mats inside the tent; they make room for me excitedly. Sass sits on the ground with the men, and I notice that his body is tense. I'm beginning to realize what he meant when he said he couldn't escape his background: here sits a sociologist with his driver, but at the same time he is a man from a prominent family with a man from a lower caste. No matter how hard Sass tries to carry out his research the way he learned in France, his surroundings keep forcing him back into his traditional role.

Sass's father was a typical Moorish aristocrat: he never thought about the future, and was completely indifferent to material things. He once gave his last goat to a passing *griotte* – a woman of the caste of *griots* who sing the history and heroic deeds of noble families. He tried to do good, and gained prestige in return, but didn't hesitate to ask his serfs for animals he could milk.

His father's slaves were freed when Sass was quite young, but they continue to make claims on the family. Sass's brothers have hired a few as drivers, and others still come by to ask if Sass has any work for them. He keeps his distance: he eats pork, drinks alcohol and doesn't pray – he wouldn't want his godlessness and disobedience to the laws of his tribe to become common knowledge. He slips them a little money now and then, just to be rid of them.

One of Abdallah's elderly uncles has unfolded a piece of yellowed paper: a poem for the Prophet written by one of his late relatives. While he reads it aloud to Sass, the women examine my hands and feet and offer to dye them with henna. Abdallah goes to look for a goat to slaughter.

But Sass doesn't want to eat here. Once the old uncle has read his poem and the ritual three glasses of tea are finished, he stands up resolutely. Abdallah pulls himself away reluctantly, and all the way to Tamchekket he sits in the backseat sulking.

※※※

I thought we'd left the civilized world behind in Kiffa, but Tamchekket is a cozy little mountain town with cupolas and gentle contours that make the ocher-colored houses look like sand castles. A strong wind is blowing, and here and there the yellow is broken by a stooped figure in a blue *boubou* scuttling along close to the houses. White and yellow banners wave from the buildings.

It takes me a while to figure out why it feels like we're driving onto a movie set. Sass looks around too, a bit lost. "It's pretty dead around here, isn't it?" We pass one car, a jeep tightly packaged in an army-green wrapping. "Well, look at that," Sass grins. "Christo's been here."

Only a few wooden stands at the market are still occupied, and the saleswomen look at us inquisitively. Abdallah knows a lot of people in Tamchekket; he's been 'naturalized', as Sass puts it, into one of the local tribes. From here on, Sass sighs, it will be a circus of favors and counter-favors.

We stop in front of a walled house with a wooden gate banging in the wind. The courtyard is deserted, but Abdallah goes looking for the owner. A little later the guest room has been swept clean, carpets rolled out, cushions produced and a young boy in the corner is stoking coals for tea.

Our host is the local town clerk. He speaks fluent French and flutters around us with theatrical gestures. Sass watches him out of the corner of his eye.

"*Asalaam alaykum!*"

"*Wa alaykum as-salaam!*"

A big man has walked into the yard. "The mayor of Tamchekket," our host whispers. The mayor kicks off his slippers and steps into the room. "*Ayak labass?*"

"*Labass . . .*"

This time Sass can't avoid the ritual greetings that fill the air with a pleasant buzzing. *Peace be with you. And with you. No trouble, I hope? No, no trouble. Everything fine? Everything is just fine. Allah be praised. Any news? Only good news. Allah be praised. How are things? Not bad.*

They scan each other's pasts thoroughly, in search of common acquaintances. Things become uneasy when it turns out that one of the mayor's cousins was executed thirty years ago on orders from Sass's brother Ahmed, but the air clears when other dignitaries from Tamchekket arrive to pay their respects as well. They sit down beside the guest from the capital, slurp tea, play with their toes and are soon lying together in a clump, casually using each other as pillows.

Our host tells a story about Bujadrah and the dragon, a long, drawn-out tale in which kings and women are the great villains. Sass is only half-listening – he tells me that the man is mixing up all kinds of legends.

Lazy from the heat, the singsong voices and the charm of this place, I look out through the open door. The sky above the ocher-yellow houses is a clear blue. The wooden door at the far end of the yard squeaks open. A man in a blue *boubou* crackling with starch comes towards us, tossing the wide sleeves of his robe over his shoulders. I suddenly understand why nomads wear such exuberant blue – it's the reflection of the sky in the monotony of sand.

The men tell us why it's so deathly silent in Tamchekket. During the municipal elections a few days ago, the two rival parties came to blows and the winners pelted the losers with glowing coals. Since then the atmosphere has been so tense that most of the inhabitants have fled to oases in the surrounding countryside. Some of them are bold enough to return to town during the day, but when evening comes they take to their heels.

Our visitors belong to the winning party, and they do their best to convince Sass that they're in the right. I enjoy the change that comes over him in the company of Moors. He listens, asks questions, occasionally says "Aha," and encourages them to go on by making a clucking noise at the back of his throat.

He tosses me knowing looks the whole time, translating the occasional phrase or directing my gaze discreetly to the teaboy, who turns out to be wearing a pistol in his belt. Sass puts on his half-glasses – his 'old man glasses', as he calls them – and jots down a few notes in a big exercise book. This political wrangling doesn't have much to do with his study of the village schools, but in his experience everything is related around these parts.

When a big platter of meat is put on the floor, everyone crowds around it. Abdallah cuts off the tastiest morsels and tosses them in our direction, but Sass barely eats. A Moorish aristocrat is supposed to remain aloof – the choicest cuts of meat are set aside for him, but he must show no interest in them.

***

Abdallah is sitting peevishly in the back of the jeep. This morning we pulled him away from his wife and children; now, just when he was about to arrange a few things in Tamchekket, Sass decides it's time to start visiting the local schools!

We drive even deeper into the desert. There are almost no roads – cars don't come here often – but amazingly enough we see another little outpost pop up on the horizon. Hearing the jeep, an old man comes outside. In one corner of his humble one-room dwelling lie a copy of the Koran with a pair of spectacles next to it, a transistor radio, a half-open bag of clothes and a pile of torn books. The rest of the room is empty. But not for long: old men with weather-beaten faces soon come shuffling in from all directions.

I'd been wondering how Sass's brother Ahmed, the former cabinet minister, could ever go back to living in a tent. The answer is right here in this room; the old man sitting in front of us was once a cabinet minister himself. Now he's the mayor and administrator of the municipal coffers, which were fattened last year with an international loan for a new school building.

Sass dons his spectacles and pulls out his big exercise book. He works his way through a list of questions, carefully jotting down the answers. He writes with a fountain pen – a ballpoint wouldn't work around here, because within a few seconds the paper is covered with a fine layer of sand.

The old men look on, accompanying his writing with a murmur that's punctuated regularly by the words '*Alhamdu lillah*,' Allah be praised. The mayor's answers don't amount to much, Sass tells me later, but he doesn't dare push him too hard. It would be thoroughly improper for him to say to this respectable old man: "How about showing me these invoices you keep talking about?"

Everyone gets up and goes outside. Some of the men drop down in the sand and start praying, while the others wait patiently. Part of the village belongs to a Muslim sect that believes in praying at unorthodox times. Ten minutes one way or the other – in a remote place like this, that's enough to create a schism. Sass smiles mysteriously. We've arrived in his favorite territory: the fields of heresy.

When he first started traveling as a sociologist, he always feared those moments when everyone started to pray. He could get out of it once, maybe even twice, but the third time people would start to wonder. Mauritania is one hundred percent Muslim; there are no unbelievers here. The first time he prayed along with the rest, he felt like a terrible hypocrite, but the next time wasn't so hard. Since then he falls to the ground without a second thought, like everyone else. He can see how his brother went from fervent atheism to mysticism: if you want to live among these people, you have to adapt to their customs or be an outcast. He wonders how long it will be before he starts feeling like them. It would solve a lot of his problems.

The men rise and use their *hawlis* to wipe the sand from their foreheads. Then the procession heads towards a rectangular construction with wooden shutters on the edge of the village: the new school. The principal, a fiery-eyed man with a heavy beard, leads the way. He's the head of the Muslim sect with the peculiar praying times, Sass whispers.

One of the two classrooms is opened for our inspection. The table at the front is covered in a thick layer of dust: school hasn't started again here either. Scattered everywhere are dirty rugs, pieces of cardboard and scraps of paper – apparently the children sit on the floor. There's a cane leaning against the wall. In the semi-darkness, my gaze crosses that of the principal. His eyes flash meanly. That's right, he says laughingly to Sass, she understands what the cane's for.

His inspection completed, Sass closes his notebook, shakes hands all round and climbs back into the jeep. If we hurry, we can visit the next school before dark. We race off, half the village gaping after us.

About a kilometer down the road, Sass suddenly pricks up his ears. "Do you hear that?" I listen, but notice nothing out of the ordinary. He tries to shift gears, then frowns. The transmission is too stiff. It could be the four-wheel drive – he's had problems with it in the past – and before I realize what's happening, we've turned around.

"Where are we going?"

"Back to Tamchekket – I can't afford to have the car break down on a deserted road like this."

Abdallah leans forward from the backseat and he and Sass become entangled in a heated discussion.

"Can't he take a look at it?"

Sass laughs. "Him? He knows even less about cars than I do!"

Abdallah keeps on talking. Amid the flow of words, the name Sidi Boîte bobs repeatedly to the surface. Sidi Boîte is a mechanic in Tamchekket who owes his name to his phenomenal knowledge of the *boîte de vitesses*, the gearbox. Mister Box will solve our problem in no time flat, Abdallah assures us.

When we arrive back in Tamchekket, our host, the town clerk, is about to leave for his camp in the oasis. With a sweeping gesture, he tell us the house is ours. Sass asks about Sidi Boîte. Of course he knows him, but he doesn't think he's in town at the moment. In fact, a messenger has already been sent to fetch him; someone else with car trouble is looking for him too. I recall the wrapped-up jeep we saw on our way in. Could that be the someone he's talking about?

Sass clambers onto the roof of the jeep and starts unloading our things. We lie two mattresses across from each other in the big yard to make a sitting area. Dates, oranges, milk, drinking water – we'll survive for the time being.

"Where's Abdallah?"

Sass gestures vaguely. "He'll probably sleep down at the oasis with the others."

A cool wind blows through the yard as dusk approaches. Shivering, we pull on our coats. "I hope Sidi Boîte really exists, and that he actually knows something about cars," Sass says. He sounds worried. The Toyota has to be in perfect condition; the terrain we'll be crossing in the next few days gets rougher all the time.

This is the first time we've been alone together, and for a moment we're uneasy in each other's company. I don't think I'd mind so much if we got stuck here, but it's clear that Sass feels differently. "Well, there isn't anything we can do tonight." He lies down on his back and clasps his hands behind his head. As darkness settles in, only his *hawli* still catches the light.

"Did you know that Abdallah started going on about his wife and children again on the way back? He didn't say it in so many words, but I know what he's thinking: by failing to respect their hospitality, we've called down a curse upon ourselves."

"You're kidding."

"Didn't I tell you we live in the Stone Age around here?"

The sky is full of twinkling stars. I find the Big Dipper right away, but don't get much further than that. I think back to the lunch I had at the Paris offices of *Le Nouvel Observateur* just before I left for Africa. Someone was talking about stars and they asked another person at the table to name their favorite constellation. I laughed to myself about it at the time, but now that I'm lying here and the heavens are open above me like a book full of letters I can't read, I regret my ignorance.

"*Le Nouvel Observateur* – we used to call that the Club Med of French culture," Sass comments dryly.

I'm amazed, as I've often been in the last few days. Sass was obviously no outsider when he lived in France. The cultural obstacles he must have encountered! He seems to have taken them with such ease. When I say something about it, he laughs. "I'd read Racine and Corneille, so I wasn't out of my element at all when I arrived. On the contrary, I felt like I knew everything, that there was nothing left for me to discover. It was all so familiar, it made me despair!"

In St Etienne he became the darling of the leading citizens, and soon after he moved to Paris he met his wife. They lived in an apartment building full of elderly ladies who often complained to him about the foreigners living in the neighborhood. "As though I weren't a foreigner myself! But they seemed to forget that. I still haven't worked out why. Maybe because my French was so good, perhaps that made them feel less of a difference."

Last year, when he went back to France for the first time in ages, he heard a Frenchman scolding an Arab in the metro. "I almost had to agree with him," he says hesitantly.

"Why?"

"It's so easy for me to imagine what a Frenchman could have

against an Arab." Sass is quiet for a moment, and then says: "On the whole, the people here are ten times more racist than the average Frenchman. Towards Westerners, but also among themselves. Just look around: this place is full of prejudices against Christians, slaves, blacks."

He'd originally planned to write his thesis on the image of the Moor in French literature, but he was afraid it would turn into an exercise in self-justification. So he settled for a study of precolonial Mauritania, from the eleventh to the nineteenth century. While working on it, he discovered how little had changed since then, how light the French colonizers' footsteps had actually been across this landscape.

He used to think that Mauritania was on its way to becoming a modern country. When he was still at school, the students ridiculed the Arabic teacher: the language of the future was French. But when the great drought came and the nomads began leading sedentary lives, they too began to send their children to school *en masse*. The new students had only been educated in the Koran; French was something so remote, it seemed more logical to teach them in Arabic. This resulted in a much greater role for Islam, and in the entire society's return to the past, to a time when the West was seen as a threat.

High above us, the biggest star of all suddenly swerves to the right in a huge arc. Could it be a satellite? Sass sees it too: "They're watching us up there," he says. "They're keeping an eye on us."

"How much do you know about the stars?"

"Nothing. No more than I do about cars." He laughs. "As you can tell by now, I'm totally unsuited to be a sociologist of the dunes. I should at least be a Sidi Boîte who knows everything about the insides of a four-wheel-drive Toyota, as well as a bit about the stars for nights like this!"

He's the kind of person who never finishes anything, he admits. "I make a hole in the sand, get tired of digging, and start again a little further along. With me, everything runs dry like a *wadi*. I'm a born dilettante, a parasite: I can't come up with anything on my own, and wind myself around existing structures like a climbing vine."

There's a pattern to these self-critical sketches, I realize. He means what he says, but still – coming from him it sounds almost like coquetry.

Darkness has fallen. The tree under which they roasted the goat this afternoon has turned into a giant, ominous bird with wings spread. I can hear Sass grumbling. He's trying to light a candle, but it keeps going out. "What time is it anyway?" He clicks on his flashlight. "Barely eight o'clock. Shall we go for a walk?"

We sneak into the quiet town. Not everyone has left, and there are little lights dancing here and there. Could that be the vigilante committee the men were talking about earlier? Sass is afraid to turn on his flashlight; next thing you know, they'll start shooting at us.

We pad along, sticking close to the walls around the yards. When we stop for a moment I think I see a roof swaying back and forth, and hear a slight flapping. "Hey, it looks like the houses are moving."

"They are."

Some of the nomads live in a cross between a tent and a house: they lash canvas between the walls in lieu of a roof, so they can open and close it at will.

On the edge of town the ground begins to slope. I take one step at a time, unsure of my footing, envying Sass's ability to see in the dark. I wish I could take his hand, but I don't dare. We walk down the path until the last house is behind us and the wind is blowing freely in our faces. The oasis of Tamchekket lies below; between the palms we see the campfires burning, the fearful townspeople sitting around them. Our host must be well into his endless repertoire of stories by now.

Muffled voices are coming from the house behind us. It's a man and a woman, probably in bed already, under the canvas that serves as their roof. Why did they stay in town – aren't they afraid? And what could they be talking about on a night like this?

"Can you hear what they're saying?"

Sass listens. "They're talking about their animals." He doesn't sound particularly interested.

"Come on, keep trying."

He does his best to tune in to the intimate chatting. "He's asking her if she remembers the night they lost the little black goat."

I could stay here for hours, eavesdropping on this nocturnal conversation, but the voices keep getting softer – no matter how Sass tries, he can't pick up anything else worth repeating.

Our house isn't hard to find; it's the only one with a white Toyota parked in front of it. Inside, we make our preparations for the night. As I'm crawling into my sleeping bag I see that Sass has put on a blue *boubou*.

"So you *are* a real Moor, after all."

"I wear this to make sure I have Saharan dreams." His voice sounds theatrical, like the creaking, ironic stage voice of an actor in an old French movie.

"You poke fun at everything."

"It's the only way to beat others to the punch, before they start poking fun at me."

In the morning when I wake, Sass is sitting upright in his sleeping bag reading, his half-glasses down on the tip of his nose, the water already on the burner. Just as we've finished straightening up the room, our host comes striding into the yard.

"Well, if it isn't the weaver of legends," Sass mumbles into his steaming cup of coffee. "What insights might he have for us today?"

Our host remains standing in the doorway, arms held wide, and calls out in a resonant voice: "Did you know I'm the head of pluviometry in Tamchekket?" I was prepared for anything, but not this. He beams at me. "Come with me!" I follow him into the yard, where he shows me a rudimentary rain gauge: a pole with a bucket on top. He carefully lifts the cover off the bucket; there are holes in the lid to let the rain through. "See, when it rains I have to measure the water and pass the information along to the head office in Nouakchott." He hesitates for a moment. "At least, if the radio's working." He gets one thousand *ouguiya* – seven dollars – a month for his services. "Every month, you understand. Even if it doesn't rain!" he gloats. *Even if it doesn't rain!* That's a good one. I'll have to tell Sass – it'll cheer him up.

Here comes Abdallah, looking like he's had a rough night. His *boubou* is wrinkled, his hair mussed, but he's in fine spirits. Being among his own obviously does him good.

The guest room is humming. They're all sitting around Sass, and the name Sidi Boîte is on everyone's lips. The teaboy comes in, followed by the woman who roasted the goat for us yesterday. We're starting to become quite settled here.

Sass catches my eye and laughs tiredly. "The plot is thickening." Sidi Boîte hasn't shown up, nor has the messenger who was sent to find him; a car will have to go and pick him up. The townspeople have a car, but it's out of gas. If Sass wouldn't mind them taking some of his . . . "I don't mind, but now it turns out no one knows where the driver is!" Sass gets up. "Shall we go for a walk? There's nothing we can do anyway, not for the time being."

As soon as we get outside, he begins spluttering. Abdallah has been singing the praises of his adopted tribe for the last half-hour. During the elections, his family came in from the desert with twelve camels to support the party that finally won. They were given a rousing reception that lasted three days, and look how generously we've been received! "As if that's what we came for! I just wish they'd help us get out of here!" Sass scuffs his sandals in the sand. "It must be *mektoub*, fate, don't you think? I'm afraid we can't do anything about it."

The white and yellow flags on the houses have lost their innocence: they show which camp the inhabitants belong to. All over the country, the campaign propaganda has been taken down, but here it's been left hanging as a sign that the battle still rages.

We walk past the gift-wrapped car, looking so much a fixture that it's hard to imagine it will ever run again. Our Toyota, I just noticed, also looks like it's becoming part of the landscape.

At the door to one of the little shops, a man is lying on a carpet, peering outside. He raises his hand in greeting.

"Who's that?"

"Don't you recognize him? It's the mayor. That's his lookout post."

We follow the path we took last night, and soon the enchanting oasis is lying at our feet. At the pond near the edge of the palm grove, nomads are bringing their camels, cows and goats down to drink – it's a scene straight out of the Bible.

"Shall we go down there?"

Sass nods. When we get close, he sniffs the air loudly. "Camel piss." He likes the smell, it reminds him of his childhood. He was five when he began to herd his parents' animals. Later, during the school vacations, he would go into the desert with the camels to let them graze. At night he would tether the animals to keep them from running away. One morning he woke up to discover that one of them was missing. It was the season when the desert bloomed, a time when camels can sense water and greenery from far off, and make a beeline for it. "I never got that camel back. I was traumatized for years."

We're close to the watering camels now, and I try to locate the smell Sass was talking about – all I can pick up is the diffuse odor of a zoo.

"That story about the runaway camel is true, but you realize I've blown it up a bit over the years," Sass says as we head back to the house. "Casting myself in the role of herdsman makes me sound pretty exotic."

"You don't have to make yourself sound more exotic for my sake, do you?"

"Force of habit, I'm afraid. I know how it sounds when I tell it. I'm aware of its effect." But those days are so far behind him, the herding of camels belongs to such a different life, it's as if he's talking about someone else.

I'm starting to get used to those two people inside him. It's like

77

the narrator's voice dubbed over his own: at first I was startled by it, almost offended, but now I know it's a part of him, and I sometimes wait in secret for it to appear.

When we get back to the house, they still haven't found the driver. As the morning wears on, the name Sidi Boîte assumes increasingly mythic proportions. The more we talk about him, the harder it is for me to believe that this roaming miracle man will ever find his way to this insignificant corner of the globe.

Then Abdallah comes up with a suggestion: why don't we go back to Kiffa? We'd have a much better chance of finding a Sidi Boîte there. If we leave this afternoon, we can spend the night with his family and go on in the morning.

Sass hesitates. Wouldn't it be better to wait? Maybe Sidi Boîte really will come along. But after the midday meal, as everyone prepares for the siesta and the coming hours loom in all their lethargy, he gets up and says: "Let's give it a try. Anything's better than wasting away around here."

It's great to be back on the road again, racing over hills and watching landscapes shift outside the window. Sass is making up for lost time. "We could easily drive on to Kiffa," I say, "at this rate we'd be there before dark." After our eccentric host in Tamchekket, the two Tunisians at the Hôtel de l'Amitié seem like paragons of cosmopolitan society.

"That's right, we could." Sass nods discreetly towards the backseat. "But I'm afraid I can't refuse his request. Then we'd really be 'maraboutized' – hexed!"

"I'm surprised at you."

"Why?"

"For doing this. For letting him push you around."

Sass shrugs. "I'm hounded by the guilt feelings of my class."

I dread spending the night in a crowded tent with Abdallah's family. As it turns out, however, Sass has no such intention. "I suggest we camp out in the desert," he says. "That is, if you don't mind."

Before dropping Abdallah close to his family's tent, Sass tells him where he can find us in the morning. Disconcerted, Abdallah remains standing at the jeep's open window. Should he have his wife bring us some food? Sass shakes his head. "No, no, we have everything we need." When Abdallah and his hunting rifle finally disappear over the hill, we both breathe a sigh of relief.

Sass turns the car around, drives into the desert and parks at the foot of a dune. I kick off my shoes and climb to the top. There's not a living soul as far as the eye can see. I'm glad he's brought me here, but I feel a bit uncomfortable at the same time, like last night in the yard in Tamchekket. He's usually alone in these kinds of places. More than ever before, I'm on his turf.

Sass has climbed onto the roof of the jeep and tossed down the mattresses. The sky isn't as clear as it was yesterday; we'll have to find a place out of the wind, for there could be a sandstorm coming tonight.

"These aren't really the dunes I like best," Sass says, looking around critically. "Too many camels come here; it's still too close to town."

"Thus spoke the city dweller."

"You're right," he smiles apologetically. "I'd like to be sedentary, but I'm not. I'm fundamentally at odds with myself."

He wraps himself in his sleeping bag to ward off the evening chill and peers out across the dunes. "I feel a bit like the main character in Flaubert's *L'éducation sentimentale*," he says. "He stands on the barricades, takes part in everything that happens, but doesn't really have much of an idea where he's headed."

An American research center recently tried to commission Sass to work on a study about slavery. He didn't like the terms of the contract: he had the impression they were trying to buy him outright, and he wouldn't stand for that. "I prefer to sell myself off in parcels, like a shopkeeper." Besides, he wonders whether he'd be worth much if he sold himself in a single go.

A lot of people in Nouakchott labor under the impression that he has an opinion worth listening to on any number of subjects. He's been asked to sit on more advisory committees than he can remember. He always says he has nothing to teach anyone. He's barely taught his children anything, because he doesn't know what to think himself.

"I don't want to build up anything – I don't want to provide for my old age, I don't want to think about my children's future." He traces his finger absentmindedly in the sand. "But I also know how unrealistic it is for me to want to leave cars, computers and machines behind and go back to living in a tent. I'm too alienated from my old social setting to ever do that. My desire for knowledge has made me lose my ability to deal spontaneously with the people around me. I feel like a spy when I'm with them; my role has something decadent about it."

Moors who hear him speak French think he's a foreigner. They're amazed to discover that he not only speaks Hassaniyya, but has also studied the old texts and knows a lot about the issues they discuss: the gender of angels, the hours of prayer, the precise moment that Ramadan begins. "It's an Aristotelian style of discourse, very refined and complex." He sighs. "But who cares about Aristotle these days?"

Still . . . he wishes he'd been born into a wealthy family, then he could have spent his life reading books and old manuscripts about completely impractical subjects.

"What good would all that knowledge do you?"

"It's the only way to stay in contact with people here. I'd like to be a font of knowledge for them to fall into! The danger, of course, is that I might fall in myself." I hear him laughing. "Next time you come to Nouakchott, there will be a shingle above my door. *Sass: Prophet.*"

Darkness has fallen without warning, and above us hangs a yellowish pall of sand that makes the stars look dull and infinitely far away. I'm amazed by Sass's honesty and lucidity. So many intellectuals in this part of the world have been confused by their studies abroad, but they do everything they can to disguise how uprooted they are. Sass isn't afraid to peer into the abyss. But when I say that, he laughs. Even his eloquence is a pose, he warns me. "Have you noticed how hazy it is this evening? The sky is full of the dust I'm trying to throw in your eyes."

We've barely crawled out of our sleeping bags when we see Abdallah coming towards us in the distance, wrapped in his blanket. He watches sullenly as we roll up the mattresses, his gaze full of disapproval. Sass has put water on to boil, but suddenly the burner stops working. No matter how he tries, he can't get it going again.

After everything has been loaded onto the roof, Sass climbs behind the wheel and turns the key in the ignition. There's a weak spluttering, nothing more. "Oh no, please." He tries again. A soft, whining, slightly infantile sound is all that the Toyota produces. All three of us stare at the indecipherable tangle of cables under the hood. Sass wiggles something here, pulls something there, but there doesn't seem to be much method to his attempts. He looks at me searchingly. "You wouldn't happen to know anything about the insides of this car, would you?"

We try to push-start the jeep, but it's impossible with just the three of us. Sass curses himself for having listened to Abdallah. We could be in Kiffa, and now we're here, further away than ever!

Abdallah offers to go for help. We'd be able to get the car started if there were six of us, wouldn't we? Once he's gone, Sass pulls the Toyota instruction manual out of the glove compartment. "Let's see if there's anything in here." He starts flipping through it, but not very convincingly. When he sees the look on my face, he grins. "My first lesson in Sidi Boîtism!" He can't make head or tail of it.

He pulls out his toolbox, and for a moment I find myself hoping that his technical ineptitude is just another pose. But the box contains only a jumble of wrenches, screws and nuts – he slams it shut in disgust.

The first helpers show up. An old man and a little boy greet us shyly, sit down in the sand, peer at us furtively, then roll themselves up in their *boubous* and go to sleep. "They're obviously no Sidi Boîtes," Sass says, "more like Sidi Camels."

Then Abdallah arrives with a good-sized delegation. There are women among them as well; they perch on the side of the dune like veiled birds and deliver a loud commentary on everything they see.

One of the boys who came with Abdallah has a big bag with him. If he helps out, will we give him a ride to Kiffa? Sass tugs at his beard. "We're making real progress now – we've already got ourselves a hitchhiker. We can't really refuse him a hypothetical service, can we?"

All attempts to push-start the jeep are fruitless. The sun is pounding down mercilessly, and Sass and I look at each other: what now? Abdallah tells us about an old shop nearby that the locals use as a storage place. If we want to, we can rest there while he goes looking for . . . well, for what, really? "We'll figure that out once we're there," Sass says. "You see how impossible it is for me to be independent?" He sounds almost triumphant. "I'm the king of roadside disasters!"

We toss a few essentials into a bag and follow Abdallah and his helpers. I'm still amazed at how little buildings keep popping up out of nowhere, offering relative comfort to passers-by. By the time we arrive, two men are already busy pounding the red floral cushions of a dusty couch.

Sass inhales deeply and looks around. The room is piled to the ceiling with camel saddles, carpets and burlap bags full of beans and rice. "Hmmmmm . . . a granary. There are bound to be lots of vermin in here. Good thing my ecological sister-in-law sent me one of those black stones against snakebite."

"Are there snakes here?"

"Yes, of course!"

I think about the black stone that's been in a little basket on the mantel at home for years. "How are you supposed to use those things?"

"You take your knife and carve a cross on the place where you've been bitten, then you press the stone against the wound until . . ." His voice sounds earnest, but I can tell from his eyes that he's exaggerating at best.

Abdallah's wife arrives with the tea set. She smiles happily – she's had to wait forever, but now her time has come. Abdallah looks around contentedly as well: later on he'll kill a goat, and perhaps I can finally have my hands and feet dyed with henna.

Sass draws Abdallah's attention to the fact that we are stuck here against our will, that we were on our way to Kiffa, and that it might perhaps be wiser if we were still to try . . . at this Abdallah suddenly recalls a man back in Tamchekket who owns a large number of wrenches and who, in his own modest way, knows a great deal about cars. Tamchekket is only fifteen kilometers from here; he could go there by camel.

Sass has pulled out his notebook and is writing a letter. "There are more mechanics in Tamchekket than you'd expect for such a little town," he mumbles. "Do you think they're holding a symposium?" He tears the page out of his book and folds it twice down the middle. "And now let's hope that this second-string mechanic isn't illiterate!"

After Abdallah has left, Sass turns somber again. He frets about spending two weeks in this place, has visions of a tow-truck having to come all the way from Kiffa, makes a mental checklist of our provisions.

Abdallah's wife and children are also waiting. School started a week ago, but the car that will take them to the capital is stuck in Tamchekket. A messenger was sent to Kiffa, but she's not sure if he's come back yet.

Sass asks her how often cars come by here. Twice a day? "Quite a busy intersection by the sound of it," he says sarcastically. "But at least *you* can go to Kiffa today. None of this is working out. You're just wasting your time with me."

I'm stunned. I've considered every possibility – except the end of this trip. We were going to go east . . .

"But you were planning to go on to Mali, weren't you?"

"That's right," I say, crestfallen.

"Well, what's keeping you? You'll see: this is going to get really boring, really soon."

I think about the Hôtel de l'Amitié. Arriving there alone, the two Tunisians in the yard – it suddenly seems a lot less appealing.

"What do I care if I have to hang around here for a few days?" I object. "It's not so bad." Sass is lying on the flowered couch, his exercise book open beside him. He's in for days, maybe even weeks, of wretched waiting, he says. That doesn't matter to him, he's used to it; but I come from a different world, he can't put me through this.

I remember all the times he's told me about his fear of being pulled back into the past. If I left, his car would be the only thing distinguishing him from the people around him – although, in its present condition, that would be a pretty abstract distinction. How could I desert him at a time like this?

The haste with which he's trying to send me back to that other, faster world offends me. Haven't we been good traveling companions, wouldn't it be more pleasant to spend these lost days together? But while he does his best to convince me, I start to suspect what's really behind his insistence: he doesn't want me to see him sink away into lethargy.

"A car! Quick!" Sass jumps up from the couch. I didn't hear a thing, but when we run outside I see a little white dot in the distance. I have no shoes on, so before long the soles of my feet are covered in thorns. Sass takes off his sandals: "Here, put these on."

"What about you?"

"My feet are callused." He laughs: "Come on, keep going. When he sees a Western woman, he'll stop. You're our calling card!"

The driver of the shiny Toyota is wearing a starched *boubou*, a snow-white turban and Ray-Ban sunglasses. For a moment it looks as though everything is back to normal. We tell him about our car trouble, and Sass asks if I can ride along with him to Kiffa to get help. The man looks us over indifferently. He has to pick up a sick woman who lives nearby and take her to Nouakchott, he says. He can't take another passenger.

When Sass asks if he knows Sidi Boîte, the man sniffs conde-scendingly. "Sidi Boîte! Sure I know him! If you let him fix your car, it's guaranteed to break down for good after only two kilo-meters."

He waves farewell and takes off. Dejected, we shuffle back to our storehouse where mice, snakes and other vermin await.

Abdallah's wife has been watching from the doorway. "That man was from the opposition party," she says disapprovingly. "I'm sure he recognized you as the mayor's guests. That's why he wouldn't give you a lift."

"As you can see, this an excellent place to observe Mauritania's celebrated altruism," Sass grins.

Inside, the room smells of the local incense called *lebkhur* that Abdallah's wife has been sprinkling on the burner's smoldering coals. The women who watched us from the dune are here too. While Sass pulls the thorns out of his feet with a pained expres-sion, one of them starts talking to him. Doesn't he have a brother named Hassan, a doctor? He treated her years ago, when she was still living in the north of the country. "Even here," Sass says, slightly amazed. His brothers Hassan and Ahmed are rivals; Ahmed is not only interested in mysticism, but also in medicine. He treats his patients with modern, not traditional, medicine. Hassan claims for all to hear that his brother should be taken to court for practicing without a license.

We make a pilgrimage to the car. How quiet and forlorn it looks, sitting there at the foot of the dune. Sass climbs behind the wheel and tries to start it, but it no longer even produces the infan-tile sound it made this morning.

Two camels come galloping toward us, nomads in flapping *boubous* sitting proudly on top of them. This, it occurs to me, is something I never would have seen if we hadn't broken down. And how right I am, because one of the riders turns out to be our very own Abdallah, back from his mission to Tamchekket. I don't recognize him for a moment, sitting there so graceful and self-assured on his dirty blanket. What a contrast with the uneasy way he sits behind the wheel of the Toyota! He smiles broadly at us from his throne and announces that the mechanic will arrive tomorrow morning. And he has more news: Sass's brother, who was running for mayor in a city up north, has been defeated. Sass is unmoved by the news.

Sass caught a cold last night out in the desert, so we sleep in the storehouse. He tosses and turns uncomfortably in his *hawli*, and I lie awake for hours as well. I'm not thinking about snakes, but I do have the unmistakable impression that a mouse in one corner of the room is scratching itself behind the ear.

※※※

There are four of them, four men with grimy turbans and shining faces. The battery is dead; they'd figured as much when Abdallah told them our story. They're busy for a few minutes, words like 'air filter' and 'fuse wire' surfacing amid the flow of Hassaniyya, before the car roars to life. It's an unexpected pleasure to hear that sound again, and to see the jeep spinning broad loops in the sand.

Abdallah has already agreed on the price: twenty liters of gas and five thousand *ouguiyas* – a hefty fee, but one Sass is quite willing to pay. As soon as the transaction is complete, they disappear; they have lots of work to do. We load our things into the jeep, and yesterday's hitchhiker gratefully tosses his bag in as well.

Sass races over the sand dunes as though the devil were after him. Away from this forsaken place of tea, henna and sluggishness. Now that we've given Abdallah a chance to spend two nights with his wife, our souls are out of hock for at least another three weeks.

"The world of Sidi Camels is behind us: behold the kingdom of Sidi Boîtes," Sass shouts in relief as we see the Road of Hope looming up in front. "Civilization is a paved road!"

We drive straight to the marketplace in Kiffa, where everyone we talk to points us in the direction of Baaba Sow. Sass is tickled. "A Senegalese! They have car repair in their genes!"

We find Baaba Sow in his workshop, where little boys are busy inflating car tires with a bicycle pump. He looks awfully grimy, which Sass says is a good sign. He climbs into the driver's seat, plays with the gears for a minute, then hops out again. What we need is a new transmission, and there aren't any to be had in Kiffa. We'll have to drive back to the capital; if Sass is careful and doesn't use the four-wheel drive, he might make it to Nouakchott.

∿∿

Just like the last time, the Tunisians are sitting on the steps across from the Hôtel de l'Amitié catching the last rays of sunlight. They wave excitedly. School has finally begun, they shout.

We sort out our things, which have become jumbled together during the last few days. When Baaba Sow explained how matters stood, yesterday's feeling of shock at the thought that our journey was over didn't return. With no more room to maneuver, it's time to move on. The Tunisians take me to a merchant at the market who knows all the back roads into Mali. He's willing to send me along with the first load of sugar headed in that direction.

∿∿

Sass knocks on my door at five in the morning. He's holding a flashlight; the hotel generator doesn't work at this time of night. He places a pile of things on my bed. "You'll be needing these." I walk out to the car with him and wave to a beaming Abdallah: for the first time during this trip, he's allowed to sit up front.

It's light by the time I wake up again. I look at the things Sass left behind: cans of French fruit salad, a box of Kellogg's cereal, cartons of milk. Precious items these, from a world racing away from me at breakneck speed.

I take Sass's blue *hawli* and walk to the bathroom at the end of the hall. Wrapping it around my face carefully, the way I saw Sass do, I look at myself in the mirror. The material is so thin that I have no trouble breathing, and it lets light through as well. Sass had it washed last night, but beneath the soap I can still smell the odor of the last few days.

That same afternoon I leave for Mali in the bed of a pick-up loaded with two tons of sugar, Sass's *hawli* wrapped around my head. There's room for a third person in the cab next to the two Moors, but they weren't keen on having any female company. Through the open windows comes the sound of monotonous Moorish music, reminding me of Islamic chanting, and the smell of the tea the man in the passenger seat is making on a little gas burner.

My fellow passenger is lying next to me. He speaks nothing but Hassaniyya, and barely looked at me before rolling himself up in his *boubou* and becoming invisible. I turn my face to the wind, look down the Road of Hope and think of Sass. Here I am again, back in the Stone Age.

THE MAN FROM SOKOLO

J UST before the border between Mauritania and Mali, we pass a
nomad camp. People rush out to look at the pick-up truck with
a white woman in it. "*Nasraniyye!*" they shout – literally, 'woman
of Nazareth'. Only when they come closer do they see that I'm
wearing trousers. "*Bantalon, bantalon,*" I hear them whisper. The
women laugh and point at the blue *hawli* wrapped around my
head.

Then I see the boy. He must be about eleven, barefooted, thin
face above a soiled *boubou*. Something in his eyes makes me look
at him longer than at the others. He doesn't turn away giggling,
the way African children usually do: he stares at me boldly. The
car starts to pull away and I'm about to smile at him when he
tosses his head back, purses his lips and blows contemptuously in
my direction.

What nerve! I'm startled and delighted at the same time.
Suddenly I see Abderrahmane Sissako atop his old-fashioned
black bike, cycling through the streets of Amsterdam, not
about to let himself be intimidated by anyone. Legs rigid, back
straight, an African beret with yellow motif perched on his
head – my bicycle repairman gave me a knowing look as we
cycled past. "They're not used to doing that back home, are
they?"

Across the border, the landscape fills with color and life:
the clay huts are painted; women sway past in lavish *pagnes*;
the air hums with cheerfulness and tittering. This is the bright
Africa I know from earlier trips. Behind me, a door has
closed.

The Africa of calabashes and straw huts didn't interest him
much, Abderrahmane told me once. He was drawn more to the
sobriety, the spirituality of desert life. Mauritania, that was the

culture of the *unspoken*. It had had more impact on him than he'd realized. Both cultures must have made their mark on him; maybe that combination is what's made him special.

꧁꧂

I first met Abderrahmane amid the bustle of an African film festival in Amsterdam. He was a stately, enigmatic figure, his skin light, his features more Arab than African. A Mauritanian, the festival-goers murmured to each other. When we struck up a conversation I learned that although he was of Moorish descent, he'd grown up in Bamako, the capital of Mali.

His black-and-white film *Octobre* was set in Moscow, where he'd studied. Monumental landscapes, slow action – you could feel the influence of the old Russian school of cinema, even though it was a modern love story about a Russian girl and an African boy. A doomed affair, smothered by prying neighbors in a desolate row of flats.

It was a message from an unknown world, startling in its authenticity. The Russians were real people, their lives filmed from the inside – they didn't resemble the one-dimensional whites you see in so many other African films. You could tell the director wasn't just an African who had studied in Moscow, but a sensitive man who had tried to understand where he found himself and why he had remained a stranger all those years. The language of the film left no room for words like 'racism'.

While Abderrahmane's colleagues held fiery speeches in the foyer about Western neo-colonialism and its corrupt African stooges, he remained silent. It was as if he'd landed in this company by chance and felt out of place. He complained about the festival audience, who were more Afrophiles than film buffs.

His self-confidence intrigued me. What had made him so different? The question didn't seem to surprise him. "I believe it's because of my father." His father was a meteorologist who had traveled extensively in Africa and Europe. He taught his children to be independent. There was no water in their swimming pool in Bamako, and they were never driven to school: the swimming pool and the car went with his job, so they were temporary, their father explained. He didn't want his children to become accustomed to such uncertain comforts.

Abderrahmane never got a bike, no matter how much he pleaded. If he gave in to him, his father sighed, what would he do about the other children? To say nothing of the nieces and nephews he had under his wing.

Abderrahmane didn't understand at the time, but he later realized that his father was right. So many civil servants had bettered themselves at the state's expense, but his father never played that game. He was a man who valued simplicity. He would come back from a conference in Geneva, hang his suit in the closet and travel straight on to his native village of Sokolo.

He wanted his children to get to know Sokolo as well. His two oldest sons went to school there for a while. They stayed with family, and their father occasionally sent them presents: colored plastic covers for their notebooks, even a soccer ball. An aunt mistook the ball for a calabash and cut it right down the middle. The boys didn't dare say anything; the two halves were used as peanut bowls.

When he retired, their father announced that he was going back to live in Sokolo. He asked if anyone wanted to go with him, but neither his two wives nor any of his fourteen children did. They'd seen it coming, but his leaving still surprised them.

Abderrahmane had been to visit him recently, and he barely recognized the man he met at the marketplace in Sokolo. He was wearing a grimy *boubou*, and didn't seem too concerned about the rest of his appearance either. Abderrahmane hugged him, then looked down at his feet. "Papa, you're not wearing shoes!"

"Oh, I guess I left them at home," his father mumbled.

But Abderrahmane soon discovered that his father rarely wore shoes in Sokolo.

He stayed for three days, and the trip seemed to have confused him. How easily his father had shed the comforts of city life!

"I'll go and visit him," I said. The words were out before I even thought about it.

Abderrahmane laughed. "There are almost no roads, and there's only one car a week."

That same afternoon, we bent over the map of West Africa. I saw that Sokolo wasn't far from the legendary Malian city of Ségou. When Abderrahmane's father was born, this area was still part of the French Sudan. Merchants traveled back and forth between Oualâta, where his father's family came from, and Sokolo, where they later moved. But now Oualâta was in Mauritania, Sokolo in Mali.

Abderrahmane's life was shaped by these new borders. In Mali he was considered a Moor, but when his father left for Sokolo and he moved to Nouakchott with his mother – a fully fledged Moor from a nomadic tribe in the heart of Mauritania – he found himself in an alien world. He didn't speak Hassaniyya, he wasn't used to wearing a *boubou*, and his name didn't sound Moorish. Moorish surnames begin with *ould*, meaning 'son of'. But, for the sake of convenience, Abderrahmane's great-grandparents had changed their name from ould-Hamid to Sissako after the influential Malian trading family they'd moved in with.

I was starting to understand why Abderrahmane wouldn't use a term like 'racism' lightly. His first bout with alienation hadn't taken place in the Soviet Union, but on the African continent.

A strange pall hangs over Bamako – as if the red sand blowing through the streets never settles, as if the light is being filtered through mica. I peer down the sandy road, and through the red haze I see a white Mazda sports car heading my way. The man who gets out has a broad, African face – no trace of Abderrahmane's light skin and Arab features.

I point to the street full of potholes. "Is it practical to have a car like that around here?"

Bako laughs apologetically. "I bought it second-hand – you can't really choose the model."

I've just arrived in this noisy, unfamiliar city after a rough trip – it's a joy to recognize Abderrahmane's smoky voice and rolling 'r'.

Bako's proud look when he climbs behind the wheel tells me how pleased he is with his car. Children beam as we drive past. They all think we're pretty lucky, of course, but I don't like sitting low in a car and, to my dismay, the window on the passenger side won't open, even though it's blistering hot inside.

I'm surprised by how little Bako resembles Abderrahmane – they have different mothers – but then Abderrahmane himself never talked about brothers and half-brothers. Bako doesn't seem to draw that distinction either. I've been sent by 'Dramane', as he calls him, the only member of the family who lives in Europe. It's good that someone is interested to see where he comes from. It helps balance the scales, which are otherwise tipped pretty heavily in one direction.

Ramadan has begun, and a sleepy hush descends over the city during the hottest part of the day. We drive to Hamdallaye, a neighborhood of clay houses surrounded by walls. Bako stops in front of an open gate, behind which two boys are snoozing under a verandah. "Those are my brothers, the high-school students," Bako says. "They're on strike for more grant money, which means they spend half the day in bed." He's right; a little later, wakened by our voices, a third brother appears sleepily from behind a curtain.

It's an African home. The pastel-blue walls and rust-colored doors must have been clean once, but years of dirt cling to them now, and here and there the plaster has fallen from the walls – leaving craters that look like bullet holes. They plan to build more rooms on the other side of the courtyard, but work has been postponed and the unfinished cubicles serve as sheepfolds.

Bako shows me to a darkened room containing an impressive dresser with a mirrored door. It takes a while before I make out the shape of a woman lying on the bed. It's N'to, Bako's mother. When Sissako's second wife moved to Mauritania, she and her children stayed here. She murmurs a greeting in Bambara. She's dark and heavy, her face beaded with sweat. She's just come home from the mosque.

N'to is Moorish, but doesn't look it. Her family comes from the border area between Mauritania and Mali, where Moors have intermarried with black Africans for generations. I'm a bit ashamed of the appraising look I give her. Moors think in terms of color: the lighter the better. I distanced myself from it while I was in Mauritania, but I've noticed that ever since I crossed the border, I've started thinking in color too.

Outside, a group of women and children are sitting under a tree. Little girls in blue dresses come back from school, ribbons in their hair and satchels on their backs. These must be the family members who've drifted in over the years. A girl brings us a bowl of rice and meat with peanut sauce. Bako has someone fetch me a spoon, and we all gather round the bowl. One of the students is observing Ramadan, but I'm relieved to notice that this doesn't keep the others from eating.

The CFA, the West African currency, was devalued a few days ago, and students from all over the region have taken to the streets. While politicians hold helpless monologues on television, cars are torched in Dakar, and students in Bamako toss up barricades and drag foreigners out of their vehicles. The embassies are advising their citizens to avoid the center of town. And here are the notorious demonstrators, napping in the sun!

They grin. They've done a lot of striking this year. The government is threatening to close down the schools until the end of the year, but they don't seem worried. The youngest of the three sits flipping through a paper, looking bored. At first I thought it was a striker's pamphlet, but it turns out to be a back issue of a satirical publication from neighboring Burkina Faso.

In 1991, students on strike in Bamako vandalized strategic buildings. They raided the homes of corrupt civil servants, and ultimately brought about the fall of Mali's president, Moussa Traoré. Since then, the tactical strike has gained considerably in prestige.

A bare-breasted woman is standing at the tap in the middle of the yard, staring at us. It's Bobo Mouso, the deaf-mute – Abderrahmane told me about her. She came wandering into the courtyard ten years ago and never left. No one knows where she's from. She's lost her memory, and she can't hear or speak. She wears big rings in her ears, and when I walk over to greet her she laughs and hands me a yellow plastic cup of water. I make a gesture of refusal, but Bako says: "You can't refuse, she wouldn't understand." She nods encouragingly as I put the cup to my lips.

A scooter drives into the yard. It's Bako's younger brother, Amidou. He and Bako are in their thirties and have rooms in town, but they come by every day. Being the only real bread-winners, they often bring food with them. Their aunt earns a little money selling grilled meat at the entrance to the high school. "But as long as they're on strike, she doesn't earn a thing," Bako says with a glance at his younger brothers. His mother sells plastic bags of icy lemonade to the children in the neighborhood, but he suspects she only does it for the company.

I take a look at Amidou's scooter. "Do you ever take anyone on the back?" He nods. "I bet it's a lot more pleasant than Bako's suffocating Mazda," I say. They all laugh. Amidou's scooter will become my favorite mode of transportation in Bamako.

In fact, the whole town seems to get around by scooter. Neatly dressed men with attache cases, coquettish women with handbags on their laps – I wonder how they manage to keep clean; I'm always covered in dust by the end of the trip. While Amidou confidently picks his way through traffic, I can't stop looking around. The stands selling grilled meat along the Route de Koulikoro are painted with graphic depictions of razor-sharp knives and animals dripping blood. One of them is called the Rôtisserie de la Democratie. Around the decaying colonial buildings in the center of town, outdoor barbers are cutting their customers' hair on reed mats, and boys are playing with home-made pinball machines.

Close to the marketplace, a crowd has gathered around a game I first saw on the beach at Nouakchott, the players throwing rings at objects inside a roped-in area. In Nouakchott the prizes stood in the sand like abstract works of art: a roll of cookies, a plastic yo-yo, a toy car. Here they're throwing for basketball shoes and other luxury goods.

Amidou has no qualms about the chaotic city he lives in. He once traveled with a German tourist in a bush taxi from Ouagadougou to Bamako. A man from the Ivory Coast sat bragging to her the whole way about the skyscrapers in Abidjan. Amidou was embarrassed. Skyscrapers – why would a European come to Africa to see skyscrapers?

One afternoon we end up in a student demonstration. It looked harmless enough from a distance, but as soon as we move into the crowd I recall the embassies' warnings. Some students are carrying slingshots with big rocks in them, and are looking around grimly. As a white person, I'm an easy target. I hang on to Amidou, who maneuvers cautiously through the crowd. "Stay calm," he whispers

Someone behind us asks whether I'm French or American.

"Neither!" I call out.

"Then help us destroy this country!" he screams.

By the time we leave the demonstration behind us, my hands are clammy. Amidou picks up speed. "No problem," he says reassuringly.

We're on our way to the Meteorological Institute, where his father worked for decades before becoming director-general at the end of his career. The staff's homes surround the institute, scattered loosely in an empty landscape.

"When we were little, everything was green around here," Amidou says.

"Green?" I look at the straggly little bushes poking up out of the soil here and there. The houses look like they were built at random, but they once stood behind rows of shady trees that have now all been cut down for firewood.

"That's where we lived." The house is back from the road a little. Two families live there now; the swimming pool has been filled in and there's nothing left of the garden where his father grew corn and tomatoes. But it's easy to imagine the young Abderrahmane coming down the sandy path on his way to the playing field behind the house. A proud little fellow, even then. He was so good at soccer that they called him Ahmed Faras, after the Moroccan star of the day.

One of his father's French colleagues lived across from them. They played with his children, so at school they were seen as a bourgeois family. When their classmates walked past their house, they would sing:

> *Suraka Mohammed, taal ila.*
> *A te kurusi don, taal ila.*
> *A te duloki don, taal ila.*
> *Julakolon ba, taal ila.*

It was a Bambara song making fun of Moors.

> *Moorish Mohammed, come over here.*
> *You without underpants, come over here.*
> *You with no undershirt, come over here.*
> *You in your bare butt, come over here.*

Their classmates also parodied the singsong exchange of Moorish greetings: "*Mohammed, break open your calabash, shave your mustache!*" they would shout. Coming from a Moorish family in Mali and playing with French children as well – Abderrahmane must have grown used to another, bigger world quite early on.

Every two years their father attended a meeting of the World Organization of Meteorologists in Europe, and brought back presents. A bar of chocolate – they dreamed it would last forever. One time he bought velour suits with white shirts and ties for Amidou and Abderrahmane. They were much too warm for Bamako, but they wore them proudly.

Their father had a plot of land on the edge of town where he raised cows and chickens, and experimented with growing fruits and vegetables. Other civil servants wouldn't have given a second thought to driving the office car to their fields, or irrigating their land with tanks of water from the municipality, but he never did that. Every morning one of his children had to walk out there to get fresh milk; he sold the eggs to the local hotels.

"Lots of civil servants tried to stay in their state housing for years after they retired," Amidou says, "but my father was in a hurry to move." He's like Abderrahmane, it occurs to me: he understands that with a father like his, he might be rather special.

The Prosper Kamara high school lies at the foot of a mountain, close to the family's house in Hamdallaye. The buildings are deserted because of the strike, but there's a soccer game going on behind them. At the time, the school was still run by the White Fathers. Prosper Kamara was the first bishop of Mali; his portrait hangs in the foyer, next to the class timetables. "If Father Didier were still here, you could ask him to show you Abderrahmane's records," Amidou says. But the last priest left two years ago, and the staff they have now . . . no, Amidou doesn't think they'd be efficient enough.

He has no more regrets about it than he does about the ravaged landscape surrounding the Meteorological Institute. The plaintive tone I sometimes hear from the colonial generation is foreign to him. He takes things as they come.

The students are frustrated, he says; they're not interested in going to school, because intellectuals and civil servants aren't appreciated around here. You can earn more by working as a boy for a white person. The future belongs to businesspeople, and they don't always have much in the way of brains.

During the trial of former President Moussa Traoré, in 1991, the defense accused the students of having been drugged during the riots. "That's right, we were drugged," a student leader said.

The people in the courtroom held their breath: now the truth would come out! "Drugged by hunger, and poverty."

We climb the broad stairs to the top floor. The evening sun casts a soft glow on the mountain. The soccer game in the red sand is more intense than I'd imagined – it's as if the players are struggling against the coming of the night.

Amidou leans over the balustrade. "Did you know that Dramane was one of the instigators of the student strike when he was eighteen?"

I nod – he'd told me about it. His older brothers warned him to be careful. A Moor getting involved in politics in Mali was in for trouble, they said, but Abderrahmane didn't let that stop him. Amidou, who is two years younger, was also caught up in the fever. One afternoon, he came home to change before going to a demonstration Abderrahmane would be leading.

"If you see your brother, tell him to come home," said his father, who had caught wind of what was happening.

Amidou went on changing his clothes.

"Did you hear me?"

"Father, this is none of your business. I'm not going to say anything to him, and what's more, I'm going to demonstrate too." Amidou laughs to think of it. "That's how we talked to him! Other children shook in their boots when their father said something, or snuck around behind his back. We were used to discussing things with him, we just told him what we thought." His father knew he couldn't do anything about it, and let him go.

"Dramane was a good public speaker," Amidou says; "he knew how to whip up a crowd." On that afternoon he stood at this balustrade and spoke to the students. Suddenly, someone shouted that the soldiers were coming. Panic broke out, and the students started running towards the mountain, where they had a hiding place. "And do you know what was strange? Dramane, who was standing up here and needed time to get down, was suddenly running way out in front of us!" Blessed are those who leave home, I think, for heroic stories shall be told about them.

It's starting to get dark now and the soccer game is barely

visible from the balustrade, but the players' excited cries continue unabated.

"What happened then?"

"Didn't he tell you?"

"I don't think so, no." In the streets of Amsterdam, these things sounded different – they're only beginning to fall into place now that I'm here.

"The government decided to break the strike and went looking for the three ringleaders. Abderrahmane had to go underground and he escaped across the border to Mauritania with another student leader. He'd disguised himself as a girl; his friend was dressed like an old lady."

"What about the third one?"

"He went into hiding too, but he turned himself in when they started threatening his family." The soccer players have abandoned their struggle against the twilight. They pat each other on the back and laugh in relief. "Cabral – everyone in Mali knows his name. He died in prison. Tortured to death."

Suddenly I'm ashamed – I'd taken these strikes so lightly until now. "And what about the boy Abderrahmane escaped to Mauritania with?"

"He went to France. After the fall of President Traoré he came back and became minister of foreign affairs."

And Dramane went to stay with his mother in Nouakchott. He'd told me about that period. They lived in a room without electricity, but the light from their neighbor's room shone through their window. In the evening he would sit studying in that beam of light, while his mother kept her neighbor talking for as long as possible. "But I couldn't concentrate on my books," he confessed. "I was trying to imagine what they were talking about all evening." It took years before he dared to go back to Bamako. Meanwhile, he patiently began ingratiating himself at the Russian Cultural Center in Nouakchott. He tried to become a Mauritanian. I had thought of him as being more innocent in those days, but now I realize he wasn't just a student whose life was yet to begin – he already had a whole life behind him.

The soccer players have gone, the square below us is empty, and with the darkness a breath of wind wafts over the balcony.

"What was Abderrahmane like when he came back to Bamako?"

Amidou stares into space. "He was quieter, more careful. When you see him now, you can hardly imagine him ever speaking to a crowd. Europe has changed him. Sometimes you don't know what he's thinking anymore." Amidou seems to be searching for tangible proof of that change. "Maybe it's because of his profession," he says hesitantly. "Ever since he went to study in Moscow, he hasn't come back to Bamako without a camera."

Paris was cold and wet the second time I met Abderrahmane. We walked through the city hunched up in our coats. It reminded him of when he first went to the Soviet Union, he said. He laughed: the day he left for Moscow, his mother fluttered around him endlessly. Finally she told him: "If you run into anyone there who's in trouble, always try to help them." As if he, with barely two hundred French francs in his pocket, could help anyone!

He arrived in Moscow at night. They took him to a hotel with twenty-six floors. He only discovered the next morning how high up he was. He saw a crowd of little dolls bustling around down there in the depths.

The next day he waited with a group of African students for the train to Rostov-on-Don, where they would be taught Russian for a year. A streetwise Angolan began hawking jeans right there in the station. Abderrahmane barely knew what a rouble looked like, but the fellow pulled a big wad of bills from his pocket and sent someone to buy beer for them. Alcohol – Abderrahmane hadn't grown up with it, but he was fascinated by the Angolan; he couldn't take his eyes off of him.

Most of the African students hung out together and were fairly indifferent to what happened outside their academic ghetto, but Abderrahmane explored his surroundings. Later, in Moscow, when he mentioned something to a group of African postgraduate students about an opera he'd seen, he realized that no one knew what he was talking about. Whenever he went to the theater, he was the only black person in the audience.

But he was a foreigner in Moscow too, dependent on his compatriots. One evening he wanted to visit a Malian friend. The doorwoman sitting at the entrance to the student flat was reading Bunin. She looked up at him wearily and said: "It's past ten, visiting hours are over."

He remained standing in front of her, crestfallen. His friend was waiting for him, he had to see him. "Look at all those lights," he said, pointing to a block of flats where Russians lived. "Over there they can visit each other whenever they want to, but I'm not allowed in because I'm a foreigner. The only person I can visit is my Malian friend."

The woman shrugged and went back to her book. But Abderrahmane wasn't about to leave it at that. "You're reading Bunin," he said, "but what good is being well read if you have no sympathy for someone who's lonely and wants to visit a friend?" The doorwoman was pleasantly surprised that he knew who Bunin was, but she still wouldn't budge.

He walked back to his flat, thinking bitterly: they're so proud of their literature, but what good is it if they turn around and slam the door in your face?

The father of one of his Muscovite friends was amazed that Abderrahmane had so many female visitors. And pretty ones at that! "It was because I was nice to them," Abderrahmane said to me. "I made tea, helped them into their coats and walked them to the door. Their own men never did that." In a documentary about mixed marriages in the Soviet Union, Lumumba University, which was established to propagate friendship among different peoples, was referred to as 'the Planet of the Apes' and 'the university of savages'. A young Russian woman told him she had always thought Africans were barbarians until she met one and discovered he was kinder and more intelligent than the average Russian.

"Did you ever fall in love there?" I asked.

Abderrahmane nodded. But he'd known it couldn't last forever, and he considered himself lucky that – unlike some of his fellow students – he hadn't married a Russian. "Russian women stick to you like glue," he said, "they won't let you be free, and I could never love someone like that. My mother loved me, and she let me go away for ten years."

The last few years in Moscow were hard: he no longer felt safe. Russians were jealous of Africans because they had foreign currency, and therefore more money, but they looked down on them as well. He didn't like their appraising looks when he walked down the street: it was is if they were estimating how much his clothes had cost.

In 1991 – after he had graduated and moved out of his student flat – a man in a paramedic's coat rang his bell and asked if he'd called an ambulance. Suddenly another man appeared behind him, and together they pushed Abderrahmane inside and tied him to a chair. When they tried to stuff a gag in his mouth, he told them that wouldn't be necessary: he wasn't going to scream. He was so calm, they thought he had a hidden alarm system. After he told them where the money was, they left. From that day on he always carried a revolver, and later he even had a bodyguard. It was time to leave. Ten years – he'd been there too long. But only after he'd finished *Octobre* was he able to say farewell.

The Sissakos don't live indoors, I discover, but in the yard. Because of Ramadan, the evenings are particularly animated. Around sundown, mattresses are dragged into the yard and the air shimmers with expectation. Food is cooking above little fires, and everyone is seated with wooden spoons at the ready.

As soon as the *muezzin* on television breaks into song, gourds filled with sorghum porridge and ginger juice are passed around and the diners throng around them. Amid all this, N'to, the woman of the house, is lying on a mattress. She lets herself be served, while at the same time making sure that everyone else is served as well.

Neighbors drop by with little pans of special dishes; acquaintances pop in for a visit. Women clothed in rustling white dresses come to take N'to to the mosque, leaving a cloud of *wousoulan*, the local incense, in their wake. Against the wall, cousins sit braiding each other's hair, little fluffs of which tumble through the yard. The sheep bleat mercilessly throughout the popular French quiz 'Lettres et chiffres'. When the power goes out, the audience groans. They wait for the problem to be solved, lit by the moon's sickle and the glowing coals.

What would *le vieux*, as his children call the old man, be doing on an evening like this; where would he be sitting? He lived here for a few months after he retired, but he couldn't stand it. The old men in the neighborhood, who spend all day playing cards, talking and drinking tea, bored him. He needed something to do; he missed his garden.

Sometimes, during Ramadan, he comes to Bamako for a few days and ends up staying for a month, just as he sometimes leaves to spend ten days in Sokolo and stays there for half a year. But Amidou isn't expecting him this time. The rice harvest is under way in Sokolo, his father is a busy man.

There are about thirty people sitting in the yard now. One of the students is so preoccupied with his Gameboy that the tea on the burner boils over and hisses on the coals. Shrieks of alarm wake him from his trance.

The warmth of this family – doesn't Abderrahmane miss it? I picture him in Paris, hunkered down in the collar of his winter coat, his face gray with cold. How can he bear Western loneliness after having lived like this?

But later that night I think: look what he's escaped from! The coziness of this nest leaves no room for being by yourself. The Gameboy goes from hand to hand, but as for reading a book in these surroundings – forget it. The striking students sometimes flip through the newspapers I bring along, but they don't really read them. Even the television is nothing but background noise.

"Reading is a bourgeois activity," Amidou says.

"What do you mean?"

"You need money to buy books."

"But you can borrow them from the library, can't you?"

Bako grins: "Don't you worry – Amidou has never read anything but Tintin."

"Yes I have!" Amidou jumps up and names a couple of French authors.

"What about African writers?"

They don't get far. "We don't have much time," Bako says, "and the little time we do have, we spend around here. Besides, Dramane isn't a great reader either." But their brother is good at telling stories, everyone agrees about that. Whenever he ventures into Bamako he comes back with new ones.

Bobo Mouso is staring at us. She can stand still for a long time in the middle of the yard, like a pillar. Then she starts pacing back and forth again, sweeping the ground with a little whisk broom, washing her feet at the tap or walking to the shower with a bucket in her hand. She didn't eat with us, but now she's holding a mango, taking bites of it and spitting out the skin.

Abderrahmane had told me that Bobo Mouso just wandered into the yard one day, but Amidou says she comes from Sokolo. Years ago, she was found standing alone in the square after the weekly market, a baby tied to her back. One of their aunts took pity on her, thinking that someone would come to claim her the next week, but no one did. She broadcast her description on the radio, sent notices to the newspapers. No one responded. When their aunt fell ill about ten years ago, Bobo Mouso came to Bamako.

"With her child?"

"Oh no, she drowned the baby by accident while giving it a bath in an irrigation ditch in Sokolo." It sounds like the kind of thing they'd expect to happen to a deaf-mute.

Bobo Mouso is now sitting down, which she seldom does. One of the students says: "She's crazy."

"How do you know?"

He laughs. Can't I see that she never dresses properly? She always walks around in rags and bare feet. Lately she's been on a sweeping binge, but there are days when all she does is lug water back and forth. She'll wash her feet ten times a day, and God help you if you leave any clothes lying around: they'll vanish straight into the suds.

"She observed Ramadan for three years once," Amidou says.

It's strange: they don't pay much attention to her, but she still belongs here, and no one questions her presence. After their aunt took her under her wing, Bobo Mouso had two more children by unknown fathers. Mindful of the drowning in the irrigation ditch, their aunt sent the children to be raised by her daughter in Bamako. The older girl is twelve now; she knows who her mother is, but she's ashamed of her.

Bobo Mouso gets up quickly: the women have returned from the mosque. When they plop down onto the mattresses, she begins to wander around the yard once again.

Amidou has picked up on my inquisitive looks. "No one in Europe could support a family like this," he says.

"That's true, but we take care of ourselves – we don't need our families as much."

He turns up his nose. Those are the kinds of ideas his brothers brought back from Europe. When Abdallah – who studied in Florence – comes to visit, the gate always remains closed. People shouldn't just come walking in here, Abdallah says. The last time he was here they talked about the rooms on the other side of the yard, that should really be finished off soon. "But first we have to deal with all these intruders," Abdallah said, meaning the people who had found their way into the yard over the years.

Intruders! Amidou was shocked. He'd never thought of them that way. They were part of the family – most of them came here through his father. "They don't ask for much," he says. "They don't want clothes or things like that – they just don't have enough money to rent a house, or even to buy rice. Staying with us is their way of surviving."

Amidou's father's youngest brother recently wrote him a letter from Sokolo; or rather, being illiterate, he had a letter written for him. He'd spent his whole life herding cows and sheep, he wrote – including those belonging to Amidou's father – and he asked Amidou for some money, referring to his years of service and how it had ruined his feet.

Amidou asked his father what to do. He said: "How often do you spend five hundred francs on trifles? From now on, you could give that money to him instead." It sounds like a typical message from *le vieux*, whose judgment trembles like a compass needle in his children's subconscious.

But Amidou has doubts at times about his family's noble sentiments. A friend of his who's lived in France claims that Africans are merely more hypocritical than Europeans: they act as though there's no difference between family members, as though a nephew is as dear to them as a brother – but when it comes down to it, they'll opt for the latter.

One afternoon, Amidou suddenly disappears. "He's gone to his *grin*," Bako laughs knowingly. A *grin* is a group of friends who meet regularly to talk, drink tea and play cards. They're often former classmates, or boys who grew up together in the same neighborhood. It's a way for old school friends, threatened with separation by their jobs or families, to regain something of their boyhood intimacy.

The next day, when Amidou announces that his *grin* is meeting, I ask if I can come along. He smiles broadly. He's already told the boys about me. A *grin* is a male affair, but since I'm a foreigner he doesn't think anyone will mind.

I'm getting to know this neighborhood that lies in the mountain's shadow. There's the house where the Soninké businessman lives with his four wives; further along sits the girl who repairs plastic buckets, and even gourd bowls, with needle and thread. Many people here sell things in front of their houses. They fry bananas and *beignets* for passers-by, or have a wooden display case set up with cigarettes, matches and chewing gum. Wandering tailors traipse through the neighborhood with sewing machines on their heads, clicking their scissors to attract attention. It's the hour before sunset and the whole neighborhood is poised for action. The toy vendor, decked out like a Christmas tree, walks past the houses, squeaking a fluorescent green crocodile to lure the children.

Amidou's *grin* meets in his friend Frankie's yard, but it can easily overflow into the street, or even across it, where part of the group is now squatting down to a rousing game of cards. Frankie is sitting in an easy chair at the gate, a tea set within arm's reach. He has someone fetch a few chairs, then hands us little glasses of strong tea. 'Saddam tea', Amidou calls it. A student leader who's causing a furor at the moment also has the nickname 'Saddam'. "Because, as you know, Saddam Hussein is our big hero."

"Why's that?"

"Because he gives the West a hard time." Amidou laughs. "Didn't Dramane tell you? Our family originally comes from Iraq."

There's a fight going on behind us in the yard. Frankie's brother lashes out at his sister and slaps her hard. Amidou scolds him. "It's because of Ramadan," he says. "He's edgy because he hasn't had anything to eat, so he takes it out on his sister!"

When a boy cycles past, Amidou comments: "He's just become a father, but he's not allowed to see his child!" The boy is a Muslim, his girlfriend a Christian – her parents won't let him into the house.

Amidou waves to a passer-by, who walks on at a brisk pace. "You should spend a few minutes talking to that guy," he chuckles. "He thinks he's the prime minister. He has a solution for everything. Last month he dealt with the problem of devaluation; this week he's busy solving the school crisis."

Bako tends to criticize his brother for spending his time this way – he gave up his *grin* long ago – but I think I understand Amidou. The *grin* is a larger world than the one in the yard where his family sits together every evening.

"Did you know that today is the fifth anniversary of the *fatwa* against Salman Rushdie?" he says suddenly.

"Where did you hear that?"

"They were talking about it on the radio."

After his remark about Saddam Hussein, I'm on my guard. "So what do you think of the *fatwa*?"

"I don't know – I never read the book."

Frankie stares broodingly at the cardplayers across the street, without saying a word. Only when Amidou tells him I'll be going to Sokolo soon does he turn and look at me.

"I hope you brought your boots with you."

"What for?"

They laugh. A group of tourists arrived at Bamako airport once wearing knee-high boots – they'd heard Mali was full of snakes.

"Frankie's done a lot of traveling too," Amidou says, "he's even been to Libya."

"To Libya? What were you doing there?"

Frankie answers evasively. "Oh, nothing much. I had a job as a technician in a spaghetti factory." Just as he was putting together a little nest egg, Gaddafi decided that Libyans could do that kind of work as well. From one day to the next, all foreign workers were thrown out of the country.

Things have gone badly with Frankie ever since, Amidou tells me later: after coming back to Bamako, he ran through his savings in no time and then fell into a depression. He was in a psychiatric hospital for a while and still hasn't recovered. He can be extremely aggressive, but there are also periods when he just turns his back on everyone and doesn't say a word. One day, not long ago, Frankie's parents couldn't find him. Amidou found him on the road to Koulikoro, about twenty kilometers outside Bamako. Frankie was walking along with a determined stride, a blank expression on his face. Amidou had a lot of trouble getting him home again.

"Frankie is going to visit his brother in Brooklyn soon," Amidou says paternally. "Maybe he'll have more luck there than he did in Libya." But the way Frankie sits there hunched beside his tea set, he barely looks fit to walk down the street.

People here travel so differently from Westerners, I realize. They go looking for work or to visit family. None of them have ever been to those cities that draw tourists to Mali – Mopti, Timbuktu or Djenné. Amidou knows Ségou because his oldest brother, Aziz, lives there, and because it's on the road to Sokolo.

He's the only one in the family drawn to Sokolo. He's pleased with my plans to visit his father, even though he teases me about it. When I pulled a stick of mosquito repellent out of my bag one evening, he said: "Don't you think you should save that for Sokolo?"

I've got a rough journey in front of me, he says. When I remind him that his father often makes the trip, he laughs heartily. "My father! He's a real Saharan! When the French were still here, he rode his camel up to the far north to set up weather stations. He worked in Tessalit and Kidal!" I've seen those names on the map – tiny dots in a frightening sea of sand.

Amidou was in Sokolo recently, and he spent six months there once when his father needed him in the rice fields. No one understood how he stuck it out, but he got along fine. He cycled around in a *boubou* and a pointy reed hat, and soon noticed he was starting to think differently.

One day a parliamentary delegation from the capital came to talk with the farmers in Sokolo about their problems. Amidou was in the audience and heard the decrees they read aloud, none of which had anything to do with the farmers. When he drew this to the politicians' attention, a spirited discussion arose.

The notables from the city came up to him afterwards. They found him very interesting. Was he a farmer? They invited him to dinner with them, but Amidou turned them down. "I have to get back to my fields," he said. He laughs slyly: he obviously enjoyed putting the men in their place.

But he rarely sided with the farmers either. They were always complaining that they earned so much less than the civil servants in town. "That's because civil servants work eight hours a day," Amidou told them, "while you people spend half the day drinking tea."

Frankie is still staring at the cardplayers across the street. He barely moves, even when the call comes to break the fast. When we say goodbye, his look is clouded: being reminded of Libya doesn't seem to have done him much good.

On the way home Amidou tells me that once, when he was coming back from his *grin*, he saw an angry crowd running towards his house. It took a while before he found out what was going on: a thief had tried to steal one of the students' scooters, but the man across the street had caught him. A furious crowd gathered in the yard. They wanted to club the thief to death.

Fortunately, old Sissako was in Bamako at the time. The thief ran into the house to hide, and Sissako ordered them to lock him in one of the rooms. While the frenzy outside was running its course, he sent one of his sons to fetch the police. But the people didn't want to let them through, and they had to use tear gas to disperse the crowd. Peace didn't return to the yard until the thief had been led away by two policemen – with the whole Sissako family standing by to make sure he wasn't molested.

⚬⚬⚬

Bako takes me to see his half-sister Kady, who lives with her mother in a new neighborhood on the edge of town. Though no one says it in so many words, the family fell apart after *le vieux* left. His second wife, Mariem, moved to Mauritania. Her four children – Abdallah, Kady, Mokhtar and Abderrahmane – all followed. Mariem only returned to Bamako after Kady had moved back.

I notice that Bako becomes slightly irritated whenever his family's Moorish background is mentioned. He considers himself one hundred percent Malian, and doesn't think he has a single Moorish habit. That doesn't go for Mariem and her children, though. When Kady comes back from visiting Nouakchott, she sometimes walks around for months in a *melahfa*, a translucent Moorish veil. "She has different faces," he says.

"And what about Abderrahmane?"

He has to think; it's obviously a touchy subject. When *Octobre* was discussed on a Malian television program recently, all Abderrahmane's friends were proud, until they heard him being called a Mauritanian. They looked at each other in amazement. Abderrahmane was Malian just like them, wasn't he? "I don't know, maybe there are sides to Dramane I don't know about," Bako says cautiously. But isn't it that way with everyone? Whenever his mother has visitors from Mopti, he sees a change come over her. She starts talking like them, and says things she never would otherwise.

Bako is a conscientious fellow. He's less playful than Amidou and when I first met him I didn't quite know what to make of him. Until the day he took me to the battery factory where he works as an engineer. He made a little excursion of it, almost a field trip. We put on smocks and he explained the whole production process; by the end, I pretty much knew how batteries were made. But it was the way he dealt with the other workers, the respect he showed them, that made me like him. It would have been so easy to use a visit by a foreign guest to puff himself up, but he didn't.

Bako pulls off the Route de Koulikoro and stops in front of what looks like a shop. Kady opened it a while back, but it hasn't been a success. The people who live in this suburb all commute to work in Bamako: her only customers turned out to be the watchmen from houses in the area. They came in to buy minuscule quantities of tea and sugar, and most of them were in such pitiful shape that she slipped them something extra.

The wooden shelves are almost empty now, and Kady is sitting on a plastic mat on the floor, playing with her baby daughter. She's pregnant for the second time and looks fragile. She struggles to her feet to get a bag of icy lemonade for the girl who walked into the shop after us. "That's the only thing that still sells," she says with a sad smile. She and her mother are gradually eating their way through the remaining stock of canned goods.

The back of the shop looks out on a modern villa. A thin woman in a white *melahfa* comes shuffling towards us along the garden path. It's Abderrahmane's mother. Her eyesight is poor, but when Kady tells her I've been sent by 'Dra', she takes my hand and begins murmuring in French, pressing me to her and not letting go. I suddenly think of the unlit room in Nouakchott where she lived with Abderrahmane. I feel shy, touched. She's not holding me, she's holding her son.

Bako leans against the counter with a bag of iced lemonade. He's obviously not planning to stay long. This house isn't like the one in Hamdallaye, where you can blend into the crowd: here, you're a visitor. "Do you think you can find your way back on your own?" Then he closes the door of the shop behind him and drives off in his white Mazda.

Kady's mother has settled on the floor. She pulls a handful of cowry shells out of her pocket, tosses them onto the mat and studies them carefully. "She tells the future," Kady says with a little laugh. "Sometimes she spends all day doing it." She tries to tell my future as well, but sweeps the shells back onto a pile irritatedly each time; she can't see a thing.

There's a gourd bowl full of sorghum and a packet of sugar cubes on the floor beside her. "She passes them out to the beggars who come by every morning," Kady tells me. "If no one's come in by ten o'clock, she starts to worry!" Her mother has always done this, even when she was young. Because she almost never went outside, but had the reputation of being a real beauty, men dressed up like beggars just to see her.

Kady has long, kinky hair and soft, almost translucent skin. She looks like Abderrahmane, but at the same time she's so different that I feel like I've come upon an unknown side to him. This pretty, fragile-looking woman on the plastic mat amid all these empty shelves – I've been aware of something tragic ever since I came in.

When her mother hears that I'm going to Sokolo, her expression clouds over. "Why? There's nothing to eat there." She went to Sokolo with Kady. It wasn't a successful visit.

"We should go again too," Kady says teasingly.

Her mother turns up her nose. "Not me!"

"We'll take enough food for a week!"

But her mother shakes her head. There are Tuareg rebels in that part of the country. Fortunately, her husband speaks Tamacheq, the Tuareg language. If they ever raid Sokolo, that might save him.

She turns and looks at me through her spectacles. Have I ever been to Nouakchott? Isn't everything there much better than it is here?

"My mother is a Mauritanophile," Kady says with a wink.

An old Moor has come in, a plastic carrier bag in his hand. He murmurs a greeting, lies down on his back on the mat and closes his eyes, using his bag as a pillow. Mariem tosses her cowry shells without looking up. It's a scene straight out of Mauritanian life – I can't take my eyes off it. Kady laughs. The man walked by one day and saw his mother sitting in the doorway. Since then he comes in regularly to eat or take a nap during the hottest part of the day.

Kady shows me around her house. In the living room we watch a video Abderrahmane made of a visit his mother paid to the house in Hamdallaye. She sits there against the clay wall like a sphinx in her white veil: a queen visiting the slums. The camera hovers around her – as though Abderrahmane is challenging her to take part in the chaotic life from which she so obviously distances herself.

"My mother has character," Kady says. Old Sissako didn't want her to move to Mauritania, and he went after her to try to change her mind. But Mariem refused to go back with him, saying she'd rather beg in the streets of Nouakchott than return to Hamdallaye.

That afternoon Kady and I lie in the grass in the back garden. Her German turns out to be perfect, and she speaks fondly of Munich, where she went to hotel school. She's like Abderrahmane: she's really been there. She had friends in Munich and could have gone to work in a hotel right away if she'd wanted. But all those years she knew she'd be coming back here, so when she fell in love with a German boy, the relationship didn't stand a chance.

"Why not? What stopped you?"

She looks at me sadly. "It's easy enough for a man, but for a woman . . ." The German boy said she didn't really love him because she wouldn't sleep with him. Not long afterwards, she met a Sudanese film maker who became extremely fond of her. "I worked in a café during the weekend to earn some money on the side, because I sent part of my grant money home to my mother. One evening he saw me there . . ." Kady shudders at the memory. "You should have seen the look on his face. Me, a girl from a good Moorish family, working in a bar! I knew right then that it was over between us."

Caught between a German who found her too prudish and a Sudanese for whom she was too liberated – Kady didn't know how to free herself from the situation. The Mauritanian government had given her a grant, but one day she would have to repay it by working at home, she'd told herself. And then there was her mother in Nouakchott: she didn't want to leave her alone any longer. While Abderrahmane was busy postponing his departure from Moscow, Kady was pondering her return.

Back in Mauritania she got a job in a hotel, but what had once seemed such a plausible choice of study turned out to be quite wrong: a woman working in a hotel in Nouakchott – that was almost like prostitution. She'd reached marriageable age, but no one proposed to her. Moorish men didn't consider her a real Moor. They could tell by her accent, by the way she wore her *melahfa*, even by the way she walked, that she'd been abroad. Men found her arrogant.

Her older brother Abdallah, who lives in Nouakchott, decided it was time for Kady to leave. She and her mother were holding each other prisoner: if she didn't move on, she'd become an old maid. So she went back to Mali and found a job in a little provincial hotel. That's where she met her husband, a businessman. He's been good to her, and her mother likes him, which helps; she moved in with them after the wedding. But she doesn't tell me what Bako let slip in an unguarded moment – she's not her husband's only wife.

Kady lies in the grass, deep in thought. She has a poetic way of talking, and Abderrahmane told me she writes poetry. But when I ask her about it, she says almost apologetically: "That was a long time ago." She doesn't complain, and yet I sense an enormous loss. Her brothers have found their way in life, but because she's a woman, she has ended up between a rock and a hard place. And now she's assumed the responsibility of looking after her mother – at least, that's what she thinks. Her mother whispered to me that she was only staying in Bamako to help Kady – otherwise she would have returned to Mauritania long ago. Back in Germany Kady had verve, but here her life has become bogged down. "She's sacrificed herself," Abderrahmane will tell me later, "she's the bird with the broken wings."

She walks with me part of the way to the Route de Koulikoro, a shawl draped over her shoulders. Watching her shuffle back through the sand, I feel dejected. But my admiration for Abderrahmane has grown in the last few hours. More than ever before, I realize how hard it was for him to leave the family nest and start a new life elsewhere.

* * *

Amidou took me to the bus station in Bamako on his scooter, and now an older, heavier version of Amidou rides up to meet me at the terminal in Ségou. Aziz, how could I miss him? The stickers on the front of his scooter, which looked like eyes from a distance, turn into two pots of mayonnaise as he gets closer.

I have piles of baggage with me; fortunately it's not my own, as my bags are full of things for his father. Bako helped me do the shopping. I've brought plantains, mandarins, coffee, cheese, olives, even *sirop de menthe*. Aziz balances the cardboard box on the tank in front of him, and I climb onto the back with a bag hanging from each shoulder and a suitcase propped between us. While the dust of Ségou billows up around us and cafés with names like *Tanti, j'ai faim* and *Soir au village* go zipping by, I feel like a pathetic goat, lashed to the back of a bike on its way to market.

Aziz is a school inspector in Ségou. He's the oldest in the family, and his whole being radiates dignity. As soon as I saw him I knew I'd left the capital far behind. His brothers in Bamako dress in Western clothes, but he's wearing sandals, a gray *boubou* with yellow embroidery, and matching trousers.

Like Bamako, Ségou is on the Niger, which makes for a lot of activity: sand is being sifted and made into bricks on the waterfront; bare-breasted girls are swimming between the fishing boats; men are playing checkers on the beach. The passenger ferry to the upriver towns of Mopti and Gao has just come into dock.

During French colonial times, Ségou was the seat of the *Office du Niger*, which coordinated rice cultivation along the river. After all these years, the colonial homes of the governor, the prefect and the bishop are still impressive, hidden behind the acacias along the waterfront.

I'm reminded of *Ségou*, Maryse Condé's two-volume epic portrayal of this city in the nineteenth century. Back then it was the capital of a powerful Bambara empire, which was brought down by Islam and the white man's arrival. Aziz has never heard of Condé. Of course, he knows the history of the area – the last king of Ségou lies buried just outside the city – but he's amazed to learn that that same history is the subject of books popular in the West.

Aziz lives in a plain house with an open yard. He began building it four years ago; two bedrooms and a living room are already finished. The floors are made of concrete, and everything is spick-and-span. The bricks for the next phase are stacked in the yard.

He has three children, and a number of children from his family in the interior live with them as well. "*Famille africaine*," as his wife notes laughingly. The clothes in the children's room hang next to empty Marlboro packets and photos of soccer players. Aziz asks if I have any children. When I shake my head, he says: "According to a Bambara proverb, someone who dies without children isn't *dead*, but *finished*."

119

That evening we sit out in the yard, under the stars, surrounded by a pleasing silence. Aziz's wife, a midwife, talks about her work. Mothers here never stay in the maternity ward long, because of the mosquitoes. Many babies used to die of suffocation at birth, but fortunately, Ségou's French sister city, Angoulême, donated a respirator to the hospital. Since then infant mortality has dropped sharply. Specialists from Angoulême occasionally come to teach courses in hygiene, and once in a while a Malian nurse goes to France for practical training – a rare opportunity that everyone tries to grab.

I listen and feel the world becoming simpler. This is life in the African interior after independence. Those fortunate enough to live in a place that isn't too remote maintain contact with the outside world through projects such as these.

Aziz doesn't understand why Bako and Amidou, both over thirty, are still single and seemingly uninterested in getting married. When he was twenty-three, his father asked him if he should look for a wife for him within the family. He said no, he wasn't even thinking of getting married yet. Four years later he married a woman he had chosen himself, but she was still the daughter of one of his father's friends.

The traditional system of arranged marriages no longer works, he admits, but aren't his younger brothers taking things a bit too far? Whenever he starts on about it, Bako only laughs. "My fiancée's mother hasn't been born yet," he says.

I talked to Bako and Amidou about their bachelor status. Girls are only interested in money, they said, and money is one thing they haven't got. They don't seem particularly bothered by it – all their friends are in the same boat. But seen from this home, where everything is arranged so neatly, I can imagine how chaotic life back in Bamako must seem.

Abderrahmane moves in a world that is beyond Aziz's ken. When Aziz visited his father in Sokolo last year, Abderrahmane was there too. He said he was planning to make a movie about Sokolo. Aziz used to do some amateur theater, and his brother promised him a role. "But first you'll have to lose weight," he joked. Now Aziz wants to know: do Europeans like African cinema? That's as hard for him to imagine as Europeans being enthusiastic about a book set in Ségou.

※※※

The car that goes from Ségou to Sokolo once a week is an old Peugeot pick-up with wooden benches under a cloth canopy. In a surge of enthusiasm, Moussa, the owner, has painted the words 'Air Sokolo' on the door. By the time I turn up the first passengers have already arrived, but Moussa looks doubtful. People don't travel much during Ramadan, and no one seems to be spending any money since the franc's been devalued.

Six passengers – a meager harvest, but after Moussa has lashed our baggage to the roof, he decides to set off. We stop on Ségou's main street to buy French bread. Moussa ties the loaves to the roof of the cab, making them look pretty sorry from the start.

Just when I think we're really on our way, Moussa stops again. He dashes into a house and comes out with an old man dressed in a white *boubou* with red piping, who takes a seat between us. He's an impressive-looking gentleman with a red felt fez and thick glasses. His skin is as rough as a lizard's, lined like the cracks in a mud wall. His laceless shoes are smashed down at the heels and look many sizes too small. Straight as a ramrod he sits next to me, his cane clenched between his knees.

Barou is his name; he's eighty-three, and he speaks the beautiful French that old men in this part of Africa use. He never went to school: he learned it from his friends. He's traveling to his rice fields close to Sokolo. It's hard for me to imagine him out in a field in the burning sun, but he says he often goes out on inspection; sometimes he stays away for weeks.

He radiates enormous strength as he sits there, a smile playing across his lips. The world is good as it is. I'm reminded of the late writer Amadou Hampâté Bâ, who was born not far from here, in Bandiagara. He was raised in the oral tradition and became one

121

with the history of this area. "An old African dying is a library going up in flames," Hampâté Bâ once said.

I sneak a glance at Barou and wonder whether Sissako looks like this as well. When I got up this morning, I was suddenly snared by doubt. Will *le vieux* appreciate my visit? I wish I could have taken Amidou with me, but he couldn't get away from work. He called the post office in Sokolo, though, to tell his father that I was coming. He also gave me an envelope of money for him, and a letter with the names of a few people I should meet in Sokolo. "My father isn't interested in the same things you might be interested in," he said with a knowing laugh, "in any way, shape or form!"

Barou's presence reassures me. Since he climbed into the cab, I have the feeling that this trip is blessed. It's as though the spirit of Sissako is already traveling with me. Everything he sees pleases him. Mangoes, papayas, guavas, pomegranates, rice, sugarcane – whatever you plant here, it grows. The land is so fertile that the farmers sow rice twice a year. "This soil likes trees," he says. But when we pass a plot of woodland, he looks doubtful. "They should plant fruit trees everywhere, then this would be just like Guinea or the Ivory Coast."

Pleasant as it is to listen to him talk, I know his story isn't completely accurate. The soil here isn't as good as he claims, as it has too much iron in it. Since the French left, the irrigation system has been neglected, and now the drought has come along and made things worse. Development experts are frantically trying to curtail the damage. Isn't Mali one of the poorest countries in the world? Isn't it propped up by the hundreds of organizations you keep tripping over in the capital?

"That's because we're still being colonized," Barou says. "The colonizer is gone, but the system remains; our leaders have taken it over." He doesn't think too highly of the democracy that descended on the country in 1991.

It's the tragedy of his generation, one you also sense in the writer Hampâté Bâ: wise as they might be, epic as their stories about the past might sound, their ancestors lost to the French and they've been left with the pieces. Hampâté Bâ's French friends encouraged him to write, but when he did, it was in French. Children today are no longer interested in the old people's stories; they sit in front of the television and dream of scooters, careening away from their parents at the speed of light. Barou's son, who went to school in Germany, is married to a German woman and has no intention of returning to Mali.

We stop along the way to pick up more passengers, but also for Moussa to take care of all kinds of business. He paces around worriedly in his *boubou* and headcloth – he's probably doing his best to turn this trip into something lucrative after all. When we pull up to a military roadblock, I look questioningly at Barou. He laughs. "We're at the crossroads between any number of countries: Mauritania, Burkina Faso, Senegal, the Ivory Coast. People could be trying to smuggle goods from one place to the next." Some of the countries he mentions are a long way from here, but his naming them reflects his broad view of the region. He says nothing about the Tuareg rebels and bandits I've been hearing about for months, who hold sway in the north, along the border with Mauritania.

Twenty kilometers past Ségou we get our first flat tire; the second puncture comes less than an hour later. Moussa stops at an open-air garage along the road, and we take shelter under the thatched reed roof of a nearby café. They serve cola, but Barou doesn't want to drink anything. He's observing Ramadan. No, he's not thirsty; he's used to fasting. But he's worried about me: shouldn't I eat something?

The tire gets a primitive patch job. To locate the leak, the tube is dunked in a water basin made from half an oil drum with legs welded onto the bottom. A boy goes by on a donkey cart, an umbrella shielding him from the sun. Kids pull empty sardine cans along behind them on strings; one of the children is wearing a pair of improvised sunglasses made from a strip of black-and-white film.

Turning from this second-hand world to the road, I see a brand-new Toyota jeep drive by, followed by an open bus with a remarkable lily-white entourage on board. They look down at us, laughing from their high seats. I can barely believe my eyes, but Barou isn't surprised at all. Tourists, he says, most likely on their way to Dogon Country. They're probably traveling in an open bus so they can take pictures, or make movies.

As always, I'm amazed how easily Africans accept material differences. Here we are, stranded in our bush taxi with hopelessly worn tires while a surrealistic carnival float full of rich white people passes by, and no one says a thing about it. White people have everything.

I peek impatiently at my watch, but Barou sits calmly on the wooden bench beside me, leaning on his cane. When the car is ready to leave, he says philosophically: "I believe we've experienced a slight delay."

The paved road ends at the town of Niono; I'm starting to see what Abderrahmane meant when he said there was no real road to Sokolo. We drive on along a narrow, bumpy trail of sand. It's like being carried down a tunnel, away from the civilized world, and the claustrophobia I felt when I climbed into Bako's Mazda returns. What if I become ill in Sokolo? Will I have to be evacuated down this dusty road full of potholes?

Barou has been murmuring prayers, letting his beads glide through his fingers, but now he seems to feel that the time has come to ask me a few questions. Are there illiterate women in France? And what about mangoes – do they grow in France? When I tell him I live in Holland, not France, he changes tack. "Are there Muslims in Holland?" My answer seems to please him. "That's good, it's becoming richer." He thinks Islam is a good religion when it's practiced correctly. Unfortunately, that's not always the case; he made a pilgrimage to Mecca once, and thinks the Saudis are hypocritical.

"I suppose they grow a lot of rice in Holland."

"No, we've got the wrong climate for that."

"But in Niono, Dutch specialists teach us how to grow rice!" He can't get over it: people coming all the way to Africa to grow a crop they don't even have in their own country!

But when I tell him that there really are Dutch farmers, he's amazed. "I thought all Europeans were intellectuals. The French who lived here let the blacks do all the work."

A short time before this we saw some Chinese people, little men in pointy reed hats driving tractors around in the fields. They work with their hands, Barou says, and speak perfect Bambara, but they don't mix with the local population.

"Don't they have children here?"

He shakes his head resolutely. "No, the Chinese are serious people."

We pass merchants on bicycles, peddling their plastic buckets, enameled pans and colorful fabric from village to village. It reminds me of my mother, who used to cycle from the Grote Hei to Neerpelt with a basket full of chicks and eggs on her carrier. The merchants greet Moussa enthusiastically, and sometimes he stops for a chat.

When I ask how far we have to go, neither Barou nor Moussa seems to know. "Another half-hour," Barou says when I persist, but I can tell he isn't sure. "In any case, we're getting closer," he smiles. He told me that a laborer would be waiting for him along the road to Sokolo, to take him to his fields. Just when I start to wonder where his helper could be hiding, Moussa slows down. Barou peers out across the fields. In the shade of a tree, a man is sleeping on a donkey cart. "That's him." Moussa helps him take down his baggage, then Barou leaves us, sitting majestically atop his cart, an umbrella held above his head.

Herds of cattle are grazing in the distance. Behind them rises an orderly little village of clay houses. Sokolo. Moussa immediately relaxes, and drives through the streets honking, one hand resting casually on the wheel. People greet him from all sides, and inquisitive glances stray in my direction.

The mosque on the marketplace gleams in the late-afternoon sun. A *muezzin* in a white *boubou* appears on the roof and begins singing hoarsely. Life goes on uninterrupted at his feet. A few passengers climb out of Moussa's taxi and mingle with the graceful figures in flapping *boubous* who are crossing the square.

I look around breathlessly. This is where Abderrahmane saw his father again after so many years. This is where he embraced him, looked down and saw to his surprise that his father was wearing no shoes. I've finally arrived.

❧

By the time Moussa has dropped off all the passengers, we've passed through the whole village and everyone knows a white woman has arrived. We stop in front of a clay house where a thin man with spectacles is squatting in the sand. That must be Sissako's youngest brother, who's always lived in Sokolo and who wrote to Amidou asking for money. He stands up, takes my bags from Moussa and leads me into a yard with cows, donkeys and chickens, past an old woman with wizened breasts lying in a doorway, to the back of the house.

Sissako isn't home, but once we've stacked all the baggage under the broad verandah, I hear hurried footsteps and turn around to find him standing there. His brother only nodded to me in greeting, but Sissako shakes my hand, briefly and firmly – I can feel his vitality right away. He's shorter than I'd imagined, and one of his eyes is smaller than the other, giving his face the irregularity I'd noticed in photos but was unable to pinpoint. My gaze travels involuntarily to his feet. He's wearing cowhide sandals – the kind Tuaregs wear.

He stands there as if he owes me an apology, as though I'd asked him why we were meeting here amid the cows and donkeys, rather than in the capital. He gestures to indicate his modest dwelling, and says Bamako, with its noisy cars and television sets, doesn't interest him; he'd rather be here.

There's a mattress lying under the verandah, and an iron bed with mosquito netting tied above it. This is where Amidou usually sleeps, and I can sleep there too, if I like. Unless, of course, I'd rather be inside . . .

"No, no," I say quickly. To live here the way Amidou does, that would be excellent.

I hear a rustling under the eaves. The whole ceiling is full of birds' nests! It's a real ruckus up there, and occasionally a tiny feather comes floating down amid the peep and flutter. Sissako shrugs apologetically again. "Swallows," he says. "They were here when I came, and I didn't have the heart to chase them away. So we've lived together ever since."

My father is a man of few formalities. Amidou hit the nail on the head. Sitting on his mattress, Sissako tears open the letters I brought him, glances at them and sticks Amidou's money in his *boubou*, mumbling now and then. Finally he stuffs the envelopes under his pillow, where he keeps his flashlight, his pocketknife, his pen and keys. That's where the letters will stay for the rest of the time I'm in Sokolo.

"And what have we here?" He pulls the cardboard box over to him, inspects the contents briefly, pulls something out and holds it up to the light. "What's this?"

"Peanut butter."

"Hmm. Did you find this in Bamako?"

I nod. It's in a plastic bag, local goods. I brought it for myself, to keep from starving the way Abderrahmane's mother predicted.

He's pleased with the five loaves of French bread. He doesn't like the bread they sell here in the market; it's too soft and tasteless, and doesn't keep for more than a few days.

The box goes into the side room, but it has to be sealed so the mice won't get to it. I put the rest of my baggage in there too. The room has a bed, and in one corner I find a dusty stack of documents, reports and school notebooks filled with a child's handwriting, letters drawn carefully between the lines. Could these belong to his oldest sons who went to school here?

Sissako refers to the room in the middle as his storeroom; it's the only one he keeps locked. At first glance, this room with its wobbly chairs and rotting crates doesn't seem to contain much that anyone might want. But as time goes by, I find it's a real treasure trove. His *boubous* are in suitcases, neatly ironed and folded, and one day he even comes out with an egg-beater. In one of the photos lying around I recognize Kady at the official opening of a hotel. She's looking festive, but the photo is crumpled and fly-specked.

Sissako is so unflappable, so very much his own man, that I take to him right away, and yet I feel more reticent than ever. You could live around someone like this for a hundred years and never get one step closer. I'm glad his children told me about him – he doesn't seem much in the habit of talking about himself.

I think back to my first meeting with Abderrahmane: his economical movements, his deliberate manner of speech. I was the Westerner, heir to a culture that considers itself dominant, yet I felt brittle and vulnerable in his presence. I was somewhat prepared for the effect that his father would have on me, but once again I'm amazed. To think that I'm in a continent that the rest of the world is prepared to write off!

The wife of Sissako's youngest brother, who lives on the other side of the house, brings me a bucket of warm water. I lather myself in a roofless cubicle, out in the open air. The tingling aroma of woodsmoke wafts my way; I hear children laughing and talking, and in the distance I see people walking down the street. The final rays of sun slide down the walls as I toss water over myself with a plastic cup. I can tell I'm going to be happy here.

When evening comes, Sissako puts together a few of the things I've brought him and we go to his friend Sori's house, where he usually eats. The inhabitants of Sokolo shuffle slowly through the streets, but he walks with a determined stride, the tails of his *boubou* swept back, hands clasped behind him. People are waiting in front of their houses for the *muezzin*'s call of deliverance, and now and then he stops to introduce me. Everyone remembers Abderrahmane's video camera, and they all ask if I have one with me as well.

We pass the square where the weekly market is held. This is where Bobo Mouso was wandering around, her baby tied to her back. It was Sissako who decided to take her to Bamako.

"Everyone thinks she's crazy," he says, "but I don't believe it. She's clean and she works hard. If she'd always eaten from the same plate with the rest of them, she would have turned out differently. But they cast her out. That's what's made her strange."

He speaks in short, staccato sentences. This must be the way he talks to his children: he gives them his opinion, and they can do with it as they please. That's how he deals with the inhabitants of Sokolo as well. "He looks like a normal villager," Amidou told me, "but as soon as he opens his mouth, everyone knows he's different." When Sissako arrived here after he'd retired, he discovered that one of his old schoolmates had been chained to the tree in front of his house – a common fate for aggressive village madmen. Sissako went to visit the man often and, to everyone's amazement, got along well with him. His friend told him he felt threatened, and that was why he sometimes flew into a rage. A marabout recommended he leave Sokolo and never return. The man began a new life elsewhere, but since then Sissako has had the reputation of being a bit mad himself.

The market stalls – little awnings propped up on thin poles – are deserted, but some of the shops around the square are still open. There used to be lots of Moorish shopkeepers here, Sissako tells me, but most of them fled for fear that the villagers might confuse them with the Tuareg rebels terrorizing the north. Recently, a car going to the market in nearby Nara was forced to stop; the passengers had to get out, and then the rebels took off with the car.

"But you're a Moor yourself. Aren't you afraid?"

Sissako shakes his head and shoulders at the same time, as if trying to ward off my question – a movement I'll see him make often when he hears something he doesn't like. "I was born here, the people know who I am."

The leaders of the Tuareg, who fought for autonomy for years, signed a treaty with the Malian government in 1992, but the robberies, thefts and mysterious disappearances in the region continue. Sissako says the culprits are rebels who disagree with their leaders, but there are also common bandits among them who

129

have taken advantage of the power vacuum created by the rebellion.

We've arrived at a large, walled house of rough concrete that breathes the same sobriety as Aziz's house in Ségou. Sissako opens the gate and steps into a broad hallway, where a man in an easy chair is listening to the radio. He gets up and walks over to us, smiling, the last light falling across his dark, handsome face and cobalt-blue *boubou*. The last thing I'd expected on the edge of this village was to meet such a distinguished figure.

Sori leads us to a room he calls *le salon*, but which looks just as bare as the rest of the house. In the dim light of an oil lamp I can make out three cane chairs and a table with magazines and books. In the next room, Sori's wife is setting out bowls of food. Sissako isn't observing Ramadan – he feels he's gone without often enough in his life – but Sori is fasting. As soon as he hears the *muezzin*'s cry on the radio, he gestures for us to be seated.

The table is a sheet on the floor with all the dishes grouped together: rice porridge, couscous, fruit. Sissako serves himself by the light of a flashlight. He occasionally glances at my plate, and when he thinks I've taken too little of anything, he dishes me up more without saying a word. Sori's wife doesn't eat with us – she's retired to the yard at the back of the house.

Sissako and Sori studied meteorology together when they were young, but then they went their separate ways. Sori ended up in politics, occupying several ministerial posts and other top government positions. Now that both of them are old, the hubbub of the world reaches them only by way of the radio or the occasional visitor.

They eat hurriedly, obviously not in the habit of talking at the table, except about the food itself. They share a passion for gardening – in Bamako, Sori once raised strawberries, and the melons on the table come from his garden as well. He cuts them in half, grumbling: they turned out too small.

After dinner we move back to the salon. Sori is concerned about the student strikes in the capital. The atmosphere is becoming grimmer with each passing day; today the radio reported that students had once again attacked a man. "When the French were here, there was order in this country," he says, "but now it's nowhere to be found." It's just like the rebellion in the north: during colonial times, French soldiers were stationed everywhere. These days, the Malian army is conspicuously absent along the border, which leaves room for all kinds of rabble to do exactly as they please.

Sissako leans back in his chair and laughs. Just before independence, when Sori and his friends came to tell him that their party had won the elections, he'd said: "Setting up a democratic and prosperous country is a task far beyond your creative powers." They'd thought that a nasty remark, but it turned out he was right. He's for democracy, but he doesn't believe the people in power are up to it, and the population doesn't really seem to want it either.

He speaks softly, but with authority. I hear Sori sigh – they've probably gone over this many times. Sissako is leaning forward now, and the light of the oil lamp casts his silhouette on the wall. I've searched his face in vain for traces of Abderrahmane, but now I recognize his profile: the sunken eyes, the pursed lips, chin resting on folded hands – an attitude of extreme composure. Even the way he runs his fingers through his hair is familiar.

I hadn't noticed before, but there's a fourth person in the room; he must have come in during dinner, and is lying on the bed behind us. It's Sori's son, Amadou, who lived in the Ivory Coast but is back now to help his father with the rice harvest. Amadou, Amidou, Mamadou – they're all African variations on the name of the prophet Mohammed; every family has one.

Amadou addresses Sissako as *l'homme*, 'the man'. Sori laughs when I comment on it. They all used to call Sissako *l'homme chic*, because he'd been to university and had such an aristocratic bearing. The shorter form, *l'homme*, has stuck. When I look over at Sissako, I see he's fallen asleep.

Outside, the moon illuminates the broad sandy path leading to the center of the village. Sori accompanies us part of the way. During the rainy season you sink to your ankles in the mud, he

131

says, and sometimes Sokolo is cut off from the outside world for months. He wasn't planning to stay for six months when he arrived in Sokolo last summer, but that's often how it goes: once he's here, life in Bamako no longer appeals to him.

Sissako and I walk on in silence. Children are playing along the road in the moonlight. A woman shouts something that makes Sissako laugh.

"What did she say?"

"She asked whether you were the daughter who arrived with Moussa this afternoon."

◢◣◥◤

Sissako is sitting straight up in bed. He took off his *boubou* last night, and now he's pottering around a charcoal burner in his underwear – a pair of white drawers and a shirt. He usually drinks hot milk in the morning, but in my honor he's dug up the Italian espresso pot Kady brought him from Germany. He's firing up the coals with a fan.

I wrap a *pagne* around my waist and slip out of bed. Sissako's brothers come into the yard. Every morning they run through the day's work with him – a sign of respect for their eldest brother. With their pointy reed hats and weathered faces, they look much older than him, but their feet are what fascinate me. There's something animal about them: blunt toes, cracked nails, callused, deeply grooved soles. Sissako is well on his way to getting feet like that too.

He cuts a piece of French bread for me, then hands me the jam and a bowl of coffee with warm milk and sugar. Everyone else in Sokolo eats warmed-up leftovers from the night before; he's the only one in town who has a Continental breakfast.

Translucent lizards race across the walls, and life is in full swing above our heads. Swallows swoop past, fledglings peep in their nests, and the occasional bird dropping lands on Kady's coffee pot or on the old radio.

Sissako asks me questions, apparently at random, just like old

Barou in the *taxi-brousse*. Is there unemployment in Holland? How many meters below sea level are the Netherlands? Does Holland import French cheese? And they have so much cheese themselves! It seems like total nonsense to him.

He also tries to find out about Abderrahmane's life in Paris. Whose apartment does he live in, and why did he go to Mongolia recently? What was he doing there? I know what he's angling for. He's probably heard about the French woman in Abderrahmane's life. I answer as evasively as I can – taking into account Amidou's remark that his father is a born journalist.

Sissako is quite well informed about Abderrahmane's trials and tribulations in Moscow, although he didn't hear it all first-hand. He knows Abderrahmane had a Russian girlfriend, whose name was Lina; through Kady, Abderrahmane once asked if his father would object if he married her. He's also picked up something about the robbery in his son's Moscow apartment. He suspects it influenced Abderrahmane's final decision not to get married.

Still, he's not concerned about Abderrahmane – maybe because Abdallah went to visit him in Paris recently and came back with no alarming reports. His son Mokhtar is the one he's worried about. He works for the Red Cross, with Liberian refugees in Abidjan, and sometimes he doesn't write or call for months.

"I think I'm going to pay him a surprise visit soon – I don't trust it."

"What don't you trust?"

"Mokhtar drinks!" The word sounds so strange in these surroundings that he has to laugh. I'm surprised he knows about it – it's the kind of thing a son usually hides from his father.

"Of course, he doesn't drink when I'm around," he says. "He doesn't even dare to smoke in my presence."

"So how do you know about it?"

In Bamako, Mokhtar came home drunk one night with a barkeeper on his heels: he didn't have enough money to pay his bill. Sissako stayed inside, but his children told him about the state Mokhtar was in.

"He learned to drink when he was studying in the Crimea, and he's gone crazy ever since." After finishing medical school, Mokhtar did postgraduate work in psychiatry in Abidjan. He'd proudly showed his father his doctoral thesis. "You'll never guess what the title was: *Alcoholism in the Ivory Coast*! I told him: you should be a real expert on that!"

Sissako's brothers, who only speak Bambara, have left without a word. A worker comes bicycling into the yard to report that something's wrong with the rice mill, which is running at full capacity these days. Sissako gets up quickly. "Do you want to come along?"

He walks even faster than he did last night, preoccupied as he is with his machine. I'm reminded of what Kady told me: *My father loves only his rice fields.* We pass the pharmacist and the butcher waiting for customers in front of their shops, and the school principal, who has nothing to do now the government's decided to close the elementary schools as well. But there's a lot of activity around the workshop where Sissako has his milling machine. People come in from the fields with donkey carts to have their rice processed. They pay in kind: they use measuring cups on their way out to toss rice into a big gourd.

Bales are piled high in the yard, and in one corner the machine stands shuddering and shaking. Sissako got it from a niece he'd taken under his wing a long time ago. It's a great piece of machinery, he says, only people treat it too roughly. He shouts something to the dusty worker who's shoveling raw rice into the huge vibrating funnel, critically eyes the machine's spasms and runs his hand through the milled rice pouring out into sacks at the other end.

The workshop is a lively meeting place; everyone of substance in Sokolo has a rice field. On our way out we run into the manager of the collective store. Sissako teasingly calls the manager a potbelly who has become too fat to work his own fields; these days he only pushes other people around. When Sori's son Amadou cycles past in his Mexican sombrero, Sissako asks whether he's already had his bourgeois breakfast of grilled meat. Sissako likes baiting people, I notice. He does it good-naturedly, but that doesn't make it any less effective: Amadou and the manager both laugh sheepishly.

"Let's go," he says suddenly. Amidou wrote to him that I should meet Bina, who runs the post and telegraph office close to the entrance to the village, across the street from the district officer's house.

There are about three thousand people in Sokolo but only one telephone, which makes Bina a key person in village life. We find him in his office, chronometer in hand, while a customer at the counter screams into the phone. He greets us enthusiastically, without taking his eyes off the clock. He listens unabashedly to what the man is blaring into the phone, and laughs heartily at what he says. They'd agreed on a three-minute call, so when the customer's time is almost up he begins gesturing wildly.

He must be about twenty-eight, a rather heavy-set young man with a beard and lively eyes. He's left an unmistakable mark on the space he works in. The walls are hung with an amusing collection of slogans glorifying the efficiency of the Malian postal system and its conscientious officials, and above his desk a photo of Saddam Hussein in battle dress is pinned next to a postcard of the White House.

Only when the customer has hung up and Bina rolls over to lock the phone do I see that he's in a wheelchair. He maneuvers skillfully around the room. It's a brand-new model with gears, and the airline tag still dangles from the back. Bina wears orthopedic shoes. Polio, I suppose.

Sissako has disappeared without a word. Bina laughs at my amazement. "Want to bet he's gone back to his milling machine?" According to Bina, that's where *le vieux* spends his days.

Bina lives with his young, pregnant wife in rooms to one side of the post office. They can't get by on his salary alone, so she sells *to* – sorghum paste – at the market during the day. In the yard are the solar panels that power the switchboard. There's a fence around them to keep out the goats, which provide a bit of income too.

Bina draws his salary at the end of each month from the post office revenues, a real tour de force when business is slow. Fortunately, about forty families from Sokolo have moved to the Congo and telephone traffic between Sokolo and Brazzaville is at an all-time high. The emigrants do business between Hong Kong and Brazza, and are considered wealthy. They eat their evening meals together at a house with a phone, so they can easily be reached.

Riots broke out in Brazzaville a while back, so some of the men sent their wives home to Sokolo. Bina listens to French radio broadcasts every day, and the wives come in regularly to ask if there's any news. "When the end of the month is coming up and I'm stuck for money, I sometimes tell them things are pretty bad. Then they're sure to ask for three minutes that same evening!" He laughs mischievously. In a village where only Bambara is spoken, a working knowledge of French is a negotiable item.

Abderrahmane made a call to France while he was in Sokolo, Bina says, and he hopes I'll feel free to call Holland while I'm here . . . The phone rings, an unearthly sound amid the braying of donkeys, the bleating of goats and the rhythmic stamping of rice being pounded to flour in the distance.

"I'll only be a moment." Bina rolls his wheelchair outside and swings himself up onto the scooter he's had since secondary school; he uses it to let people know there's a call for them. A few minutes later he's back again.

"Why didn't you bring your customer with you?"

He climbs up the steps, dragging his paralyzed leg behind him. "Listen, I'm not a taxi driver!"

The party in question arrives on his bicycle, with the dusty worker I saw at the milling machine in his wake. Mr Sissako is expecting me for lunch.

***

Sori's house looks even barer by day. Lunch is on the table in the back room, but Sori is nowhere in sight; he must be taking a nap. After we've eaten, Amadou drives us home in his father's pick-up. The sun is high in the sky and the streets of Sokolo are deserted.

In the yard the air is stiflingly hot, but under the swallows' nests it's cool. Amadou stays for a while, and Sissako lies on his back on the mattress, his knees pulled up, full of good humor and laughing readily at the stories Amadou tells. A little later, though, he suddenly falls asleep and snores so loudly that Amadou and I don't know where to look. But his nap doesn't last long, and when he awakes he effortlessly picks up the thread of the conversation.

From under my bed – where a host of precious things seem to be stored – he pulls out an enameled pan in which he keeps stale bread and peanuts. He and Amadou sit across from each other, cracking nuts fraternally like two blissful monkeys. Raw peanuts are good for his digestion, Sissako has discovered. There's no doctor in town, so he's become his own physician. The other villagers consult him as well; mothers even bring their sick children to him for advice. Abderrahmane sent him a book about medicine once, but unfortunately it never arrived.

He takes the morning's milk and mixes it with water, sugar and sorghum flour to make *zrig*, which they use in Mauritania to fatten up marriageable daughters. He pours a big glass of it and hands it to me. The flour has gone mildewy, making the beverage taste like sawdust, but I'd probably hurt his feelings if I refused so I drink it all. Ten days later, when Abderrahmane's mother sees me again, she'll home in on me from behind her thick glasses and say I've put on weight.

Sometimes Sissako laughingly translates Amadou's words, or comments on what he's just said, but afterwards the conversation automatically switches to French. Amadou seems to have led a worldly life in Abidjan. He ate breakfast every morning at an establishment he says was as good as any Parisian *brasserie*. He had a black American girlfriend, and he tells tall tales about the nightclubs they visited. To him, Abidjan is the Paris of Africa.

Amadou told me he'd come back to Sokolo to help his father and see what effect the devaluation of the franc will have. But

137

Sissako tells me an altogether different story. Sori bought his son a truck so he could trade goods between Abidjan and Bamako, but Amadou ran through so much money that his father finally called him home. Sori has been trying to get him to do some work ever since, but so far the switch from Abidjan to Sokolo hasn't gone smoothly. Amadou can't talk to his father, and I have the impression that Sissako has taken over the task.

Amadou is a dreamer, Sissako says. He's always talking about Paris, even though he's never been there. I should ask him sometime about the fiancée his father found for him; Amadou anxiously keeps her under wraps, but still lets her grill meat for him every morning.

As a matter of fact, Amadou is disgusted by this place where he sits cracking peanuts with such relish. He knew a French woman in Abidjan who was afraid of cockroaches, and he assumes that dusty Sokolo horrifies me as well. When he turns on the radio and I laugh at the horrible static it produces, he says with annoyance: "You probably think it's full of cockroaches or mice." He asks me to write down the Dutch words for 'mouse', 'dust' and 'cockroach'.

Amadou looks up to Sissako, but he has a hard time understanding how he puts up with things around here. "*L'homme* can live anywhere," he says while Sissako rummages around under my bed for his glasses.

Sissako fishes a few more peanuts out of the pan. "Amadou thinks I've come here to go primitive," he says, tossing the shells carelessly on the ground. "And he's afraid his father brought him back here to go primitive as well." He laces up his Tuareg sandals, prompting another of Amadou's disparaging remarks. "He thinks I'm a savage because I wear shoes like these." Sissako laughs. "The only thing he'll wear are fancy brand-name shoes!" Of the three of us, I realize, Sissako is at heart the youngest, and certainly the most free.

A gangly young man comes wandering into the yard. It's Djéry, whom Amidou mentioned in the letter he wrote to his father. He has all the time in the world and would be pleased to show me around, Amidou said. Sissako takes advantage of his arrival to disappear noiselessly.

∿∿

Like Amadou, Djéry is no normal village boy. He attended school in Bamako and planned on becoming a civil servant. He couldn't find a job in the capital, though, so he left in the hope of reaching Brazzaville, where other adventurers from Sokolo had done so well. He'd been in Abidjan too, but his experiences were quite different from Amadou's. Abidjan is like the Wild West, he says: he saw a robbery in broad daylight, and after that he didn't dare go out at night. From the Ivory Coast he hitchhiked to Nigeria, where he found work. But he couldn't save enough money for a plane ticket to Brazzaville, so he returned to Sokolo without a penny. Now he's the trainer of the local soccer team, and his father is trying to buy a shop for him, or else a display case of merchandise he can sell in the market.

He met a number of women during his travels, and even lived with one of them for a while. There was one city girl he would have liked to marry, but he couldn't afford it. Now, his father has found a fiancée for him in Sokolo. She's fourteen, half his age, and has never been to school; Djéry talks about her like a child. The problem is, she's starting to cost him money too. Before Ramadan is over he has to buy her new clothes and all kinds of *tralala*, like braids for her hair and cowry shells to hang in them.

As we walk through the village, Djéry greets the pharmacist, who he calls 'Bernard Tapie' because he sponsors the village soccer team. Balls, cleats, uniforms: all the equipment comes from him. "His brother is the governor of Timbuktu," Djéry whispers, as if that explains everything.

The road stops at a pond where women and children are washing clothes. Djéry isn't sure when the pond was dug. "It was here before I was born," he says – Africans often say that when they don't know the particulars. About ten years ago there was a rumor that the pond water had healing properties, and people came from all over to bathe in it. The miraculous powers are worn out now. On the other side of the pond is a marsh where children are catching little fish in nets and with their bare hands. The scrawny little minnows give flavor to the sauce they put on their rice.

The ocher-colored wall around the graveyard was donated by the expats living in Brazzaville. The graves bear few markings, but Djéry says there's an old man in Sokolo who knows where everyone is buried.

"And what's this?" I've stumbled upon a grave with *Drissa Coulibaly, 12.6.92* written on it. "That was the district officer's watchman, who was killed when the rebels attacked Sokolo," Djéry says.

Rebels attacking Sokolo? Sissako didn't tell me about that. They came at night, planning to murder or kidnap the district officer. But he was away on business, so they shot the guard instead. They fired their guns in the air and made a lot of noise, causing people to flee in panic. Some of them ran into the bush; others swam across the river or hid in wells.

"The rebels are very powerful," Djéry says. "There are those who can even stand up to bullets. In Gao, the rebels had a marabout who traveled with them. Whenever they left after a raid, he'd summon up a sandstorm to cover their tracks." There isn't the slightest trace of skepticism in his voice. "Fortunately, the army killed the marabout."

During the days after the rebel attack on Sokolo, local Moors didn't dare venture onto the street. Everyone thought they were accomplices, even though the rebels had also shot a Moorish shopkeeper who tried to run away. After the villagers slaughtered all their camels, the Moors left Sokolo one by one.

"Tuaregs used to live here too," Djéry says, "but they all left in 1990, after one of them was killed. Someone recognized him as being related to the rebels who had murdered a Peul close to here."

He talks calmly about the rebels; from the sound of it, Sokolo has learned to live with them. But people no longer cultivate their rice fields to the north, and the Peul – who herd the people's cattle – are afraid to go too far from the village. The former district officer left Sokolo, and his replacement rarely sleeps in his own house.

Darkness is falling – Sissako will be waiting for me. I walk back to the house deep in thought, realizing I'm on the edge of one of those no-man's lands that have become so common in Africa. When I first spoke of wanting to travel from Mauritania to Mali along the route Sissako's grandparents had taken, everyone had warned me against it. The map showed a border post, but they assured me it had long been shut down.

I finally came into the country along a smugglers' route. The driver of the pick-up had suddenly grinned and told me we were in Mali. He dropped me off at the police station in the next town. No one seemed surprised by my arrival, and my passport was neatly stamped. The customs posts had moved to safer ground, leaving border towns like Sokolo to the rebels' whims.

It's quiet when I walk into Sissako's yard. The machines have been taken inside, and at the back I can hear the regular breathing of the cows. I come around the corner and find Sissako kneeling on a cowhide in the light of the new moon. Is he praying? He isn't making the mechanical movements Muslims do; he's just kneeling there, quiet and solitary, his head raised slightly, prayer beads between his fingers. Only the serenity that surrounds him makes me think he's praying.

The way I came barreling around the corner – I feel frivolous. I slip past him hesitantly, onto the verandah where the oil lamp is flickering.

✺

"You brought peanut butter, but you're not eating it," Sissako says one morning at breakfast. When I tell him Americans eat peanut butter on bread with jam, his eyes light up. "Shall we try it?" I ask.

He nods. "Why not?"

Under his brothers' watchful eyes we smear the brown, grainy substance on our bread and spread jam over it. The bread is hard as rock, and we have to wash it down with coffee. It doesn't taste bad, Sissako thinks, only a bit rich.

Sissako is at his most talkative in the morning, and I learn to value those moments when all he needs is a little prompting to launch into a story – even to laugh freely – for he can be moody as well. When I ask a question, he'll pretend he hasn't heard, or he'll swing the conversation off in a different direction. "Why aren't you eating any fruit? It'll rot otherwise," or: "You still haven't asked me to try your cheese." He regards the things I've brought as my property, given to him only for safekeeping.

A few days ago, when I told him about my visit to the graveyard, he skirted the subject. But now he asks whether Djéry also showed me the former slave market in the old town, on the other side of the pond. When his paternal grandfather used to travel back and forth as a trader between Oualâta and Sokolo, the market still existed. He brought textiles and salt from Oualâta, and left Sokolo with slaves, captured during raids on the surrounding villages. The Moors would storm a village on their camels, shooting into the air, and take any children who were playing down by the water.

One day, Sori's grandfather informed Sissako's maternal grandfather, Kimbéry, that a stunningly beautiful Peul girl of noble birth was left at the market, unsold. The raiders had seized her while she was at the well with her slaves. She was crying, because no one wanted her: she was too skinny. Kimbéry paid for her in gold dust, and married her. They had one daughter: Sissako's mother.

The year his mother was born, slavery was abolished. "The slave market in Sokolo was closed down, but the trading went on for a while, of course," Sissako says. Not long afterwards, Kimbéry asked his wife if she remembered where she came from. She told him the name of the village, and he took her home on horseback. She married a Peul and had a number of children.

Abolition was a major blow for the noble Moorish families. Masters who'd treated their slaves badly and forced them to work at gunpoint ran into trouble when all of them left. Fortunately, Sissako's grandfathers had been good to their slaves, so most of them stayed on.

In the course of time, Sissako's paternal grandfather settled in Sokolo and became the local Moorish leader. The French demanded that the local chieftains send their children to school, but like all true Muslims his grandfather was vehemently opposed to white Christian schools. He used his influence to send the children of other Moors or their slaves. When the French found out about it, they forced him to send his eldest grandchild, Mohammed.

"That was me," Sissako says. "My friends all laughed at me. One of them, a Peul, got out of going to school by acting deaf and dumb for three days. He was considered a real hero." Sissako was good at science so he finally ended up studying meteorology in Bamako. In 1938 the French sent him to Aguelhok, a barren outpost in the far north of Mali, close to the Algerian border. He traveled around on a camel loaded with meteorological equipment. That must have been when he went to Kidal and Tessalit – the reason his son Amidou spoke of him admiringly as 'a real Saharan'.

He spent five years at Aguelhok, where he lived with two white people and three blacks. Supplies were flown in once a month. Sometimes the wind was so fierce you couldn't see your hand in front of your face; they ate under mosquito netting.

Later he opened weather stations at Gao, Ségou and Kayes. Kayes was famous for being one of the hottest cities in Africa. The French district officer had a barrel of water installed in his office and would sit in it, chair and all, up to his midriff. Sometimes he'd dip a towel in the barrel to wipe the sweat off his forehead.

One day, when Sissako was stationed at Mopti, there was a celebration for the hundredth birthday of an American who had fought against slavery. The French came to pick up all the local officials and take them to the festivities. "But I refused to go."

Sissako suddenly stops talking. Sitting on his mattress amid the remains of our breakfast, he refills my cup of coffee.

I've been listening to him quietly, afraid to interrupt his flow of words, but now I cautiously ask: "Why didn't you go?"

"Because it wasn't my party."

"Why not?"

"No one ever reimbursed my grandfather for his freed slaves," he says defiantly; "that was a huge loss for him!"

I secretly admire him for his honesty. People around here know how Westerners feel about slavery, and they usually do their best to avoid this touchy subject.

Sissako takes his pocketknife from under the pillow. He's trying to make a new rubber gasket for Kady's espresso machine, and before long he's completely absorbed in his work. I'm not quite sure how to get the conversation going again. Later, when I learn about his relationship to Sori, I understand that he has no reason to feel any guilt.

Sori's ancestors were the slaves of Sissako's grandfather. After abolition they became part of the family, as often happened in Moorish society; some freed slaves even became tribal chieftains. Sori was born a free man – he had the same opportunities as Sissako – but he couldn't compensate for the social disadvantage of his past in the space of a generation.

The conversation at Sori's had been animated during the first days of my stay, but gradually it's fallen silent. The distinguished presence that impressed me so much at first hides a bitterly disappointed man. Having made his career under the socialist president Modibo Keita, Sori also served for years as advisor to his successor and rival, Moussa Traoré. He was one of the founders of Traoré's system, but was shoved aside while that regime was still in power. Events in this country have raised Sori to the heights, then brought him down again just as easily. Sissako, who always remained his own master, clearly came out the stronger of the two.

And Amadou, the spoiled boy who got everything he wanted from his father, hasn't made it either. Sissako seems to feel responsible – that's why he tries to steer him in the right direction during those lost afternoon hours they spend eating peanuts together.

In retrospect, even Abderrahmane's self-confidence becomes more plausible: he belongs to a family of rulers – there's no reason why he can't look a Russian or Frenchman straight in the eye.

"I worked with white people all my life," Sissako says. "I've learned to appreciate them, even though they often have a hard time accepting that a black can do something as well as they can." At one of the remote outposts where he was stationed, his white colleagues once tried unsuccessfully to repair a short circuit. When a Guinean finally succeeded, they called it a stroke of luck.

Sissako had looked forward to independence, but he was skeptical once it arrived. He knew the men who were going into politics, and had no faith in their sense of democracy; they, in turn, resented him. He and Sori often discussed it– but they never agreed.

"You were a meteorologist. That doesn't have anything to do with politics, does it?"

"That's what you think! The party wanted its pawns everywhere. They tried to control the meteorologists' union by saying the secretary had to be a party member. We quickly put a stop to that."

Suddenly I remember something Abdallah told me in Nouakchott. When he was about fifteen, his school went to a big rally at the soccer stadium in Bamako. During the meeting, the crowd began chanting his father's name. Sissako had opposed the party's desire to exclude Israel and South Africa from the World Organization of Meteorologists. It was his belief that every country had a right to meteorological information: science was an international commodity. A marionette was thrown into the air, and the speaker on stage shouted that this was the fate of enemies of the people like Mohammed Sissako. Abdallah was frightened. While his classmates stamped their feet and screamed along with the crowd, he tried to make himself as small as possible.

Sissako waves his hand dismissively when I remind him of the incident, but admits that Modibo Keita's regime was hostile to him. At a party conference in Mopti in 1968, they decided to teach him and his comrades a lesson. Smiling, he adds: "But before the party bosses got to Bamako, a military coup put an end to their regime." The new leaders wanted to make him a cabinet minister, but he declined. "I don't believe I could work with soldiers," he'd told them. And he was proven right about that as well.

Malians live beyond their means, Sissako says. He always had a car at his disposal, but the country couldn't really afford that kind of luxury. His son Mohammed had a Vietnamese classmate in Leningrad who came back from vacation with the glad tidings that he'd been able to buy a bicycle, so he was no longer dependent on public transport. If only Mali could learn from that!

"People always try to profit from a family member who's in a position of responsibility," he says. "There's a Bambara proverb that goes: 'He who stands close to the fire must warm himself'. You see it here in Sokolo as well. The village associations set up to borrow money from the bank all go bankrupt, because the secretary puts his own interests before those of the community. In colonial times, fraud was severely punished. I knew a man who went to prison for five years for stealing thirty-eight francs." He smiles. "Not that such punishment kept people from stealing, mind you!"

He himself never tried to avoid his family responsibilities, and he still has lots of relatives under his wing. "That's why I'm happy to be in Sokolo. Not only because I enjoy myself more here, but because I can make myself useful by sending rice to my family."

Yet he's taught his children to be independent. The world is changing; he saw it during his travels in Europe. Western individualism is on the rise in Africa as well. "Could you imagine Amidou living with Bako once he was married? In this day and age? It's unthinkable!"

But still, the situation in Mali makes them rely on each other more than ever. Almost all of his older children received grants to study abroad, but the younger ones can't count on that anymore. He's worried about his three youngest sons: what will become of them if all they do is strike? He'd like to bring them to Sokolo, but what does he have to offer them? To put them to work here, he'd have to have money to buy more machines.

The young people in Sokolo suffer under unemployment and instability, and they're all waiting for a chance to strike it rich. "The Soninké, a trading people who often go out into the world to seek their fortune, have a saying: 'Riches or a distant grave'. They want to come home wealthy, or else be buried far away."

Sissako looks up. The worker who runs the milling machine has come cycling into the yard. He has a permanent look of dissatisfaction about him. When I say something about it, he complains about his measly pay. So what would he rather be doing? His reply is grim: "I have two ambitions: to become a drug dealer or a mercenary."

Sissako has put his pocketknife and the rubber ring back under his pillow. The spell of our morning's conversation is broken.

***

My days in Sokolo have quickly become filled with minor rituals and pastimes. After our daily visit to the rice mill, we drop by the post office – sometimes because Sissako is expecting a call from Bamako, or simply because he wants to hear the latest news from Bina.

This morning he contacts the home front himself: the rice mill keeps breaking down, and he wants his son Jiddou, who goes to technical school, to come to Sokolo and help. "That'll teach him to go on strike!"

Bina just heard on the radio that the market in Nouakchott has burned down. "First the market in Dakar, then the one in Bamako, and now Nouakchott – you people must get a real kick out of it!" he shouts in my direction.

"What do you mean?"

"Don't you see what's going on? First the French force the devaluation on us, and now they go on to destroy the African economy!" Comments like these are Bina's stock-in-trade whenever I'm around. He's from Markala, a village on the Niger close

147

to Ségou. A lot of foreigners worked in Markala, and that has shaped his attitude towards whites. Every time a sum is mentioned in local currency, he converts it to French francs, just to rub my nose in the consequences of the recent devaluation and prove that the French still run things around here.

I shrug. "White people have other things on their minds besides burning down your markets."

"That's what you say!"

Sissako has been listening to our bickering, and says calmly: "It's true, the French have had a hard time coming to terms with our independence. But I can tell you the exact reason why the market in Nouakchott burned down, because every market in Africa works the same way: one of the merchants has electricity, which is tapped off by a neighbor who knows nothing about electricity. One short circuit is enough to send the whole place up in flames." He looks at Bina and laughs mildly. "With all those wooden stands, it doesn't take long, does it?"

Le vieux has spoken; Bina and I are silent for a moment. I envy Sissako's quiet powers of persuasion. I get wound up too easily by Bina's conspiracy theories.

But Bina already has his sights on something else. Would Sissako happen to have a hundred francs for him?

"What for?"

"To buy some grilled meat."

"Don't you get paid for what you do? Don't you receive a salary?" Sissako asks in feigned amazement.

"Of course I do, but you know that's never enough," Bina complains.

"Don't put up with it then!" Sissako laughs. He's used to Bina inventing all kinds of reasons for him to call Bamako when he's had another lean few weeks. "By the end of the month, Bina is capable of absolutely anything."

Sori comes in, and he and Sissako begin gesticulating wildly, talking in Bambara. They clearly disagree about something, and I see Bina's eyes twinkle devilishly: an argument, that's grist to his mill. Suddenly Sissako seizes the tails of his *boubou*, flaps them aside and walks out of the post office with a determined stride. Sori sighs and shuffles off after him.

"What was that all about?"

"Oh, it's a little routine they go through," Bina gloats. The elementary school in Sokolo will soon be celebrating its hundredth anniversary, and the festivities are in the hands of a certain Kamara, who was appointed by Sori. Sissako says there's nothing to celebrate: the school building is in a miserable condition, the pupils are a bunch of savages, and Kamara himself is the biggest zero of all. He accuses Sori of appointing an illiterate because he's easy to manipulate: a typical politician's trick.

"They fight like cats and dogs in the morning," Bina says, "but when evening comes they're back sitting across from each other at the table, the best of friends!"

Bina is fond of *Bâ Sissako*, Father Sissako, as he refers to him respectfully. "Old pans make the best sauce," he says. Without *le vieux* around, his life in Sokolo would have a lot less meaning. The villagers are backward, that's Sissako's eternal complaint, and they have no desire to move ahead. Sissako doesn't talk to me about these things – he probably sees them as internal affairs, none of a white person's business.

Amadou comes to take me to the weekly market in a neighboring village, where he has to sell six hundred kilos of rice for his father. In his jeans, shirt and trusty Mexican sombrero, he cuts a bizarre figure amid the other merchants in their *boubous* and headcloths. But he bargains skillfully and gets the price he wants; whatever else Abidjan did, it made him streetwise.

To celebrate his successful transaction, we drive to the canteen at a nearby army base where they actually sell beer. There are three refrigerators, but the beer's still lukewarm. This isn't the first time he's been here, I notice, and it goes without saying that our escapade is to remain secret from *l'homme*.

We find him waiting at home, slightly worried: I didn't eat any lunch, he says, and I probably got too much sun. When he hears that Amadou wants to take me to Sori's fields north of town the next day, he says: "Not on your life. It's too dangerous."

149

It's Djéry who finally shows me the fields around Sokolo. Bina insists we take his canteen, for I wouldn't be the first white person to keel over from thirst on a walk like this. It's a gold-colored flask a pilgrim brought back for him from Mecca. As soon as I sling it over my shoulder, I feel like I'm on a school outing.

"Aren't you going to put on gloves against the mosquitoes?" Bina asks. According to him, the white people in Markala wore shoulder-length gloves and wrapped their feet in plastic bags when they sat outside at night. The Portuguese nuns confessed to him that they'd thought blacks were born with tails, which they had cut off when they arrived in Europe.

Jumping over ditches, Djéry and I pick our way through a flat landscape where Dutch threshing machines are winnowing mowed stalks of rice. Groups of women with sticks move through the field, threshing what the machines have missed. They walk behind each other in rows, so nothing goes to waste. The women are paid in rice.

Squinting, I see the painting in my parent's house, in which my mother – a small, stooped figure in a blazing yellow field of wheat – is tying sheaves into bundles.

The chaff is loaded onto donkey carts and taken to the village. It's used for fodder, or mixed with cow dung, soil and water into a paste that's plastered onto the houses before the rainy season comes.

Along the way we meet children carrying slabs of clay with threads stretched across them. "They bury them just under the surface and put a few grains of rice on them," Djéry says. "The birds that land on them become hopelessly tangled in the threads."

"And what do they do with those birds?"

"Eat them." They add a bit of flavor to the food, just like the little fish we saw them catching in the swamp. Djéry did it too when he was a boy.

Later, when I ask Sissako whether these instruments of torture existed in his day, he nods. But he never had one himself. "I couldn't even kill a snake."

People keep stopping us along the way to talk. Young men ask me to take them back to Holland, women offer to braid my hair or dye my lips blue. But Djéry has already drawn me into his private economy. His younger sister washes my clothes in the pond, and she keeps showing up at Sissako's door with notes from Djéry full of instructions about the money I'm to give her. This time it's to buy soap, the next time to pay the man who irons my clothes. Formal notes, they are always signed '*ton Jerry*'.

When Sissako's around, Sokolo seems a solid village, but with Djéry at my side it becomes shaky ground. He's one of the only young men in the village who can read and write. In elementary school the first grade is usually quite full, but the further one goes, the smaller the classes become. Many parents take their children out of school because they need them to help in the fields.

Djéry and his friends get together every afternoon at his parents' home. Most of them have only been to Koran school, so they ask me questions through Djéry. They want to know whether there are Muslims in Holland, as they've heard on the radio that many Europeans are converting to Islam these days. There's even a prominent French philosopher who's become a Muslim. Roger Garaudy – they're delighted that I know his name.

Just as Bina knows the telephone secrets of Sokolo, so Djéry has access to its private correspondence. Parents often ask him to write letters to their children who've left Sokolo.

"What kinds of things do they write?"

"Mostly traditional instructions."

"Such as?"

Djéry laughs shyly. "I went to the white people's school, so I don't believe in it myself. But parents ask a marabout to make *gris-gris*, so their children will have good fortune abroad. I have to write and tell them what's in the *gris-gris*, and what they have to do with it."

As the village soccer trainer, he was opposed at first to his players' wearing *gris-gris,* but after Sokolo lost two games in a row his position was undermined.

Besides Islam, Djéry and his friends talk a lot about magic.

They tell me about a musician who could play his instrument without touching it. He'd been raised by the devil, and when he went blind he was given magic powers. And have I never heard of the great marabout who lived on the outskirts of Sokolo? He could make documents damning to corrupt officials vanish at a distance. Even former president Moussa Traoré consulted him.

I think of the period when Amidou lived here. He told me it had made him change his way of thinking. In Sokolo there were spirits who lived at the river's edge and pulled you into the water. Bako laughed when he talked like that: "Seeing is believing!"

When I ask Sissako about the blind musician, he smiles knowingly. "Yes, indeed, it seems he was a man of many talents." He doesn't believe in things like that. Some marabouts are good psychologists, but in his view any marabout who helps a corrupt official is a huckster who's sold his soul to the devil.

Sometimes when Djéry and his friends come to pick me up at the house they hang around under the verandah for a while. There isn't much for them to do now that the rice harvest is winding down. Sissako is one of the only elders in Sokolo who talks to them. He went to great lengths recently to explain to them that the Earth was round, but the idleness in which Djéry and his friends spend their days irritates him as well; he calls them a bunch of do-nothings. One afternoon, when one of them dares to call him 'grandpa', he says crossly: "I'm not your grandpa. In Moorish society, grandfathers wouldn't stoop to speak with their grandchildren."

Of all the people I meet in Sissako's surroundings, Bina interests me most. He has a sense of humor and a sharp tongue, and his handicap doesn't seem to keep him from bending the world to his will. His office is the nerve center of Sokolo, and I stop in regularly.

Sissako seems relieved that I can find my own way, but when Bina invites me to eat at his house one evening, I notice it makes him uneasy. The children here ride their bicycles without headlights, he says: what if someone ran into me? He sends a worker along to accompany me.

Bina is sitting outside in his easy chair and greets me in his usual minor key: "How are things . . . considering?" The chilled ginger juice with mint is standing ready for him to break his fast. It's one of the great pleasures of Ramadan: putting a glass of ice-cold ginger juice to your lips after a whole day without drinking. He buys the ice from the only man in Sokolo with a kerosene refrigerator.

Bina's wife, Rokia, is perched on a stool, cooking dinner. She has fine features and seems slender and fragile next to her husband's bulk. They have a tender relationship. Bina proudly calls her the 'Queen of *To*', because she makes the best sorghum-paste in all of Sokolo.

When the *muezzin*'s call rings out, Bina hands me a glass of ginger juice and Rokia puts a bowl of rice porridge in front of us, with two spoons. She's had a toothache for weeks, but the dentist in Sokolo won't help her because she's pregnant. And now, to make matters worse, her little goat has disappeared. "It wanted to become independent," Bina says with a sly glance in my direction, "prematurely, just like the Africans."

Bina moved to Sokolo two years ago. After the rebels raided the town, his predecessor fled and the post office was almost closed down. He felt it was his duty to apply for the job: he'd attended Koran school here as a boy, and he did his apprenticeship in Sokolo as well.

He was the only one in his family who went to school. "I have my crippled leg to thank for that," he says with a grin, "otherwise my father would have put me to work in the fields like my brothers."

At school everyone thought something special would come of him. Besides African writers, he also read Balzac, and when he came to Sokolo he hoped to finally find the peace and quiet he needed to do some writing himself. He already had a subject in mind: his father had been in politics and had made extensive use of *gris-gris* to stay in power; Bina had written down quite a few anecdotes. But in Sokolo he had less time to write than ever before. The world of reading and writing is too far away. "I haven't even unpacked my notes since I arrived!"

When darkness falls we move inside and eat by the light of an oil lamp. A man knocks on the door and asks if he can call Brazzaville. Bina comes back, chronometer in hand. He laughs knowingly. "He wanted me to leave him alone," he whispers. "As if I don't know what all those calls to Brazzaville are about: money! The only difference is the size of the sum they beg for."

Not that he isn't desperately in need of money himself. At the beginning of each month he puts six new batteries in his radio-cassette recorder. When the batteries run down, he waits until the next month to buy new ones. Meanwhile, his whole family calls on him for favors, and asks for expensive embroidered *boubous*, without bothering to ask what he actually earns. "They think: where there's room for one, there's room for a thousand!" It's one of the problems that send him to Bâ Sissako for advice: when he was a civil servant, how did he make ends meet?

"But how did you get that wheelchair?" I ask. How could someone with his salary ever afford that?

Bina laughs slyly. A long time ago, he wrote a letter to the French Association for the Paralyzed, including a photo of himself and his crippled leg. He never got a reply, but he didn't give up. His father had always said: "Life is a battle; the losers are those who abandon hope." As soon as he started working at the post office in Sokolo, he called the association at their number in France. "When I heard they were coming to Mali with three wheelchairs, I went straight down to Bamako and got one for free! The other two stayed at the ministry – they probably went to the highest bidder."

He would have had to save for twenty-five years to buy a wheelchair like this. He would never have been able to pay for the orthopedic shoes he got from the Portuguese nuns in Markala either. "I'm already worried about what will happen when the soles wear out!"

Fortunately, an ad he placed in the Association for the

Paralyzed's journal has produced a lively correspondence with a few French people. An old woman with shaky handwriting has come to regard him as her son. She regularly sends him packages from Perpignan. "Rokia, show us what she sent last time!"

Rokia disappears into the bedroom and comes back with a porcelain statue of the Virgin Mary. She carries it carefully, like a doll. "Look," she says, "one of the hands broke off in the mail."

"Does this lady know you're Muslims?"

"I believe so," Bina says with a wry smile, "but that doesn't stop her. She went to Lourdes a while back and had my name scratched into the foot of the statue of the Virgin." He reminds me of Wangrin, the main character in Hampâté Bâ's picaresque novel *L'étrange destin de Wangrin* (The Strange Fate of Wangrin), who also succeeded in profiting from the most unlikely situations.

Compared to many people in Sokolo, Bina isn't badly off. His house is neat and tidy, and it's the first time I've eaten at a table since I arrived. But he's still frustrated. He's had his dreams, of being a writer, of improving his lot, and now here he is earning a pitiful salary in some forgotten corner of the country, struggling against his family's greed.

And then there's the devaluation of the franc. I'm starting to understand what's behind his bitter jokes of the last few days. His heroes are Saddam Hussein, Pablo Escobar and Jacques Mesrine – he sees them as modern-day Don Quixotes. He follows the student strikes with interest; the grimmer the better, as far as he's concerned. Grinning maliciously, he tells me about 'Article 320', a term dating from the student riots of 1991, when a liter of gasoline cost three hundred francs and a box of matches twenty. Back then, government officials were set on fire under Article 320. Students called it the 'BV', which stands for 'burnt alive'.

"Since the devaluation, of course, it's become 'Article 440'," he says, "because gasoline and matches are more expensive."

When the conversation turns to the Tuareg rebels operating in the area, Bina moves over to the wooden cupboard against the wall and says mysteriously: "I have something to show you." He comes back with a photo of an old Tuareg man sitting in the back of a pick-up, a dazed look in his eyes. His trousers are torn and he holds a light blue *hawli* between his legs to cover his nakedness.

"Who took this picture?"

"I did!" He sounds triumphant. The man had camped for a while in a nearby village, and was suspected of being a rebel spy. One night soon after he left the area, all the cattle in the village were stolen. When he showed up again, the villagers grabbed him and took him to Sokolo, so the district officer could decide his fate. But, as usual, the district officer wasn't there. The Tuareg had been beaten badly before he even got to town, and the village chief in Sokolo gave him his *hawli* to cover himself. Bina took the picture just as the villagers were getting ready to take the man to an army base.

"But he never got there."

"What do you mean?

"I don't know. I suppose they killed him along the way."

I take another look at the man in the picture. His light green eyes are hollows in his face. He must have known what was going to happen.

"The people in Sokolo have no faith in the army," Bina says. "They solve their own problems. Why do you think they built a wall around the graveyard?"

"I don't know, why?"

"There are many marabouts and other important people buried there. The ancestral spirits have to guard them against the rebels."

"And you believe that?"

"When I first came here, I didn't. I thought they would have been better off investing the money in a maternity clinic, so there would be fewer children lying in the graveyard. But now I'm not so sure."

Bina puts the photo back in its place. Rokia has gone to bed, and I realize it's time for me to leave. Out on the patio, Bina stands looking at the moon which hangs like a powerful lamp in the sky. "You know, Rokia and I didn't sleep in our bed last night."

"Why not?"

"Because of the rebels," he whispers.

At first I think he's joking, but he's serious. Tuareg rebels have been sighted around Sokolo again. The district officer and Bina live next to the village gates and hold strategic posts – the local chief warned them to sleep somewhere else. "Rokia forgot her toothache just like that!"

"Where did you sleep then?" I've started whispering too, even though there's not a soul around.

"I'm not telling!"

"I bet it was in the well."

Bina looks at me in alarm. "Who told you about the well?"

"I don't remember." It seems I've said something wrong, but I'm not exactly sure what.

The next day Amadou remarks: "The rumors about rebels have picked up ever since you arrived. Who knows, maybe you're a spy." Sori, who lives at the other end of the village, is in equal danger, especially since his pick-up was used to bring back the wounded after the last clash.

When I get home the oil lamp is burning low, and as I tiptoe down the verandah I hear Sissako moving. He sits up in bed.

"Haven't you slept yet?"

"No."

"Were you worried?"

He mumbles something about children bicycling around without lights.

"I'm sorry," I say, but he's already asleep. I lie awake for a long time. I hear scuffling and gnawing noises; this morning I saw a rat run across the yard. Is that what's chewing on my sleeping bag? Or have I woken the swallows in their nests above my head?

⚏

When I wake up, it's still dark. Someone is rummaging around under my bed. I lie perfectly still. Has my mosquito netting come loose, and is Sissako trying to tuck it back in? Then I hear an enormous crackling sound. Reports about the elections in Togo, demonstrations in Gabon and the state of emergency in Congo whiz through the air.

The radio! We picked it up yesterday from the Moorish shop-keeper at the marketplace. His little shop looked like a hopeless clutter of wires, switches and bent antennas, but there's nothing he can't recycle, repair or rebuild.

Sissako occasionally listens to the five o'clock news on RFI, Radio France Internationale. That's where he first heard that Abderrahmane's *Octobre* had been well received at Cannes, he tells me over breakfast. He was pleased, of course, even though he'd never seen the film; movies don't interest him at all. The last time he went to a movie theater was in 1951, in Bamako. Two of his friends took him, and he fell asleep during the opening score. "You're a snake-man," his doctor said to him. "As soon the music starts, you're hypnotized, like a cobra hearing the snake-charmer's flute."

After breakfast Sissako takes his knife from under the pillow and goes back to work on the rubber ring for Kady's coffee pot. Today is the weekly market day in Sokolo, and with a bit of luck his son Jiddou will arrive on a truck headed this way.

I've reserved a seat in Moussa's car to Niono for tomorrow, and from there I'll take a *taxi-brousse* to Bamako. Only now that I'm about to leave do I realize I've gradually entered another dimension in time. Having a radio fixed, making a new rubber ring for a coffee pot, sending notes back and forth about clothes that have to be washed and ironed – such are the things that have inevitably filled my days here. Abderrahmane's *Octobre*, which brought me to Sokolo, has become a faint beacon on the horizon, emitting only the weakest of signals.

In an unguarded moment I'd promised Rokia I would make crêpes before I left, thereby unleashing a wild flurry of activity. Where would they find eggs? Around here, eggs aren't eaten – they're left to hatch. Ever since I made my offer, hunting season has opened on all eggs in and around Sokolo. Sissako has asked shopkeepers to put aside all incoming eggs, and Bina has called his colleagues at all post offices within a fifteen-kilometer radius and stated his willingness to come on his scooter and pick them up.

Djéry and I wander around the market. We stop in front of a

stand selling the dried heads of wild cats used by marabouts in their *gris-gris* – but no eggs.

"Now, let's hold our breath and hope the market doesn't burn down!" Bina says when he hears where I've been. Thirteen teeny-weeny eggs are all he's gathered. He watches as I break them, and says: "Your arrival has dealt a sensitive blow to poultry production in Sokolo." I'll make him go broke, he complains, giving his wife a recipe with expensive ingredients like milk and eggs.

When I arrive back at the house, Jiddou is sitting in the shade, his Walkman in his lap. A truck dropped him off at the village gates, so he had to walk a long way to get here. He's brought a big cardboard box too. It's the first time he's ever visited his father, and although he looks around a bit uneasily, he says he's happy that his father asked him to come. He's brought a manual for diesel motors which he hopes will shed some light on the workings of the rice mill.

Sissako walks into the yard, and takes a peek in the cardboard box. Sesame biscuits, melons, bananas. "I don't see anything of interest," he says. Then he lies down on his mattress and fires a volley of questions at Jiddou about the strikes in Bamako.

Jiddou no longer resembles the bored young man I saw in the yard in Hamdallaye; he's clearly his father's son. Nothing about this place surprises him – he knows his father and his total disregard for appearances. "In Bamako, everyone acts busy," he says philosophically. "Here, that's not necessary; everything is clear."

That evening we take a plate of crêpes to Sori's house. When we walk home in the light of the full moon, the village is teeming with life. Children are singing and dancing in the street. Halfway through the month of Ramadan, the spirits who usually roam at night are chained, making it safe for them to play outside. We pass a group of boys with cow's horns tied to their heads, who sing mockingly:

> *Have you seen the djinn?*
> *The djinn has dyed*
> *his feet with henna.*
> *The djinn has dyed*
> *his hands with henna.*

Everything is so peaceful as we walk the sandy, moonlit road home. Nothing points to the events that will take place barely one year later. Down these streets the rebels will sneak into Sokolo early one morning, heading for Sissako's house. They will rob him of the money his son Mohammed just sent him, and of all the valuables in his storeroom.

Then they will take him hostage and bring him to the market-place, shooting in the air. Along the way he will see the body of the man killed by the rebels as they made their way into the village. Sokolo is wide awake, but no one dares to show their face, not even the vigilante committee. "I always knew the people of Sokolo were cowards," Sissako will later say resignedly.

The rebels are nervous young men. He keeps talking to them, trying to calm them down. It's as his second wife, Mariem, predicted: his knowledge of Tamacheq is what saves him.

"What do we do with the old man?" one of the rebels asks after they've plundered the shops around the market square.

"Let him go," his boss says.

The telephone lines have been cut, so Sissako has to walk to the next village to call Bamako. A little later, news of the raid on Sokolo buzzes around the world: from Amidou in Bamako to Abdallah in Nouakchott; from Abderrahmane in Paris to Amsterdam, where a fax rolls in: 'The Tuareg rebels have raided Sokolo. They kidnapped Papa, but he got away unharmed. I'm at home.'

Abderrahmane sounds anxious on the phone. He'd never realized how dangerous the place was, he admits; his father always shrugged it off. Aziz is headed north from Ségou, and Amidou is on his way to Sokolo as well.

"Everyone wants Papa to move back to Bamako," Abderrahmane says. But his father has already let them know he wouldn't dream of going away. The harvest has begun; his rice mill is running at full speed. How could he leave Sokolo at a moment like this?

MALI BLUES

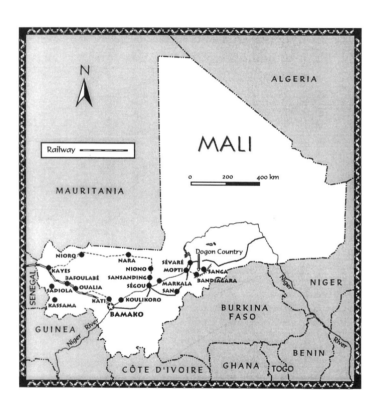

I thought I was finished. Just one more look at this landscape, I thought. But since this afternoon I don't know anymore. *Boubacar Traoré*. For months I've been listening to his melancholy music, so different from the Zaïrian pop that swamps this continent that I was somewhat surprised he'd found his way onto a British record label.

Yesterday I saw him on stage. A bluesman of about fifty-five in a dark suit, checkered cap on his head. He stood there, alone with his guitar, a microphone at his feet – he used his feet to tap the rhythm.

One song caused a commotion among the Malians in the audience. *Mali Twist* – some of them jumped up onto the stage to dance. The man next to me clapped his hands, a blissful smile on his face. "This is our youth," he said. For years, all of Mali woke to this song on the radio. It was a call to Malians throughout the world to return home and help build their country. That was just after independence, in 1963. *Kar Kar, blouson noir* they called him, because he wore a leather jacket like Johnny Halliday and Elvis Presley. Nostalgia rippled through the audience.

After the concert he was standing alone with a bottle of cola in his hand, so I summoned the courage to walk up to him and arrange a meeting. Ali Farka Touré, who had just won a Grammy in America for his record with Ry Cooder, was there too. Later I saw them leave together, Farka carrying the guitar – a sign of respect for an older colleague.

Finding his house wasn't easy. Ask for me at the New Galaxy club, he'd said, but the people there look at me, puzzled. Boubacar Traoré? Never heard of him. Only when I mention his nickname, Kar Kar, does it ring a bell. "Kar Kar, the musician? But he's in France!" The salesman at a perfume shop thinks he lives in the neighborhood. He points towards the hill, behind a factory from which a plume of black smoke is rising into the air. On my way there I pass a junkyard with a tow truck parked out the front. Children shout *"Toubab, toubab!* Whitey, whitey!" and tag along behind me, so I arrive at his house with a whole delegation.

He's lying on a mattress in the courtyard, listening to the radio – a soccer match from the sound of it. He seems pleasantly surprised that I not only said I'd come by, but actually have. The neighbor visiting him greets me politely and disappears.

Except for the checkered cap, there's little resemblance to the man on stage. He's dressed in a pair of worn orange and black striped pants and a shirt. In the shadow of a mango tree stands a blue Peugeot scooter bearing an 'Allah is Great' sticker. The metal door to his room is ajar; he's taped a poster from his concert to the cupboard door. A sheep is standing under the reed awning, and chickens are scratching their way across the yard.

His French comes from far away; I can barely understand him. Although he says three times that he's pleased to see me, my questions run up against a wall of incomprehension and suspicion. Why do I want to know when he began singing, or when he recorded his first album? What do I need that 'information' for? His face closes; the lines around his mouth harden. He seems to regard his life as a series of secrets to be guarded.

He's willing to tell me how he got the name 'Kar Kar'. In his younger days he was a talented soccer player, and he left school at twelve because he couldn't think about anything else. He was so good at dribbling – *kari kari* in Bambara – that his supporters encouraged him loudly. When he began singing, they all knew him as Kar Kar.

When evening falls, he goes into his room and lights a candle. Only then do I realize he has no electricity. There's no running water either; the drinking water is kept cool in an earthenware jug. Squatting under the mango tree, he begins his ritual cleansing before prayers. I watch in silence, but he goes on talking. Do I feel the cool breeze blowing through the yard? Down there – he points towards the center of Bamako – the heat remains hanging between the houses. But this hill is full of water, it runs over the rocks all year round, and during the rainy season it rushes downhill with growing force; sometimes the whole neighborhood is flooded.

He rolls out a sheepskin rug and turns to face Mecca. When he bends over I see that he's wearing three leather thongs around his thighs. *Gris-gris*. I look the other way in embarrassment.

In the falling darkness, the noises grow louder. Tom-toms are rolling in the distance. Suddenly a long, drawn-out scream shakes the hillside. "Did you hear that?" he asks when he's finished praying. "Holland is playing against Italy. I think your people just scored."

We walk down the hill together towards the paved road. Did I come by taxi? But the *douroudourouni*, the 'little five-five', stops right over there! A ride used to cost twenty-five francs. The price has gone up with each new president, but the name has stuck.

He laughs when I click on my flashlight. When he came back from France four years ago, he walked around at night with a flashlight too. "Kar Kar has gone blind in France!" everyone said. He'd been wearing shoes for two years – the soles of his feet were as soft as a baby's.

Before I know it I've asked another careless question. "No, I didn't go to France to play music," he snaps. "My wife, Pierrette, had just died. I had to earn money, so I worked on building sites." Pierrette – his saddest songs are about her. I thought she was French, but it turns out she was a *métisse*.

I'd like to ask more questions, but he keeps right on talking. In Paris he lived in a *foyer* – a boarding house – with other African immigrants. The Zaïrians among them categorically refused to buy tickets for the metro, because all the steel used in the French subway cars came from Zaïre – why should they pay?!

People are sitting in front of their houses, listening to the radio; here and there a television is on. Out of the darkness comes the occasional greeting. "Kar Kar, *ça va?*" "*Anitjé!* Thanks! *Ça va très bien.*" A boy comes by, pushing a cart full of empty plastic jerry cans. "Hey, I haven't seen you around for days!" Kar Kar calls out. "Have you got a girlfriend across town? I'm out of water!"

At the taxi stand he gets into an argument with a cab driver. Two thousand francs! They quarrel in Bambara. Indignant, he pulls me to the other side of the street. "That man is an idiot!"

"What did he say?"

"That a black brother shouldn't try to get in his way, that white people have more money than they know what to do with."

"What did you tell him?"

"That he's behind the times! There are rich whites and poor whites, just like black people! Anyone who doesn't know that is living in the past. When he tried to lower his price, I told him: I wouldn't let her get in your car if it only cost a hundred francs! What would he think, I asked him, if he had a guest from Holland and a Malian tried to cheat her? He knew what I meant, he realized I was right."

Once I'm in the taxi, I realize that I can't leave yet. Not yet. Just as I was about to move on, I've walked into another story.

***

It's so hard to talk to him! He doesn't understand what I want from him, but I barely know myself. His name is connected with the optimistic years just after independence, but along the way something has broken, and somehow his career has become bogged down. "I've done everything for my country," he says, "but the politicians aren't grateful. They've done nothing in return. Hundreds of musicians have been decorated – some of them weren't even from Mali! – but they've always overlooked me."

He couldn't live from his music alone, so he's had all kinds of jobs. Unlike many intellectuals in this country, he hasn't lost contact with everyday life. He buys everything from the little local shops: a couple of cigarettes, a tiny packet of Nescafé, fifty grams of powdered milk, two candles. When his pans are too hot to pick up, he uses folded-up brochures from the Dutch World Service that a journalist once sent him. Every time he lights a candle he puts a little sugar on it. They last longer that way.

All that walking back and forth between his house and the shops doesn't seem to bother him. Everyone does it; they run into each other along the way and stop to talk.

"Why don't you buy a packet of cigarettes? Wouldn't that be cheaper?"

"But then I'd smoke them all!"

He lives in an economy totally different from my own. The CDs and tapes he's released don't seem to have changed his lifestyle much. If he was a Westerner, he'd probably have made a career by now; he'd have a manager, a villa, a car, a busy life. But the world of showbiz is foreign to him. I like that, but it also makes it harder to talk to him. The most harmless questions cause him to rear up in indignation. And yet I have the feeling he's full of stories.

This afternoon we take a walk up the hill, the sheep following along behind us. It turns out there are indeed a lot of springs at the top. It's cool up here, with orchards of mangoes and bananas, and little creeks where children play. After searching for a bit, I make out Kar's house far below: the rectangular walled yard with the gray iron gate, three rooms with little windows, three young mango trees and the bush with medicinal powers that all the neighbors come to pluck. They boil the leaves and wash themselves with the extract, or make tea from it. His father taught him to pick the leaves on Thursdays – that's when they work best.

Lafiabougou means 'quiet village'. Three years ago, when Kar bought his plot of land, there were only a few huts surrounded by clay walls. Everyone thought he was brave for walking around by himself at night, because the hill was frequented by riffraff – boys who blew up the rocks with dynamite, sold the stones and used the money to buy dope. "But I wasn't afraid of them," he says. "When I was young, I was a bigger hooligan than all of them put together."

Here and there you still see a yard with a hut and an old well, where people live the way they did in the old days, but stone

houses have risen up all around. There's still a lot of building
going on; the hammering and pounding hangs in the air like a mad
symphony. Kar's house isn't finished either, and he's busy laying
the foundations for the next couple of rooms. "My children will
live here someday," he says. Since Pierrette died, they've been
staying with her family at the bottom of the hill. "I can't take care
of them as long as I don't have a wife, and after Pierrette . . ."
There's a strange intensity to his voice whenever he mentions her
name. She died six years ago. People here often talk resignedly
about their dead – death is so common in this country. But he
seems full of defiance still.

When we get back to his house, dark smoke from the factory
is blowing into the yard. They melt iron scrap down there to make
parts for trains and other machinery. In the vacant lot in front of
the foundry, a neighbor has set up a kitchen where Kar goes with
a pan to buy food. The bowls are set out on a long table. I can
barely make out what's in all of them, but Kar simply points to
what he wants, and the woman serves him without hesitating.

It's a well-organized community. The neighbors have the
scoundrels well under their thumb, and no thieves have been seen
since two of them were clubbed to death.

"Clubbed to death?" I'm always shocked by the drastic pun-
ishments for thievery around here, but Kar laughs. If you take a
thief to the police station, you spend half a day filing a complaint
and the next morning you see him walking down the street again.
"Violence came here along with democracy," he says. "When
President Moussa Traoré's regime was on the point of collapse,
people were being beaten and set on fire all over town." That was
four years ago, but everyone in Mali saw it on television; since
then they've developed a taste for it.

Back at the house he washes his hands with soap. I pick up a
plastic pitcher to pour water over them, but he stops me aghast.
"A woman isn't supposed to do that for a man!"

"Why not?"

"It brings bad luck."

"Why is that?"

"I don't know. My parents said so, and that's what their parents told them."

A bit taken aback, I leave him to it. He puts the pan of food on the ground between us and hands me a spoon. He eats with his hands.

"How much do you pay for this?"

"*Ah non!*" Questions about prices are apparently off limits as well.

After we've eaten, the sheep comes over and sniffs the remains of the rice. Kar sits looking at it. "It smells meat – it doesn't like that," he says. The sheep begins kicking at the pan and Kar strokes its head, laughing. "It thinks it can kick away the smell of meat!" He's good with animals. In Kayes, where he was born, he once had a sheep that was so fat everyone called it 'Three Hundred Thousand'. He sold it to a Senegalese man for a hundred and fifty thousand francs. His mother was so attached to the animal that she cried when it was put on the train to Dakar. "I could always become a shepherd," he says. "If I bought a ewe I'd have a whole herd in no time. I could let them graze up on the hill."

The wind has picked up: it seems a storm is on its way. Kar looks at the sky, worried. "This isn't a good wind. It's dry, empty. It comes from the Sahara." The rainy season has begun, but hardly a drop has fallen. "Still, you'd think it was going to start raining, wouldn't you? It's been this way for days. In town they're saying the road crews on the Route de Koulikoro are stopping the rain. Others think it's the revenge of the people who lived in the shantytowns that were torn down a while ago; as long as they have to sleep outside, they're making sure it doesn't rain."

"Do you believe those stories?"

He laughs. "Some people can stop the rain, that's for sure. It's not that hard, not even for a woman! But it's not good to do it."

Faint flashes of light are dancing high up the hill. At first I think they're the eyes of jackals, but Kar says they're from hunters out after partridges. Have I seen the Hôtel de l'Amitié? On a clear day it looks like it's right near here, but it's actually seven kilometers away! When he bought this ground no one wanted to live here because it was so far from town. The terrain was uneven, barren and rocky – he killed fifteen snakes in the first few days – but he saw right away that it was a spot among thousands. Meanwhile, Lafiabougou has become part of Bamako. The property prices have quadrupled, and everyone envies him.

"Look, there's the flight to Paris." He stares after the plane as it climbs. "That's the third one today. This morning one left for Moscow, by way of Gaddafi's town." When he hears another plane, he frowns. "That one's not on schedule. Must be a *wouya-wouya* plane from Mauritania."

Wouya-wouya – it's his favorite expression for anything that's no good. He doesn't think much of Mauritania, that country of nomads. In the past, they didn't even wear underpants! "But their president set the police on them – then they had to!"

Just before eight, Kar rolls the scooter out of his room; he's going to watch television at his brother-in-law's at the bottom of the hill. At the taxi stand, I nod towards the red neon New Galaxy sign. "What kind of club is that?"

"I don't know. I've never been there." He looks at me questioningly. "Do you want to go in for a drink?" He's already turned his scooter in that direction. "If you want to, we'll do it, right?"

A few men are sitting together at the bar under blue neon lights. Behind them is a dark garden with little seating areas – a place for couples. We settle down hesitantly on the white chairs. Kar is about to order a cola, but when I ask for a beer he orders a big bottle with two glasses.

"I don't usually drink," he says.

"You never have?"

"Sure, when I was young. But back then I was a vagabond!" Since he's lived in Bamako, he spends all his time working on his house. "If anyone saw me in here and went around tomorrow saying Kar Kar was at the New Galaxy drinking beer with a white woman . . ." He laughs at the thought. "You know, no one would believe them? They'd say they were lying!"

He enjoys that ambiguity, I notice. Something youthful came over him as soon as we walked in the door. I can tell he's familiar with this life, or at least he was at one time. When the waiter brings us our beer, Kar carefully fills the glasses and puts the cap back on the bottle.

"I told you before that I didn't go to France to play music," he says in a tone that tells me a story's on its way. "But I did take my guitar with me. The French customs officials just waved me through: they thought I was a *griot* coming to sing at a Malian wedding!"

In Paris he worked in a bar, then at a hotel, and later on construction sites. "I was happy with whatever I could find. I didn't go to France to become a cabinet minister: I went to earn money." During the weekends he performed for immigrants in the *foyers*, but his boss had no idea that the man up on the scaffolding was a musician. Even the Senegalese producer who'd released one of his tapes a year earlier didn't know he was in Paris.

"Why not?"

"I can't explain it to you. You wouldn't understand. Someday maybe, but not yet. After Pierrette died . . ." He pours the rest of the beer into our glasses. "My heart was full of bitterness, everyone thought I would go crazy! I'd never been able to earn money playing music, so I wanted to try another way."

A producer in London heard his tape and was so enthusiastic that he wanted to organize a British tour right away. When he called Paris, they told him Boubacar Traoré lived in the Malian interior, in a dusty town that would be completely cut off from the outside world if the train between Bamako and Dakar didn't pass through. "So he sent someone to Kayes to find me!" Now Kar is holding forth. The story, in which he plays the main role, seems to amuse him. "In Kayes they looked at the man in amazement. 'Kar Kar,' they said, 'but he's in France!'"

His Senegalese producer finally located him through some musician friends. It turned out Kar Kar was living two streets away from him. "At first I didn't even want to meet him. Why should I? I went there to work!" But his friends talked him into it, and not long afterwards he flew to England for a tour, and recorded his first CD on the British Stern label.

171

I suddenly recall the young man I met on my first visit to Lafiabougou who'd claimed Kar Kar was in France. Kar laughs when I tell him. "I never announced that I'd come back. I just bought a piece of land and started building. I spend the day at my brother's shop in the market, and the evening in Lafiabougou. Everything I earn goes into my house. Some people think I never left Kayes; others say I'm still in France. When Malian television broadcast one of my clips a while ago, dozens of viewers called the station: they couldn't believe their eyes, they thought I was long dead and buried!"

※※※

The story of this man in his courtyard in Lafiabougou intrigues me, but I don't trust myself completely. Could I be looking for a noble savage? Leaves that heal only on Thursdays, people who stop the rain, water you're not allowed to pour over someone's hands – I've never spent time getting to know anyone who believes in things like that. Yet that's one reason why he interests me. I suspect he'll initiate me into something I've only seen from the outside.

No white person has ever entered his yard, no white person has ever been in his brother's shop where I go to find him this afternoon. *Baaba Traoré*, he'd jotted down the name and telephone number in chicken scratches on a scrap of paper. Writing isn't his strong suit.

You can hardly call it a shop: there's nothing you can buy. When I come walking up, a group of men are sitting under a corrugated-iron roof, watching boys unload bales of rice from a truck. The driver is sleeping on a reed mat under his vehicle. It's stiflingly hot, not a breath of wind. I don't see Kar, but his blue scooter with the plastic handgrips with stars on them is parked in front of the store. He's just had it painted; the 'Allah is Great' sticker has been replaced by a scantily clad woman, who says in Malian English: *Shut up your mouth, amebo!*

Seated behind the wooden counter in an otherwise empty

room, Baaba is bent over a form. He's a few years older than Kar and has nothing of his brother's nervousness or impetuousness. Still, he was the first one in the family to go traveling. Abidjan, Monrovia, Nairobi – he knows those African cities like the back of his hand. He smuggled gold from the Zaïrian interior into Uganda, brought in carloads of iron and cobalt from the Shaba, owned shops in the Ivory Coast and Sierra Leone. But some shady dealings in Abidjan forced him to come back to Bamako, where business has been a lot worse.

Baaba shakes my hand and nods towards the darkness behind him. "Are you looking for my brother? He's lounging back there."

On a mattress in the corner, Kar is keeping himself cool with a reed fan. "Today it's really hot," he groans. "Are you learning about Mali? Sometimes the sun beats down so hard it knocks you off your feet."

"We all want to move to the North Pole," Baaba says without looking up from his figures. Only now do I see what he's up to: he's filling out a racing form. The telephone next to him is locked safely in a wooden box. "To be an Eskimo," he muses, "with a string of fish hanging in a creaking hole in the ice. That would be my kind of life. But the best thing, of course, would be a grave in a paradise of ice, so I could stay nice and cool until the end of time."

Kar stands up and looks over Baaba's shoulder at his ciphering. "Do you see what my brother's doing?" He turns up his nose. "The daily double! I know all about it. There's no way you can win. I keep telling him to stop, but he won't listen." He played the horses himself for a while in France, but he soon found out something was rotten. "Some French people buy computers to help them bet, and even they lose. So how can he expect to win with a ballpoint pen!"

Baaba smiles absently. He's spent his whole life chasing after money. He went looking for it everywhere, even in countries at war. When Obote was still in power in Uganda, he spent months in the area run by Museveni's rebels. Wars are made for traders, he says, everything's more expensive then. "If you gave me a plane, I'd fly to Angola tomorrow. The war's just over, so this is a good moment. They're busy rebuilding the country – there's nothing they don't need. Whoever gets there first earns the most money."

Kar has picked up a plastic bag with his things in it. "Shall we get going? I'm thirsty." Down the street is a tent where men are sitting at a long wooden table, drinking ginger juice. Sali, the proprietor, is a pretty woman with a sassy look in her eye. When she sees Kar, she shouts something that makes everyone laugh. The ginger juice she serves in big plastic cups is spicy and cold.

The atmosphere under the canvas is jovial, with jokes rocketing back and forth, and Kar does most of the talking. The playfulness I caught a glimpse of that evening in the New Galaxy has come over him again. But when Sali looks the other way, he says: "You have to watch out for women like her, they ruin men. All they want is to improve their business."

"Baaba's store puzzled me," I say. "What does he do there?"

"Oh, he and his friends are on the lookout." Kar sizes me up wordlessly, as if wondering how much to tell me. "There's always something to sell or arrange. Some cargo from a market in the interior, an imported second-hand car that needs the right papers." He laughs mysteriously. "These fellows are crafty, you don't need to worry about them. Some days they bring in a million francs. They've got credit everywhere, and don't think anyone dares to come asking for his money!"

"And what about you? What do you do there?"

He dismisses my question with a wave of the hand. "I take care of my own affairs." He falls silent again for a moment. "Sometimes I go into the country with a truck or a bus and bring things back with me." It all sounds so cryptic that I stop asking.

"You should have seen Baaba in his heyday," he says. "He had money! I went to visit him in Monrovia and Abidjan, and he had houses, cars – everyone called him *patron*. I kept telling him he should build a house in Mali, but he wouldn't listen." Now Baaba's money is *gâté*, spoiled. He rents two rooms in

Hamdallaye and keeps his food in the refrigerator next door. He doesn't even have enough money to play the horses. "You know, the first year in Lafiabougou, he didn't come to visit me once? It hurt him too much to see my house." Kar gets up and hands Sali the empty plastic cups. "Let's get going."

Baaba and his friends watch as we climb onto the blue scooter. I realize that my being here could work out well for Kar at this point in his life. Everyone knows he's been to Europe, that his career got a new start there, and after his British tour he went to Switzerland, Canada and the United States. For Baaba's friends, these are such unlikely destinations that they sometimes tease him about it. "Too late, London just called!" they shout when he pulls up on his scooter. I've descended among them as living proof of their friend's success abroad.

"Damn it!" Kar pulls over to the side of the road. His scooter is playing up. "And I just got it back from the mechanic!" Fortunately the man works nearby, in the shade of a tree on a little square, close to the Soudan Cinéma. Kar kicks up a row when we get there, but as soon as the problem's been fixed he bids the man a good-natured farewell. His mood shifts are phenomenal, and I'm relieved to see that I'm not the only one who has to deal with them. The mechanic and I exchange a sympathetic look as he pushes us onto the street.

"You have to keep a machine running," Kar says as we putter along, "otherwise it'll keep you running." That's what his father taught him. He takes care of his things, I've noticed – his yard is neatly in order. His mother had four sons: she taught them what a mother usually shows her daughters.

On the way to Lafiabougou he stops at the Rôtisserie Moderne, a dark, smoky hole-in-the-wall, and comes out with a little brown package under his arm. He gives his scooter an appraising glance. "It looks just like a Yamaha, doesn't it?"

It's our first drive together by day through the streets of Lafiabougou. White people are rare here, so our passage doesn't go unnoticed. Again I have the feeling that I'm sitting on the back like a trophy.

His gate is open, and two boys are sleeping in the shade of the mango. A ghetto blaster covered by a T-shirt spews a flood of static. The stones they've brought to level the ground are stacked in the middle of the yard. From behind the pile of rocks comes a steady knocking. "What's that sound?"

Kar walks over to the well. "Come and take a look!" About ten meters below us, a man with a hammer and chisel is busy deepening the hole.

"Do you think there's water here?"

"Of course! There are little underground streams all over the place. I told you this hill was full of water, didn't I?!" There's a white priest – a *mon père*, as Kar calls him – who'll bring his pendulum and find water in your yard for money, but Kar located this well himself. "If we haven't hit water by tomorrow, we'll toss some dynamite in it."

Albert, the young foreman, comes over to say hello, and a bit later the yard is humming with activity: wheelbarrows full of sand roll in; a boy is filling plastic barrels with water; two others are mixing cement. From his garden chair Kar comments on the work in progress, and hands out orders and compliments. He keeps a firm hand on the rudder. The boys call him *patron* and *père*. "It's a motley crew," he says. "If you don't watch out, they'll take off with your cement. And you can't pay them in advance, because then you won't see them till the money's finished. I talk and laugh with them, but I make sure they know who's boss, every minute of the day."

Albert uses a length of twine to mark off the rooms they're going to build. He's just heard on the radio that the French have arrested a Malian *griotte*: she'd set up a network to smuggle so-called musicians into France. The customs people became suspicious when a fifteen-man orchestra showed up at the airport with no luggage. A clever official had a couple of instruments brought in: it turned out no one could play a note!

"Musicians used to be the only ones who could travel without being checked," Kar says. "But that's all over now."

Albert dreams of going to France as well. "But when I do, I'll be smarter than that," he says. "I'll wait until the World Cup, and register at the consulate as a soccer fan."

Kar laughs at him: "You think the French won't be ready for tricks like that?!"

He unlocks the door to his room. "I want to show you something." While he's squatting down in front of his open suitcase, I sneak a look inside his room. A bed with embroidered sheets, a low, narrow cupboard, a table with pans and cutlery, clothes hanging on hooks. His guitar is standing in the corner. Sometimes he doesn't touch it for months, he's told me, but as soon as he picks it up it's as though he's never done anything else.

He comes out of the room clutching a pile of photographs and clippings. Announcements and reviews of concerts he's given, pictures of him with the daughter of John Lee Hooker and singer Angélique Kidjo from Benin, an interview with a French music magazine – things any manager would use to make up a press kit. But Kar holds it all nervously on his lap, and allows me only a hurried glance at the clippings. Again I have the feeling I'm on territory he considers confidential.

"What's this?" A photograph of a hotshot in a fringed leather jacket, his guitar at the ready – I'm bowled over. *Kar Kar, blouson noir.* I'm more than ten years younger than him, but this is right out of my own youth – he stares at me brazenly, straight through the years. "What's that around your neck?"

Kar takes a look at the photo. "That must be the Santa Maria necklace." Santa Maria was the most famous *grin* – friends' club – in Kayes. You could buy the necklaces from the priests at the mission; they had a medal with a picture of the Virgin Mary on them. "We bought every necklace they had. Everyone who joined the club wore one."

He has more pictures from those days. Studio photos of himself in the most unlikely poses, patched jeans and pointy shoes, guitar hanging on a rope around his neck. They all have 'Kar Kar' written on them in his chicken scratches, and sometimes the date and the place where they were taken. Here he is in Mopti in 1965 with his friends. One of them was a Ghanaian fan who'd heard his music on the radio and traveled to Mali to meet him. They're hanging on each other's shoulders, pushing each other, embracing the neon Agfa sign the studio used for decoration. They're wearing open shirts and flashy sunglasses.

Kar looks at the pictures with little interest. "Back then we were *jéjés*," he says. A *jéjé* had flair and didn't give a damn about anything; a *jéjé* drove a three-speed Vespa named 'Saturday Night' and read *Salut de copains*, a pop magazine in which the marital ups and downs of Johnny Halliday and Sylvie Vartan were subjected to careful scrutiny. On weekdays, Kar was a tailor. He had a lot of customers: all his female fans got him to make their clothes.

Another popular *grin* in Kayes was Kafa, Bambara for 'I couldn't care less'. When the members of Kafa got together, taxi drivers knew they had to take a detour; the club made tea in the middle of the street, and if anyone said anything about it, they'd shout: "*Kafa!*"

While Kar is talking, another scene comes to mind. Tough guys with sultry looks leaning against the front of a café at the busiest crossing in my home town of Neerpelt. The rattle of accelerating scooters with broken mufflers. 'The Lazy Corner' – every mother's nightmare, every daughter's dream.

"And these are my parents." They're sitting stiff as ramrods, staring with dignity into the camera. Kar stands between them, laughing. "I was the only son they could count on," he says. "My oldest brother, Kalilou, had gone to Cuba as a musician. Baaba was off on an adventure in the Ivory Coast, and my youngest brother, Maciré, was a spoiled kid. I did everything for them: I worked on the land, gathered firewood for my mother and helped her around the house."

And there's Pierrette. A pretty girl with light skin and a thick head of hair. Her mother was Moorish, her father a French soldier. "Everyone said our marriage wouldn't last because she was a *métisse*. They thought she hadn't learned how to pound sorghum, that she couldn't cook or wash *boubous*. But Pierrette could do anything. Her children all walked by the time they were eight months old!" He looks pensively at the photo. "I was young when I married her. Maybe too young. I should probably have waited until my older brothers were married, but they weren't around, and my mother needed a woman to help her."

His dedication to his parents amazes me. There's no trace of rebellion – that's not how it was with us. He and his father did disagree, though, on what should happen after independence. His father was a veteran of Indochina and, later, cook to the French district officer in Kayes. He was sorry when the socialist president Modibo Keita handed the whites their walking papers. Meanwhile, his son was singing the praises of independence and promising his sweetheart that he would bring her Malian *pagnes* and shoes.

In 1963, when Malian radio recorded eight of his most popular songs, he became famous at home and abroad. In *Mali Twist* he imitated all kinds of animals, including a crowing rooster – it became the nation's early-morning hit. "You had to be awfully lazy if you didn't jump to work after hearing *Mali Twist*," Kar says. There was a lot of enthusiasm in those years, and he did his part. *Mali Twist* became a sort of national anthem: whenever soldiers saw him, they saluted.

"We didn't know anything back then, we thought we were going to build airplanes and send men to the moon! We should have done what President Houphouët Boigny did in the Ivory Coast, we should have let the white people stay. Because the whites were right: no black person ever designed a factory, not even a box of matches." He laughs. "Modibo Keita said we would make our own matches; we found out what that meant! When you lit one, you had to call the fire department! Takala Matches – everyone in Mali remembers them. You had to hold them at arm's length when you went to light a cigarette, otherwise your hair would go up in flames. Sometimes they lit themselves in your pocket. I don't know how many houses burned down because of Takala Matches! The situation got so bad, you weren't allowed in a taxi if you had them with you. They also started marketing Malian cigarettes that made you cough your lungs out. Liberté

179

they called them, but soon they were better known under the name 'donkeyshit'."

He had *donated* his songs to the country; they were played on the radio every day but never recorded and sold, he never earned anything from them. "The Malians loved me. I was their Johnny Halliday, their James Brown, but I didn't have enough money in my pocket to buy cigarettes."

It soon turned out that his brand of patriotism wasn't what the regime had in mind. Santa Maria became so popular that teenagers from all over the country came to Kayes, and clubs of the same name popped up in other cities as well. "Some people thought Santa Maria was a political party!" In a country where all youth movements were run by the party, this was unheard of. One day an influential citizen of Kayes went to the police and told them that Santa Maria had led his daughter astray. In the weeks that followed, police cars patrolled the streets: members of Santa Maria and Kafa who were drinking tea in front of their houses were picked up and taken to the police station. When a policeman asked a member of Kafa why he was wearing a T-shirt with the word 'Kafa' on it, the boy told him it was because he came from 'Kafadougou' – Kafa Town. The policeman hit him.

While I look at the pictures, Kar keeps a sharp eye on the workers and occasionally shouts something at them, but the memories of the past have softened his features; I'm starting to see the young man who led a gang that barely knew its own strength. Santa Maria lasted for six months. It was such an intense period that it seemed like years.

"What are you doing?" Kar looks at me in alarm. I've pulled a notebook out of my bag to make a few notes. "*Ah non!*" he says, disappointed.

"What difference does it make if I do it here or at my place?" I protest. But while I'm putting the notebook away, I could kick myself for interrupting his story.

"You're in too much of a hurry," he says. "If you want to find out about me, you should go with me to Kayes."

"There's nothing I'd like more." I'd been through Kayes one

night, on the train from Dakar to Bamako. Our arrival unleashed some commotion at the station, but the city behind breathed a deep silence. Nothing made me want to get out. But that's all different now.

I read somewhere that Kayes is one of the hottest cities in Africa, I tell him. "Who wrote that?" Kar says, peeved. "I'll smack him on the head!" It's all lies. Kayes was the first place the French settled on their way into the West African interior. Back in colonial days, the people of Kayes were considered French. "They're jealous in Bamako because we were civilized long before they were. Some people even tell you it's so hot in Kayes that lizards crossing the road stick to the asphalt halfway!"

The knocking in the well has stopped. The man who was breaking rock climbs out of the hole, and the other workers prepare to leave as well. Today's work is finished. Kar sweeps his photographs back into their folder. "I used to have a lot more pictures," he says.

"What happened to them?"

"Pierrette . . ." He smiles. "I have to admit, they weren't all decent, in some of them I was with girls who . . . Anyway, we weren't completely dressed." He stares ahead thoughtfully. "Success isn't good for you. You think you can do whatever you want to, you don't care about anything anymore. You're not even afraid of the president."

When he was invited somewhere to play, fans would line the roads fifteen kilometers outside of town. He was paraded through the streets in an open jeep. Young men followed him around and offered him their sisters. In 1963, a cabinet minister's wife had her chauffeur pick him up at his tailor shop in Bamako: she wanted him to make a dress for her. It quickly became clear that she had other things in mind. When he delivered the dress to the hotel room as she'd asked, she said he was so successful – she wished she could have a souvenir of their meeting. He'd pointed to the bed: "Let's go."

Back then things happened so incredibly fast. If he told a girl: "I like your style," that was it. "No, success isn't good. You're no longer part of the world, it makes you crazy. That's why it's so easy to start drinking or taking drugs, like Jimi Hendrix. You think you can handle anything; instead of two pills you take four, then six, then eight – until you're dead."

One afternoon, ten years later, Pierrette took the box of photographs and put it on the ground between them. She went through them one by one, asked who the people were in the picture, then either put the photograph back in the box or tore it up.

"And you, what did you do?"

"I think I was listening to a soccer match on the radio. I didn't say anything, I knew we'd get into a fight if I opened my mouth." She tore up at least two hundred photos. "That evening in bed, she asked me if I was angry. I told her no, she was right. I wasn't a foolish young man anymore who had pictures taken of himself with loose women. I was married, the father of two sons. Badialo had already died."

"Badialo?" It's a name that comes back often in his songs. *Death spares no one. If Death spared anyone, it should have been my Badialo.*

"She was our first daughter. She was about eight months old, and had just started walking. One day she was tripping around happily, the next day she was dead." He sighs. "A couple of shots of penicillin would have saved her, but many Africans make the mistake of waiting too long to go to the doctor. When my father died a few years later, I could accept that, he'd had his day, but Badialo – her life had only begun. She never even got a chance. We had eleven children and only six of them survived, but Badialo's death hurt the most. Maybe because she was the first. They all disappeared the same way: one day they were healthy, the next day they were dead. We once lost two children in the same week."

Again I'm struck by the defiance in his voice. "If I told you what I've been through . . ." Kar rubs his forehead. "My oldest brother, Kalilou, came back from Cuba and set up an orchestra, Las Maravillas del Mali. They were really successful. One morning he woke up feeling bad; two days later he was dead. There were those who said someone had tossed him a *korté*. Maybe they were right. People can't stand to see someone else being success-ful. African jealousy is something terrible."

He looks at me, as if to see whether I'm still following him. "Africans are wicked," he says. "They make life impossible for each other. When a white person invents something, his col-leagues say: Let's see that, that's interesting. After the inventor dies, they try to continue his work. But do you know what they do around here?" He laughs with a sneer. "They hire a marabout to sabotage the inventor!" He shakes his head. "No, Africa, it's not worth it."

Kar gets up and walks over to the mango tree. It's time for prayer. I sit staring into space while he washes his hands, face and feet, but suddenly he turns around and says: "Someday I'll tell you a story. Maybe you've traveled a lot in Africa, but what I'll tell you, you've never heard. No man can stand so much sorrow. It will make you cry, and everyone you tell will cry too."

༺༻

Kar's made macaroni, but after he warms it up he discovers that it's spoiled. He's terribly upset. "It doesn't matter," I say, still awed by what he's been telling me, "we can get something around the corner." But he's inconsolable. He wanted to serve me a meal he'd fixed himself, he'd been working on it all morning! "And all because of this damned heat!" He sullenly grabs an empty pan and disappears into the darkness. We eat in silence. Then, with-out saying a word, he rolls his scooter out of his room. "I'm going to see my children. If you like, you can come along."

"You got all worked up about nothing," I say soothingly as he pulls the gate closed behind us.

"I have a bad character," he says. "When things don't go the way I planned, I get upset." He starts the scooter with an angry kick. "Pierrette knew she had to stay out of my way at moments like that."

But by the time we arrive at his brother-in-law Mamadou's

house, the storm has blown over. A girl of about ten leaves a group of children playing in the street and runs up to him: "*Papaa!*" She has short, curly hair and a light complexion. "This is Tanti, she loves me the most." Laughing, Kar picks her up and carries her inside.

It's a rented house, like so many in Bamako's neighborhoods: rooms facing onto a courtyard where a number of families live close together. Mamadou is sitting behind a curtain, watching television. He's Pierrette's half-brother: after her father, the French soldier, went home, her mother married a Malian.

Tanti plops down on the couch and starts talking at a mile a minute: she's holding a wallet with pebbles for coins and toffee wrappers for bills. "But she has real money too," Kar says proudly. "Tanti is a real business woman. At school she sells toffees for five francs apiece!" When the weekend comes she puts her things in a plastic bag and walks up the hill to stay with him. She washes his clothes, cooks, does the dishes and sweeps the yard. Sometimes, when he gets home, he finds her squatted down in front of the gate, waiting for him.

A smaller version of Tanti sticks her head out from behind the curtain. When she sees me she remains there, standing shyly. Kar grabs her by the arm and pulls her onto his lap. "This one is spoiled," he says, "because her mother died right after she was born. She was never breast-fed. Everyone felt sorry for her." All his children have had a spanking at some point, but he's never raised his hand to Zévilé. "Allah wouldn't like that. It's bad enough when your mother dies while you're still a baby."

For me, this situation takes some getting used to. Happy as his children are to see him, Kar acts like a visitor. We watch the news, Mamadou's wife comes in with tea, and soon the children have gone back outside to play. I think of all the complaining I've heard in the last few months about the family responsibilities that complicate life for modern Malians. Mamadou must be about thirty-five. He has two little children of his own, and he works as an engineer in a pharmaceuticals plant. I can imagine that the arrival of his late sister's children has interfered with his plans, that he'd thought his life would be different. But when I comment cautiously to Kar about this later on, he's truly surprised. Other members of Pierrette's family live in the house next to them; his children are being raised in the *grande famille*. No one has ever suggested to him that there was anything untoward about the arrangement.

As soon as the news is over, we leave without much ado. The neighbors are watching a violent video in the courtyard. In front of the gate we meet Kar's eighteen-year-old daughter Mantjini, with her girlfriends. Thick eyebrows, a high forehead, an enormous head of hair – the resemblance to her mother is striking.

Tanti and Zévilé are nowhere in sight. So young, it strikes me, and already completely accustomed to life without parents. But then I realize that this isn't so unusual. In his autobiography, the Malian writer Amadou Hampâté Bâ tells how, as a child, he constantly moved from one branch of the family to the next. That didn't seem to affect his sense of belonging.

Kar leaves his scooter parked where it is; the taxi stand is nearby. I walk next to him, thinking. "What was it like for them when you went to France? In fact, they'd not only lost their mother; their father was gone as well." I ask it hesitantly, braced for his reaction – some questions make him so angry. But our conversation during the last few hours has softened him. "No, that's not how it was," he says. "They were happy for me. They knew I was going to work for them. After a few weeks I started sending money and clothes. And I called every Sunday. That's why they love me: they know what I did for them during that period."

He was happy in France. He worked, ate, slept and didn't think about a thing. All his worries had rolled off him. "France helped me forget my sadness; if I'd stayed here, I might have died." But when his oldest son Sambou wrote to him, it all came back. Sometimes those letters bothered him so much that he had to put them aside after reading only a few sentences.

Kar insists on buying the tickets to Kayes, and he refuses my offer to pay my own way. "We Bambara don't believe in paying separately. When you do something alone, you do everything alone."

He's a nervous traveler, so we arrive at Bamako station that morning an hour too early. Right away, he gets into an argument with the boy who helps carry our baggage to the train. A thousand francs, where does he get off asking for that kind of money?! He makes a big scene, and everyone gets involved. One bystander shouts that he shouldn't pay anything; another says he should call the railway police. But after he's scolded the boy, Kar feels sorry for him and gives him three hundred francs. "A drug addict, did you see that?" he sputters as the fellow disappears into the crowd. "He was almost too high to talk."

A little later he starts bickering with a hefty business woman who has shoved some of her baggage onto the spot allotted to ours, so our own bags are pushed out of place. I laugh to myself about the way he marks off his territory. When all the commotion has died down, one thing's clear to all passengers in our compartment: this man is not to be messed with. "I've done everything for my country," he says stubbornly, "there's no way I'll let them take anything away from me!"

Women come down the aisle selling bags of *wousoulan* – a local incense. It smells so good that I reach for my wallet right away. "*Ah non*," Kar moans, "you're not going to buy that junk!" The plastic bags are sprayed with perfume, he says, and filled with odorless pieces of wood.

We step back onto the platform in search of a fan – a *ventilateur africain*, as he calls it – and ice for his plastic cooler. His concert was on television last night, and the greetings and compliments come in from all sides. He's flattered, I can tell, but he takes it all with a grain of salt. "They act like they haven't seen me for the last thirty years!"

After the whistle blows for the third time, the train groans and chugs into motion. While Kar is filling the cooler with ice and water from plastic sacks, he remembers all the things he's forgotten: his prayer rug, his comb, his toothbrush, a pan to put food in when we stop along the way. "But at least I have my plastic cups!" He brought them back from his tour of Canada: 'Vancouver Folk Festival' is written on the side. They have a lid you can slide open and closed. Kar looks at them fondly. "I've been sorry ever since that I didn't grab more of them – they were just lying there for the taking!"

The train we're on comes from France, "Because when white people get tired of a train, they give it to the Africans." All the insignias of the SNCF, the Société Nationale des Chemins de Fer, are still intact, and there's even a map of the French rail network hanging between the cars. "We're grateful when we get a present, we don't ruin it," Kar says. "If the Dutch gave us a train, we'd leave their map hanging in it too."

It's less than five hundred kilometers from Bamako to Kayes. A French TGV could make the trip in two hours, Kar says, but with this *wouya-wouya* diesel, which rides at a snail's pace and stops all the time, we'll be lucky to get there in ten. Whenever we approach a station we see the women on the surrounding hillsides running down to the tracks, baskets of merchandise on their heads. Perspiring heavily, they line up single-file outside the cars with mangoes, bananas and sandwiches. They have only a few minutes before the magic moment of the day is past. Kar peers up and down the platform in search of bargains. Looking pleased, he lugs a big bag of manioc into the train; they don't get that in Kayes.

Blind men are pushed into the train by relatives at every stop. They travel along for a while, shuffling down the aisle, calling out plaintively: "Alms, in the name of Allah!" One man is selling black stones against scorpion stings, another one shouts that he has liver for sale. "Liver! Forget it! We've heard that one before," Kar says. "If you show any interest, he puts his bowl on the floor, pulls the paper aside and it turns out he has everything but liver. But by that time you've smelled the meat, so you'll take whatever he cuts off."

Two men in front of us are engaged in animated conversation. One of them has just come back from Brazzaville, where he runs a shop. The soldiers there, who aren't getting paid by the Congolese government, started plundering the town a while back. Shopkeepers are having a particularly hard time. The man is from Kayes, and he is thinking about moving back to his home town. "Hopefully he has a house there," Kar muses, "otherwise he's in as much trouble as my brother Baaba."

A woman at the other end of the compartment is singing and swaying back and forth in a trance. At first the noise was lost in the general commotion, but now more and more passengers are turning to look at her. Sometimes her singing switches to a speedy monologue, punctuated by laughter; sometimes she bangs her head so hard against the seat that she hurts herself. The solicitous young man beside her does his best to quieten her. Two days ago she came out of the shower singing, someone explains, and she's been out of control ever since. The sedatives the doctor in Bamako gave her didn't work, so her family has decided to send her back to her native village, in the hope that she'll calm down there. Before long the entire compartment gets involved, and tall tales start going around about bizarre things that happened on other trips. A few weeks ago a man fell asleep in this train – and never woke up again.

As it becomes warmer in the compartment, the passengers grow quiet. Everyone around us is dozing off, and even the psychotic woman has grown tired of singing. We use our fans to temper the heat, and fill our cooler at every stop. We're entering warmer climes, a landscape in sepia baking in the sun. Kar looks out the window with more interest than before: we're getting close to his birthplace. When we stop at a desolate station in the middle of nowhere, he says: "This is Oualia. Pierrette and I lived here for two years." Reed huts faded by the sun, not a soul on the street. "Here?" He laughs at my astonishment. "That's right, and it wasn't so bad, not compared with where we'd been."

He didn't earn enough as a tailor, so after Santa Maria was disbanded he went out to seek his fortune, just like his brother Baaba. His travels took him to Bobo Dioulasso, in what was then Upper Volta. The white people hadn't left there yet, so you could buy jeans and other Western goods no longer available in Mali. He started trading between Bobo and Mali, and sending money home every week.

After a while he opened a tailor's shop in Bobo. Down at the end of the street was the Normandie nightclub, where the famous Volta Jazz band played every evening – he could hear them all the way down the street in his shop. His head was still filled with music, but he felt responsible for his parents. He'd left them in Kayes with his little brother Maciré, and had come to Bobo to earn money. No one knew that the tailor hunched over his sewing machine was the singer Kar Kar, whose songs were on the radio all the time.

Until a friend informed the owner of the Normandie that Kar was living just down the street. One evening he couldn't get out of it any longer; he had to play. When he was called on stage, the audience could hardly believe that Kar Kar was in their midst. After the show they didn't want to let him go, and they took him to his tailor shop in procession. That same night, the girl everyone in Bobo was in love with stopped in front of his shop on her Italian Vespa. From that time on he performed regularly in the Normandie, and his shop became a well-known meeting place.

But none of this made him rich, and he kept worrying about his parents. When he was offered a job as a technical agent at the CAC, the Centre d'Action Cooperative, in Nioro, not far from Kayes, he didn't hesitate for a moment: he closed his shop and left Bobo.

As a technical agent, he had to supply the state-run cooperatives with salt, powdered milk, seeds and rice that the farmers could buy on credit. The state also sold oxen and machinery on the installment plan. In his free time, Kar set up an orchestra in Nioro and played with them on the weekends. It was during one of those shows that Pierrette fell in love with him.

In 1968, the year President Modibo Keita was brought down, Kar was living in Bafoulabé, close to Kayes, leading a well-known orchestra. Like many singers at the time, he'd written a number in praise of the Malian president: it was taken off the radio from one day to the next.

"They transferred me to Kundia," Kar laughs. "Talk about remote! Sometimes we didn't see a single car for six months!" Two years later, one of the officials from the CAC in Bamako ran into him there. The man liked Kar's music, and was deeply shocked. "If you stay here, you'll end up killing your wife," he said. He arranged for Kar to be transferred to Oualia, the village where we just stopped. "Compared with Kundia, Oualia was paradise," Kar says. "It's along the tracks, so a train came by every day."

He's been talking for quite a while, but now he looks anxiously at his watch. The train is more than two hours late. It keeps coming to a halt, and even stops at a little station where it's not supposed to. "Someone on the crew probably has something to take care of here," Kar grumbles.

It's starting to get dark, but when I put my head out the window I notice that the evening brings no relief. It's like riding into an oven. Suddenly I remember the story of the French district officer who spent his days in a barrel of water. Wasn't that in Kayes? Kar has his head out the window too. "Hot, isn't it?" I say. He nods. "But don't go telling anyone in Bamako!"

❦

At Kayes we worm our way through the throng to the station exit. Our bags are almost torn from our hands, but Kar shakes off all nuisances with a few forceful gestures. He's on his own turf here and doesn't have to shout – as soon as the boys recognize him, they step back in awe.

Outside, he stops and looks around. A heavy man steps out of the line of taxi drivers and walks over with a broad grin. "Kar Kar, *ça va?*" He takes our baggage and puts it in his car.

The taxi is a wreck that groans under the driver's enormous weight, but that doesn't dampen his spirits any. He's thrilled that his friend, who was on television last night, has come to Kayes.

190

They met back when Kar worked in Nioro. The cabby was only a boy then, but he remembers the day Kar married Pierrette as if it were yesterday. The announcements were stuck up on every tree; sheep walked around with invitations tied around their necks, and if Kar's fans had been able to catch any stray dogs they would have decked them out as well. He remembers peering at the couple from between the grown-ups' legs. "Pierrette was so beautiful! Every merchant in Nioro tried to win her hand. Some of them were a lot richer than Kar, but she only had eyes for him." He tries to meet my gaze in the broken rearview mirror. "That's why he can't forget her," he says, more quietly all of a sudden; "maybe that's why he's never married again."

I'm surprised that Kar's private life is such public knowledge here, but when I look up I see him smiling benignly, the way people do when a *griot* sings their praises.

The taxi stops in front of a clay house along a darkened street. As soon as we climb out, shouting children pounce on us and grab our bags. In front of the house is a ditch with a few planks laid across it. "Careful," Kar says, leading the way, "everything here is pretty rickety."

Under a tree in the courtyard, a group of people are watching television. Kar's brother Maciré gets up and launches into an apology: he was at the station earlier this evening, but no one could tell him when the train would be coming in. He's tall and skinny and has a slow, rather plaintive voice. His wife Mamou, who's expecting twins, is lying on a bare boxspring. The other people watching television are neighbors. Sheep are bleating in a roofed-in corner of the yard.

Kar looks around. "Where's Abdoulaye?" Abdoulaye is the twelve-year-old son he left behind in Kayes after Pierrette died. Her wish was that he receive an education from the marabout who runs a French–Arabic school here. It's not unusual for parents to entrust one of their children to a marabout.

"*Papaa!*" A beautiful little boy with Arabic features comes running up and throws himself into Kar's arms. Kar smiles, presses his son to him, talks to him softly. Abdoulaye's marabout left for Saudi Arabia a while ago. "Next year I'll bring you to Bamako to go to school," Kar promises.

The three of us walk to a room where a mattress with a clean sheet is lying on the ground. Next to the bed is an electric fan, the only other furnishing. "Where's the hat rack?" Abdoulaye laughs. "They used it as firewood to cook with." Kar shakes his head. "These people. Barbarians is what they are." Last time he was in Kayes, he pounded four nails into the wall to hang his mosquito netting. The holes are there, but the nails have vanished. "What could they have done with them? You can't burn nails, can you?"

It takes a while before I realize that this is one of the rooms where he and Pierrette lived. They ate in the front room, slept in here. Pierrette kept her crockery in a cupboard with screen doors; on the wall hung the framed photo of *Kar Kar, blouson noir*. Even the ruined bed on which Mamou is lying once belonged to Pierrette. Kar bought it for her so she could rest in the shade, out in the courtyard, after a hard day's work.

In 1991, when he came back here to visit after two years in France, everything he'd left behind had fallen apart. The mattress that had once been on Pierrette's bed was gone, and pieces of screen from her cupboard were floating around the yard. "It was a good thing I took my photos with me, otherwise I'd have lost them too!"

Mamou's oldest daughter brings me a bucket of hot water. When she adds a little cold water and I stick my hand in it to check the temperature, Kar shouts: "Don't do that!"

"Why not?"

He takes a plastic cup, ladles a little water out of the bucket and pours it over his hand. "That's how you're supposed to feel whether it's the right temperature."

"Why?"

"That's how we learned to do it."

"I don't see any difference," I say defiantly.

"It's the way my mother always did it, and what she did . . ."

"Does the Koran say anything about it?" I ask incredulously.

"No, but when you get it from your parents, and their ancestors passed it down from generation to generation, it almost becomes a commandment, because our ancestors were closer to God than we are."

"And what happens if you don't do it?"

"Nothing special. Your *baraka* – luck – diminishes."

I drape a towel over my shoulder, pick up the bucket and walk pensively to the washroom. When Kar first confronted me with one of these ancestral decrees, back in his yard in Bamako, I'd almost laughed. Superstition! Now that I'm in the place where his mother taught him these things, I notice it's harder to shrug them off. During the next few days I sneakily stick my hand into the warm water anyway, but feel guilty whenever he catches me at it. Suddenly I can imagine simply adopting decrees like this, if only to spare the feelings of people who believe in them.

Kar's television appearance is the talk of the courtyard. Everyone's surprised that he's made such a strong comeback. They all thought he'd left music behind, that he'd lost his voice. "They should have given you a Grammy Award instead of Ali Farka Touré," Maciré says. Kar laughs distractedly. He tells them about the new CD that will be coming out soon, and about an invitation he's received to perform in the French city of Angoulême. Abdoulaye pulls up a stool and sits looking at his father with a blissful smile. Kar puts his arm around him and says he's bought a bike for him; it's waiting in Bamako.

Mamou's children are falling asleep all around us, and the neighbors leave quietly, one by one. Kar pulls a sheet out of his bag. He's going to sleep in the yard too, amid the adults and children lying on reed mats with their arms and legs tossed across each other. Exhausted, I collapse on my bed, my head in the breath of wind coming from the electric fan. Out in the yard I hear the sheep rattling the empty pans on the cooker. They're looking for the food which has left its scent there.

When we leave the house the next morning I see that the ditch isn't covered with planks, but with worn-out pieces of railroad track. Maciré's children are playing in the street, poking sticks into the brackish ditch, using cans to dish up water for making mud pies. The water bubbles and seethes, and a cloud of mosquitoes is hanging above it – I look at it in disgust.

"To think we used to hold horse races in these drainage ditches," Kar says.

"Horse races?"

"Sure! Some of these ditches go on for kilometers. We used to take little pieces of wood and whittle at them endlessly, then toss them into the ditch and run along beside them, cheering like it was a real horse race. Sometimes there were forty of us!"

"But how could you tell which horse was yours?"

"That was easy! We worked on them for hours, painting or drawing on them."

We've arrived at a dusty crossroads. This is where the circus used to put up its tents. It came from Senegal and stayed for weeks – at night you could hear the elephants trumpeting and the lions roaring. A monument in the form of an obelisk has been erected on the square. "A present from the former governor," Kar says. "No one knows what it's supposed to represent. We call it 'the candle'." At first there was a lamp up at the top. It gave a lot of light, like a beacon, but when the lamp broke the new governor didn't think it was worth fixing.

"Kar Kar!"

"Dra! *Ça va?*"

In a little shop on the square, a man sits working on a radio. Behind him rises a boneyard of electrical equipment. "Everyone in Kayes is dependent on Dra," Kar says. "If your television breaks down during a soccer match, he'll have it fixed before the game is over."

Dra is using a brush to sweep the dust out of a radio. "Sorry to keep working, but this has to be finished really fast."

Kar leans against the counter and looks out at the crossroads. The streets were paved until recently, but after they found gold at Sadiola, south of Kayes, the pavement was broken up. The South Africans want to build a factory at Sadiola, and they donated money to widen the streets in town. "But you see what happens: the asphalt has been taken away and Kayes has been covered in dust for the last year."

"Our radios are getting used to it," Dra says resignedly.

"And when are they going to repave the streets?"

"Ah! That's a very good question!" Kar says. "At this moment everyone is busy using up the money. If there's any left . . ."

Across the square lies Kayes' main thoroughfare, a busy street lined with shops. Kar keeps stopping to greet friends. I recognize the facetious tone from our visit to the market in Bamako – he's in his element. All the shopkeepers know him. He picks out a few nails for the mosquito netting; when he pulls out his wallet, the salesman waves him away.

In the fabric shop that belongs to his friend Sidi, cola is brought out for us. "Anyone with a fridge in Kayes is rich," Kar says as he inspects the contents of the refrigerator, "because he can sell soft drinks and iced water." He peers at the nylon jogging suits hanging everywhere. "Do you think any of these would fit Abdoulaye?"

The tailors work in the street. Some of them sit under a canopy or wear a gauze mask against the dust; their sewing machines are Chinese-made. We pass a man in a skull-cap who's embroidering a blue and white pattern on a pillowcase. Suddenly Kar stops and retraces his steps. "Diallo, is that you?" He shakes the man's hand delightedly. "We were in France together," he says to me, "we lived in the same *foyer*."

When Kar asks him what brought him back to Kayes, a shadow crosses Diallo's face. He came to visit his family and couldn't get away again. "My papers, I couldn't get them together." He traveled all the way to the Congo, but came back empty-handed. "I'm still hoping, but . . ." He looks at us and laughs bravely, but his eyes are sad. A moment ago he was completely absorbed in embroidering his pillow; our arrival has upset him.

A lot of people in these dusty streets dream of going abroad, I discover in the next few days. Kar is seen here as a man of the world: not only does he travel back and forth between Mali and

Europe, he's even brought a foreign woman with him to Kayes! He takes it all as his due. If people think he's still living in Paris, he doesn't spoil their illusions.

"Would you like to see my old shop?" We've arrived at the covered section of the market, in the labyrinth of alleyways where sounds are muffled and the light filters through a reed roof. It feels like an Arab *souq* and smells of herbs, tea and dried fish. Kar stops in front of a shop with second-hand clothes lying on a table and shoulder bags dangling from the corrugated-iron doors. Business went well here: when the train from Dakar arrived, Senegalese women came pouring in; he sometimes made two hundred thousand francs in a single morning.

The narrow street is filled with a peculiar odor that makes me sneeze. Two doors down an old man is lying on a mat amid dried lizards, snake skins, the claws of wild cats, monkey paws and other paraphernalia for making *gris-gris*. I sneeze again. "Was he around when you worked here?" Kar nods. "Didn't it bother you?"

He laughs. "No, not me!"

I'm glad to be out in the open air again. We walk towards the River Senegal, on the other side of which lies Kayendi, 'little Kayes'. Open canoes full of passengers shuttle back and forth, and there's a low bridge for cars and pedestrians. Every year the Peul come with their cattle from Mauritania and cross the river. Just before the rains begin, they head north again. "As soon as it starts raining, the bridge is eaten up by the water," Kar says. "But as long as the Peul haven't brought their cattle to the other side, it won't rain. They see to that."

"What do you mean?"

"They keep it from raining! Every child in Kayes knows that."

He's turned and headed up the steps of a majestic colonial building overlooking the water. "And now we're going to see what Maciré is up to." Maciré is a gofer at the BIAO, the Banque Internationale de l'Afrique Occidentale. He barely attended school – he got his job through a friend of the family.

In a little office with smudged windows, we find him writing at a desk amid stacks of dossiers. "Ah, just in time!" He jumps to his feet and presents Kar with an electricity bill. "Do you think you could . . . ?"

Kar pushes the bill away without looking at it. "Why should I?"

"But you know my vacation starts tomorrow!" Maciré usually earns a little on the side by arranging things for bank customers, but he loses those revenues when he's off work. "It's only . . ." But Kar doesn't even want to hear about it.

I watch with interest. Usually I'm the victim of this kind of sponging, and I always feel embarrassed and guilty when I refuse. Now I get to see how they handle this among themselves!

But while the three of us are walking home, Maciré convinces his brother to buy him a hundred kilos of rice and sorghum. He stands in the shop as though this were merely his due, inspecting the rice, letting the grains of sorghum trickle through his fingers and telling the porter where to deliver the sacks. I see Kar in a pose that will soon become familiar: hunched over his wallet, he carefully counts out first the bills, then the change. *L'oncle d'Amérique.*

By the time we get back to the house, the sacks have already arrived. Mamou takes the opportunity to complain about the bed she sleeps on, saying that she needs a mattress. But Kar feels he's spent enough already. "When you've had your fill of rice and sorghum, you won't even notice it," he says hard-heartedly, "then you'll sleep like a log, even on bare boxsprings."

The heat in the courtyard is so devastating that I don't know which way to turn. After we've eaten, I lie on my bed and try to read. The heat outside the range of the electric fan is infernal. Kar and Abdoulaye are in the front room. It's touching to see the two of them together. "Tanti and Abdoulaye are my favorites," Kar let slip once. "They understand me best."

Kar is lying on his back in his boxer shorts, fanning himself. Abdoulaye leans against the bed and takes the fan from him every once in a while. It's been six months since they saw each other, and Abdoulaye is full of stories that Kar will later recount in detail. At every new anecdote, he gives his father a poke:

"*Papaa!*" His classmates are described in succession. 'The Cat', who's so limber he can fight without soiling his white *boubou*; the boy with the protruding navel who didn't come to school for five days because he couldn't stop playing soccer; the girl who always wants to play with the boys; 'The Mouse', who has a little pinched face and has been bragging for months that his mother's going to buy him a bicycle (no one's seen the bicycle, though, so his classmates tease him by asking if his bicycle happens to be the size of a mouse). When Abdoulaye notices that his father has fallen asleep, he quietly puts down the fan and lies beside him.

Later, we sit in the yard with Kar's ghetto blaster. He takes a piece of plastic and whittles a horse for me with his pocketknife, then lets it bob around in a blue bowl filled with water. "Of course, this isn't as sophisticated as the ones we used to make," he says, eyeing the unsightly thing. "We used to rub them against the wall until they shone. All the horses had names: Olympic, Lam Toro, Bel Ami. We would have hopped on them if we could!"

Mamou and the neighbors are playing a Nigerian version of snakes-and-ladders. It's called 'Ludo Game', and the board has pictures of Mike Tyson and other black athletes on it. They've put it on an upturned bucket and are sitting on empty milk cans. The dice rattle loudly on the plastic, and the players scold and scream at each other. Maciré is sleeping on a mat in the shade, a badly tuned radio next to his ear, oblivious to it all.

"Look at that." Kar directs my gaze to the verandah, where a sheep is busy devouring a notebook. I jump up and tear it out of its mouth. It's one of Abdoulaye's schoolbooks. "No wonder things disappear around here," Kar says impassively.

I'm amazed at how nonchalant things are here in the yard. The laundry is slung over the line without clothespins – damp pieces of clothing fall on the ground, but no one picks them up. Mamou's oldest daughter pounds sorghum for supper in a big wooden mortar which the sheep casually eat from later on. Her little sister Bintou – a touchingly beautiful child of about seven –

can barely talk. "Wait until she gets older," Maciré said this afternoon. He has fifty-five days of leave coming up. When I asked what he was planning to do, he replied: "Nothing, just relax." And this house is in such bad need of repair!

None of this would surprise me as much if it weren't for the sharp contrast with Kar. "You should have seen this house when I was young," he says. "I did everything. I raised pigeons that people came all the way from Senegal to buy! When Santa Maria was at its peak, there were sometimes fifty people drinking tea and listening to records. We sat in the front room, which we called '*la casa*', or on the patio I built next to the street. When I lived here with Pierrette, I fixed the house every year before the rainy season. But now . . ." He looks around, concerned. "I hope the rains start soon, but I'm afraid there won't be a single room where we can stay dry."

To the people around us, Kar and I belong together, so he's started acting that way too. The antagonism between Kar and Maciré bring us closer still. Thinking back to our first meeting, to the minefield of unfamiliar codes I walked into, I realize just how far I've come in a short period.

After seeing his friend Diallo from the Parisian *foyer* this morning, Kar told me about his stint in the French building industry. His Jewish boss was quite fond of him, and kept giving him more responsibilities. One day Kar and the Italian foreman were laying a marble staircase in a luxury apartment. While they were carrying a heavy slab of marble up to the flat, the Italian threw his back out. "Goddamn Africans," he swore.

"And what about Italians?" Before Kar knew what he was doing, he'd punched the foreman in the face.

The next morning his boss came to where Kar lived. He'd been working with the Italian for more than twenty years, he said. He hated it, but he had to let Kar go.

We walked along together in silence. Someone who could get angry enough to hit a full-grown man – that wasn't the Kar I'd known up till then. He too was sunk in thought. After a while he said: "Now I've told you a story about my life in France."

When he comes back from the shower, I'm writing in my red and black notebook. For a moment I feel caught and afraid he'll scold me, but he simply peers over my shoulder and says: "Be careful your hand doesn't start swelling up from all that writing."

※※※

The hottest hours of the day are behind us; the neighbors have gone, Abdoulaye and his friends are out playing in the street, and even Maciré has disappeared without a word. "I think I know where he's hanging out," Kar says mysteriously. "Let's see if we can surprise him."

In the neighborhood where he takes me, we witness a loud ruckus in the street: a woman has pulled a traffic sign out of the ground and is threatening to hit a drunken man over the head with it. The woman's right, Kar says; from the sound of it the drunk has owed her money for months. "We call this part of town 'California'." He's automatically begun to speak in a whisper. The name comes from back when the western *A Lawless Street* played in Kayes. It's a tough neighborhood, full of thieves and prostitutes. If it's illegal, you'll find it here.

Kar pushes open the gate to an ocher-colored colonial building, the former French club of Kayes. The music that's been hanging in the air for a while comes closer. A band is rehearsing at the back of the building. On bass guitar, with a poker face, is Maciré. Kar laughs. "What did I tell you?"

It's a *wouya-wouya* orchestra, Kar says, but that doesn't keep his brother from spending all his free time here. When he sees us, Maciré sticks up his hand and grins. He's about forty-seven, balding just like Kar, but his face is still completely smooth and his body has something feeble about it. "My mother spoiled him," Kar says; "he never learned to act like an adult."

When the band has finished playing, Maciré comes over to us. "So, what did you think?" Kar shrugs, I mumble something, but Maciré says self-confidently: "You just wait, another six months of rehearsing and we'll be ready!" He's talked himself into believing that he's on his way to international fame, just like Kar. "Next year I'll send you a tape and you can get to work," he says to me. I'm not an impresario, I protest, but Kar winks at me. "Since Maciré has seen you, he's on a plane out."

We lean against a low wall and watch the boys playing football on the square. "In the days of Santa Maria, this was a dance floor," Kar says. "Some very lively dancing went on here!" When their show really picked up steam, Kar used to jump down off the stage and do somersaults through the audience with his guitar, while the bass player climbed up on his instrument like a monkey.

A soccer game is in progress under the floodlights across the courtyard. Back when the French were still here, that was the tennis court. "All the players were dressed in white uniforms, and we used to fight to retrieve balls for them," Maciré says. "For every ball you brought back, they gave you twenty-five francs. With that money, we bought cigarettes or went to the movies." In the evening the French would sit at the bar or stroll around under the lemon trees in light tropical suits, whisky in hand. Maciré looks at the weathered court and the weeds that have sprung up around it; he shakes his head and says regretfully: "Ah no, the whites, they worked!"

Kar and I steal a glance at each other and break out laughing. "What's to keep you from doing the same?" I say.

But Maciré is in dreamland. "White suits is what they wore," he says, "snow-white suits." He stares off at an imaginary vista where figures in tennis gear rush back and forth and you can hear the plunking of the balls.

"D'you suppose we could get anything to drink around here?" Kar asks impatiently. But at the open bar, with the stern admonition 'Drinking Compulsory' hanging above it, there's nothing to be had. The trainload of soft drinks from Bamako didn't come in on time, the barman explains; there's been a shortage in Kayes ever since.

"You see how cut off from the world Kayes is?" Kar says as the three of us walk home through the darkened streets. "As soon as something goes wrong with the train, there's a crisis. Our president and his predecessor both came from here, but do you think they did anything for this part of the country? Moussa Traoré didn't even have a road built to his home town!"

The river was still an important transport route when Kar was young. Boats came up the Senegal from the West African coastal city of St-Louis to Kayes, where goods were taken further into the interior by truck. You could hear the *Cap Lopez* coming from kilometers away. There was even a song encouraging mothers to go down to the waterfront and pick up the sugar and salt that had spilled on the quay when the boats were unloaded. "Some of the ships were so big that people played basketball on the deck. When they moored here, the school children were given a tour, and sometimes we were even allowed to watch a movie on board. The French wanted to civilize us."

The streets are quiet. The only crowd is in front of the movie house; the first session will start in a few minutes. Across the street women are sitting at low tables, selling beverages, apples and nuts. From the darkness on the first floor comes a whispered "Kar Kar!" It's the old man who runs the projector – Kar recognizes his voice.

The marquee posters for the film *Tremors* are curled and yellowed, but Kar says they're changed all the time; they show new films every day now. Things used to be different. He must have seen *Last Train from Gun Hill* at least fifty times. "But I never got bored, I discovered something new every time." Kirk Douglas, Anthony Quinn and Burt Lancaster were big heroes around here. When Kar and his friends were broke, they climbed over the wall.

He went to the movies all the time, even after he was married. When there was a horror-film festival he never missed a screening. Women who gave birth to devils, a baby that drank blood instead of milk, snakes that swallowed cars, dead men who rose from the grave to walk the streets and cut out people's hearts – sometimes people were so scared that the theater emptied out within fifteen minutes of the show beginning. But Kar stayed put. According to him, Americans know a lot more about devils, fetishes and *gris-gris* than Africans do. Indian productions have the best crying scenes, and they do the most lying: they even let horses and dogs fly around.

"What about French movies?"

"French movies? No, then we'd go somewhere and drink tea instead!" Kar laughs scornfully. "Nothing ever happens in French movies; all they do is talk, mostly about love. I think it's because they don't have enough money. They're still at the first scene when an American movie's already in full swing."

He pulls me up the stairs. "Come on, I'll show you the inside of the theater." It's an enormous open-air cinema like the ones I saw on the coast in St-Louis. In the depths are the metal benches for the 'Indians', as they're called: they have the cheapest tickets, make the most noise and have to run when it starts raining. A second-class ticket gets you a seat in the middle of the theater. The whites sat all the way up at the top, under the corrugated-iron roof. Kar points to the vacant bar. "They had everything: whisky, gin, vermouth – whatever they wanted."

The day he heard about his brother Kalilou's death on the radio, he went to the movies. "What else was I was to do? The train for Bamako didn't leave until the next morning, and I didn't want to tell my mother about it – I was afraid she'd have a heart attack." But he wasn't the only one who'd been listening to the radio. When he got home, he found his mother crying in the yard with a crowd of people around her.

Maciré is waiting for us outside on the steps. The silence in the streets of Kayes has become even more intense. Bare light bulbs dangle above the wooden shutters of the shops, here and there a watchman is lying asleep on a sheet of cardboard. At the dusty crossroads where we stood this morning, Kar stops and points, swaying his arms like a traffic cop: "This road goes to Guinea, this one to Bamako, this one to Mauritania, this one to Senegal." The streets are so badly damaged, it's hard to imagine them leading to a bigger world, but Kar means it: every day, trucks with names like *Earth Missile*, *The Green Sahel*, *Who Knows the Future?*, *Desert Storm* and *Fate is Fatal* begin their odysseys here, sighing and puffing. When 'the candle' was still lit, you could see it from miles away.

Shortly after independence, volunteers widened the road to Guinea. After a brief, idyllic federation, Mali and Senegal had fallen out and President Modibo Keita tried to strengthen ties with the socialist regime of Sékou Touré in Guinea. "That was back when all of Mali stood behind Modibo. If he shouted 'Left!', everyone turned left. If he changed his mind and said: 'Okay, now everybody turn right!', they followed without batting an eye." Crews of volunteers worked on the road with true revolutionary zeal, in continuous shifts. Musicians went out every morning with drums and guitars, xylophones and harp-lutes to serenade the workers. Meanwhile – as it turned out later – the mayor of Kayes had his fingers in the municipal till. "But when we'd finished eighty kilometers of road, Mali and Senegal signed a peace agreement and we stopped right there."

Not long afterwards, the Senegalese president Senghor paid a visit of reconciliation to Kayes. By that time the city was so deeply in debt to the power company that all the streetlights had been turned off. "Every citizen living close to a streetlight was requested to hang a lamp in front of his house. You should have seen Kayes, it was swimming in light, it was like a *petit* Paris!" The bare bulbs hanging above the shops in the center of town date from that time.

At the house, the neighbors are again watching television with Mamou. "Hey, my favorite program, 'Jaa Jugu'!" Delighted, Maciré pulls up a few chairs. Every evening, in 'Jaa Jugu' – 'Bad Images' – a popular actor pokes fun at Malian mores. Exuberant wedding parties, dirty streets and alcohol abuse are ridiculed in the form of comic sketches. The filthy pools of water that flow across the screen bear a striking resemblance to the ditch in front of Maciré's house, but no one in the audience seems to notice. Maciré beams, and his children know the dialogue by heart.

For months, 'Jaa Jugu' has been causing a furor. Recently, it ridiculed women who bleach their skin. They were called *tsjatsjo* – piebald women – because the products they use leave spots on the skin. The morning after the show, children all over town began following women around, jeering at them and throwing stones. The police had to calm things down. The sketch was taken off television, and replaced by a veiled woman begging her persecutors to stop what they were doing.

After the news the announcer says that Boubacar Traoré, otherwise known as Kar Kar, will be giving a concert the next evening at the Palais de la Culture in Bamako, along with other musicians.

I look at Kar in amazement. "Do you know anything about this?"

"Not me, and I'm not going either," he says. "They wouldn't even pay for my train ticket." Some of the musicians the announcer mentioned aren't even in Mali, Kar says. The organizers just use their names to draw a crowd, then take off with the box office. "You see what kind of a place Mali is? Do you understand now why it's so hard for an artist to get ahead around here? A few years ago I made a video clip in Lausanne that was shown on television right away in the Ivory Coast and Senegal, but nothing happened in Mali. After a while I realized why: they were expecting me to pay, the way *griots* do when they want to be on television." Kar sniffs in disdain. "I told them: 'Forget it! I've done everything for my country, you people should be paying me!' These days, even disc jockeys wait until you slip them a little money. You can turn the whole place upside down, but you can't earn money making music around here. That's why it's so important for us to make a name in Europe."

The children suddenly go racing out into the street. Kar laughs at my surprised look. "Don't you hear anything?" There's a dull rumbling in the distance, like a herd of animals running by. "That's right. It's the Peul taking their cattle across the river." He listens carefully. "There are a lot of them. It will start raining before long if they keep this up."

A pleasant wind is blowing in the yard, but when I go into my room it seems as if the day's heat has packed itself in there. That night I sleep outside like everyone else.

At breakfast Mamou complains that Maciré sowed sorghum on his father's land last year, and even harvested it, but then waited so long to bring in the sheaves that passing sheep ate it all. Kar listens to her lament in silence.

Maciré looks at me and says waveringly: "I don't have what I need to work the land. It used to rain a lot more, everything grew by itself, but since the drought . . ."

"Excuses, excuses," Kar says, "you're too lazy, that's all."

"Kar is the only one in our family with the gift of farming," Maciré continues, unperturbed. "God has given it to him. You should have seen him when he used to live here – he brought in hundreds of kilos of sorghum and peanuts every year!"

"The earth doesn't lie," Kar says quietly, "if you treat her well, she'll give you what you ask for." He gets up. "Let's go out there and see." He looks around. "Abdoulaye, are you coming with us?"

This time we head away from town. Abdoulaye knows the way, because he often takes Maciré's sheep out to graze. "If Abdoulaye didn't take care of them they would have starved long ago!" Kar never comes to Kayes without stopping by his father's land, he admits, even though it's been neglected since he left.

It's strange to walk around with him this morning. Everyone heard the television announcer say he was giving a concert in Bamako, so they're all amazed to see him here. "Double Kar!" someone shouts to him. "He thinks I can do magic," Kar laughs; "I'm in Bamako at the same time that he sees me walking around here."

People are listening to the radio in front of their homes, and suddenly Kar's music comes wafting towards us. A local disc jockey who was with us on the train is talking about how Kar taught him to play guitar in Nioro. Kar doesn't say a word, but he walks with the supple movements of one who knows he isn't passing unnoticed. He stops now and then to shake hands, and the charming smile he reserves for his fans never leaves his face.

Abdoulaye walks in front, and children his age call out to him as well. "My son is known everywhere he goes," Kar notes contentedly. "That's because he plays soccer. He goes to all the neighborhoods; I was like that too." Kar's mother used to put out bowls of peanuts after every match, because the supporters usually brought Kar home on their shoulders. But once, when he spent three months in bed after an injury and no one came to visit him, she said: "See what a thankless sport it is? You'd better do something else."

She took him to a famous marabout. She wanted to know what was in store for this son who, more so than her other children, seemed destined for great things. She wanted to know how she could protect him from the jealousy that his destiny would surely provoke.

In those days soccer was the only thing on Kar's mind. He couldn't imagine ever giving it up, but the marabout said he would quit, and that it wouldn't be long before he left school. Not because he wasn't intelligent, but because something would happen that would make him famous and have everyone talking about him. "My mother thought I would become a cabinet minister, or even president!"

The marabout also said there would be fighting in the family. "That's impossible," said his mother, who assumed that family feuds were always caused by other marriages. "I'm my husband's only wife!"

Furthermore, the marabout predicted, Kar would go to Europe and even make a name for himself there. "Europe! Where would poor people like us ever get that kind of money?" his mother said in disbelief.

"In the years after that, I tried to get away, but never succeeded." Abdoulaye is walking next to us now, and Kar puts an arm around him protectively. "Maybe that's how it had to be; maybe I had to get married and have children, maybe Pierrette had to die before I got the chance to go away."

He sounds grieved, and I feel a lump in my throat. It's been a long time since he's talked about Pierrette like this. "How were you able to go to France after she died?"

Kar hesitates. There are many things he talks about easily now, but the period surrounding the death of Pierrette is veiled in mist. "Mai Sangaré said I still had my voice, that I should give it a try."

Mai Sangaré – I know that name. *When you go to Santa Maria, give Mai my greetings. Mai Sangaré. Everything in good time.*

"Yes, I sang about him," Kar says quietly. "If it wasn't for him . . ." They became friends back when Kar still lived in Kayes. Later Mai left for Gabon, to work as a teacher, and only came back to Mali on leave. "A few months after Pierrette's death, he was in Bamako. When he saw the shape I was in . . . he was the one who said I should go." Kar had no money and no passport. But all the insurmountable obstacles of his younger years were suddenly solved with the greatest of ease. Within two days he had his papers. Through a friend of Pierrette's brother Mamadou, who was living in France, he got an accommodation certificate and Mai paid for his plane ticket.

"*Papaa!*" Abdoulaye wants to know what kind of bike his father has bought for him. Kar describes it, and tells him it has a bell. "A bell," Abdoulaye says, disappointed, "no one around here has a bell, they're for savages!" When Kar promises that he'll buy him basketball shoes when he gets to Bamako, Abdoulaye is disgruntled again: he and his soccer pals wear only plastic sandals! Kar pulls him towards him, laughing. "He'll have a lot to learn in Bamako!"

It's only nine o'clock, but the sun is relentless. We're close to the station now. Partly hidden behind shrubbery are three buildings where the railway personnel worked in colonial times. They're sturdy houses with thick walls and broad verandahs, built to last another hundred years, Kar says. The people of Kayes call them *cent portes*, because they have so many doors and windows. One of them houses the Hôtel du Rail, where foreigners stay when they stop in Kayes.

Behind them are the villas where the senior railway personnel live. "When the French were still here, those houses were surrounded by trees full of lemons, mandarins and bananas," Kar says. "When you walked around here you felt like it was snowing, that's how fresh it was." I can't help laughing – he can make things so palpable. "*Ah oui*," he muses, "*les blancs aimaient faire la fraîcheur.*"

He came here often with his friends; one of them would act as lookout while the others climbed over the wall to steal fruit. That's how they found out about the white people's cats. Fat, lazy animals, not like the strays in their neighborhoods that could only be caught and put in the pan after an intensive round-up.

"You ate cat?"

"You bet! Our mothers were more than happy to lend us a pan when we'd caught one, because cat meat is good for children: it makes them limber and protects them against evil spirits. Why else would they use so many cats for *gris-gris*? The skin of a black cat is particularly powerful. Too bad old people take those kinds of secrets to their graves, just because they can't find anyone worthy of passing them on to."

The tame cats in the white peoples' gardens caught their fancy, and it wasn't long before one after the other began disappearing. Kar sees me shudder and laughs. "They had so much meat on them that we had no appetite left when evening came around. Oh, they were so tender! Especially the haunches."

"Did your mothers know where those cats came from?"

"No, we didn't tell them that. My mother wouldn't have put up with it; my father worked for a white man."

Kar's story made me queasy at first, but now I'm starting to feel a bit of unholy glee. My white acquaintances' cats in Bamako eat meat their young servants could never afford, and the memory of the Amsterdam animal ambulance racing up to rescue a cat that had almost been asphyxiated by a fire in my neighborhood still makes me uneasy. That Kar and his friends dared to wring the necks of those lethargic symbols of Western wellbeing!

"The cat that belonged to the *gendarmerie* was the fattest of all," Kar says, "but also the hardest to catch. It sat on the commander's windowsill all day, purring. We lurked around for weeks, whistling, hissing, meowing, trying a thousand different tricks, but there was no way to get it to move. Until Mani, the biggest rascal in our group, came up with the idea of asking the

209

butcher for some leftovers. We fried that up into a real tasty meal and used it to lure the cat down off the windowsill. Then we threw a net over it and raced away. While we were running, Mani kept yelling: 'I get the butt!' ' "

"You were a bunch of scoundrels!"

"We certainly were. Sometimes we'd walk past the villa in question the next day and see the lady of the house wandering around with tears in her eyes. As if there'd been a death in the family! Even the commander of the *gendarmerie* was out of sorts for days after his cat disappeared." Sounding chastened, he adds: "When you're young, you don't think about the suffering you cause others. Only God can forgive us for what we did back then."

There's the aerodrome. Not many planes land at Kayes anymore, but the airstrip is still intact. This is where the real Olympic, Lam Toro and Bel Ami raced. "There was this Lebanese man – whenever his horse won, he tossed five-franc notes in the air!" The evening before the race a *griot* would walk through the streets of Kayes with a little tom-tom, to announce which horses would be running. Some of them were legends. Lam Toro drank alcohol and had to be tied to the post before the race to keep him from heading straight for home. Bel Ami was pure white and so popular that everyone cried when he died; he was given a human burial.

"Look at this." Kar has stopped in front of a termite's nest and points the tip of his shoe at a battalion of insects struggling industriously with a piece of wire. "People in Kayes say termites have secret powers. That's why they often leave something behind when they pass a nest, hoping the termites will take it." The termites' storage places are real granaries – his mother told him that people once opened a termite's nest during a famine and found at least a ton of sorghum.

"*Papaa!*" Abdoulaye is tugging at Kar's sleeve again. We've arrived at his family's field, little more than a hectare of land bordered by bushes and trees. Abdoulaye was here with a friend of his not long ago and killed a snake. He picks up a stick and shows us how he did it. Kar laughs proudly: "Abdoulaye is just like me, he's not afraid of anything. Whenever Kalilou or Baaba saw a snake, I had to kill it, and they disappeared for the rest of the day. But I just went on working."

He recently bought three *gris-gris* from a man in Bamako, which he wears around his thighs to keep from getting backache. But they help against snakes as well, he's noticed – he hasn't seen one in his yard in Lafiabougou since.

"But I've been stung by scorpions many times!"

"What did you do? Did you have a black stone with you?"

"A black stone! What would I need that for! After a scorpion stings you, it's completely numbed, you can just pick it up. You tear it open and take something out of its insides that you rub on the wound."

"Take out what?"

"I don't know exactly what you call it. Besides, when you've been stung you don't look that closely, you just tear out the insides." It makes my flesh crawl, but Kar laughs. Shekna, his son who's going to the police academy in Bamako, has often been stung by scorpions; he just tore them open and went on working as if nothing had happened. "If you recite a verse from the Koran while holding a finger on the wound, the pain goes away too."

Kar kicks at a pile of straw lying in the middle of the field. "And this is Maciré's work." He looks around: if his father could see this! "But I always knew I couldn't count on Maciré," he says resignedly.

When his father fell ill in 1975, Kar quit his job as technical agent and moved with Pierrette to Kayes. A few months later his father died. Kar opened a little shop on the marketplace and began working on the land. "It's strange," he says, "as soon as I started farming, no one wanted to know me anymore. All my old friends dropped me." He wrote a song about it in which he calls them *jéjés* and do-nothings. *That's how people are. When I was rich, I had all kinds of friends. But when I put my hand to the plow, they left me, one by one.* "People are ingrates, they look down on farmers, but they have no trouble eating corn and sorghum!"

He stopped playing in orchestras, something he'd done for years, but sometimes people invited him to play at birth celebrations or other special occasions; that way he earned a little extra money. He began singing stories, epic tales he came up with during the evening hours. They were based on local legends that had been passed along by *griots*, in which princes and poor people played a central role. When he visited his brother Baaba in the Ivory Coast, he brought back a radio-cassette player to record them. He sold the tapes in his shop. *Falaye*, *The Three Girls*, *Samba* – the local radio stations played them, and there were fanatical collectors who didn't want to miss a single episode.

Sometimes he closed up shop so he could work on the land with his mother and his children. Pierrette brought them lunch. "And this is where I sat, drinking tea." The tree looks like a weeping willow; its branches hang down almost to the ground. "It's like a little house, isn't it? You're closed in on all sides – you couldn't make a better place if you tried," Kar says contentedly. "But my father always warned me not to fall asleep here, because a *djinn* lived in this tree." One afternoon, when his father dozed off, the *djinn* tapped him on the shoulder and said: "Get up!"

Kar looks at me, sees the smile playing at the corners of my mouth, and says: "Yeah, I didn't believe him at first either, until I fell asleep one afternoon too!" He felt the tapping on his shoulder twice, and heard a voice saying: "Get up!" "It wasn't an evil *djinn*," he adds quickly, "otherwise he would have hit me."

"How do you know it was a male *djinn*, and not a woman?"

"I could tell by his voice!" Kar smiles. "If it had been a woman, I would have married her; who knows what kind of luck she might have brought me!"

The next morning he left a bowl of milk in the tree, in order to catch a glimpse of the *djinn*. But the milk remained untouched, so he finally drank it himself.

He laughs as he tells the tale, but one sign from me and he'll drop the subject. Africans know that white people don't believe in such things, and don't talk about them readily – you don't tell secrets to the uninitiated. I'd like to hear more, but does that mean I have to act gullible?

Kar picks up on my hesitation. "Don't pretend you don't know what a *djinn* is," he says impatiently, "it's like a devil, and you people know what that is, otherwise the word wouldn't exist!"

"Are there *djinn*s in Europe too?"

"Are there ever! You see them walking down the street, in the market, everywhere! They like to move around where people are, so they can tell their fellow *djinn*s everything they've seen."

"But how do you recognize them?"

"Sometimes by their feet, or by their eyes. *Djinn*s have eyes you can only look into once. When they get close, it's like a shock going through you." When he was traveling in the metro with a countryman, they would sometimes nudge each other: there was a *djinn* sitting in their compartment.

"I don't really believe in things like that," he says all of a sudden. "I believe in God. But I know they exist." Everyone in Kayes knows the story of the marabout who rented a room in a house where a *djinn* lived. When his housemates told him about the route the *djinn* followed during its evening rounds, the marabout just laughed at them. That same evening he posted himself right in the middle of the route they'd showed him and began reading verses from the Koran. But while he was reading, he fell asleep. Two hours later Kayes was awakened by a bloodcurdling scream: someone had stepped on the marabout's chest! Kar laughs heartily. If the marabout had succeeded in driving out the *djinn*, everyone would have come to him from that day on. But now he had to pack his things and leave town.

"There are good *djinn*s and evil *djinn*s. Some evil *djinn*s kill children. Usually they're old women, like witches. They form a circle, and can even make a woman eat her own child."

"Eat her child?"

"Not really eat it, of course. But one day the child becomes ill, and gradually all the life flows out of it. Just like a piece of fruit hollowed out until only the rind is left."

I listen and let him talk. Since I first came to Africa ten years ago I've heard stories about people who can turn into crocodiles, monkeys or cockroaches, and who go out at night to scare their fellow villagers. When Kar told me about the *korté* that jealous colleagues must have tossed at his brother Kalilou, I knew what he was talking about. Poison from a distance. Someone once explained to me how a fetishist goes about making sure his victim will be bitten by an adder. He takes a patch from clothing the victim often wears and puts it in a box with the adder. From that moment on he begins to starve it, poke it with pins and hurt it in all kinds of ways, so it starts associating the patch of fabric with pain. Then he sets the creature free near its victim's house.

According to Kar, some fetishists can even kill people in Europe that way. They put a minuscule quantity of poison in an insect and send it to France.

"By plane?"

"No, not by plane, come on. They have their ways. It goes as fast as a fax, there are fetishists who are real good at it. That's how it always goes with Africans: instead of applying their knowledge in the service of something useful, they only use it to destroy."

We're well on our way back to town; the first houses have begun to appear. "I'm dying of thirst, aren't you?" Kar sounds worried – there isn't a roadside stall in sight. "We should have brought water with us," he says.

At the side of the road, three little boys are sitting with a cooler. Maybe they . . . ? Kar walks over to them. I can tell by the excited look in their eyes that they've recognized him. They don't say anything, but grin happily as busy hands unscrew the cooler and fish out three plastic bags. The singer who was on television has come to buy water from them! Kar plays along, giving them material for the story they'll tell their friends later on; they'll be the envy of the neighborhood. He jokes, tests whether the water is cold enough, pulls out his wallet and carefully counts out the change.

Abdoulaye hasn't missed a moment of it. He takes one of the bags from his father, bites off a corner and winks at me.

Mamou is sitting on a stool at what she calls her *bureau* – an iron trough with two holes on which big pans are simmering above a fire. This must be where the hat rack met its end not so long ago. "See the African woman?" she says. "Always in the kitchen, always at work."

Kar, Maciré and I eat from the same enamel bowl and use a fan to shoo away the flies. The children squat around plastic tubs and finish everything, including our leftovers. Little Bintou cries a lot. Everyone teases her, and she can't defend herself because she can barely talk. This morning she put on a party dress with a tight satin bodice and a floral skirt, to take her sister to school. She was completely exhausted when she came home. The children kick her, Mamou says.

Now she's sitting against a tree, naked, and the dress is lying amid a pile of rags on Mamou's bed. Her little brother is the only one who'll play with her. She traps him between two overturned chairs and, lovingly draping a *pagne* over him, says: "We're having a good time, but you're not part of it." She repeats what the children in the street say to her. "If you try to get away, I'll kick you!" When Kar gets too close, she shouts: "Get out of here, or I'll slit your throat!"

The air is leaden with heat. Even Kar complains about it; he can't recall it ever being so hot. After the siesta he walks out into the yard in his boxer shorts and snarls: "And don't ever tell anyone from Kayes that it's hot where he lives, not unless you're itching for a fight!"

Mamou and the neighbors are bent over the Ludo board again. Mamou's bare breasts hang heavily over the *pagne* she's tied around her big belly. The twins are due in about a month. She's asked me to send her baby clothes, just as matter-of-factly as Maciré asked me to represent his musical interests in Europe.

When, for the umpteenth time this afternoon, a flurry of screeches rises up from the corner where the Ludo game is in progress, Kar shakes his head in disbelief. "Too bad you don't speak Bambara. If you did you'd never want to leave, because the things these people say . . ."

215

"Like what?"

"You can't translate it. They curse each other's mothers, fathers and children; they drag all kinds of demons into it – nothing's sacred." He peers over at the players. Some of them are old, others are young, but when you hear them play it's as if they're all the same age – the adults have no authority at all. "I talk to young people and laugh with them too, but I always make sure they know I'm their elder. There's a Bambara proverb that says: 'If you play with the uncircumcised as if they're your equals, one day they'll bring a lizard into your room'."

The television is usually turned on around this time, but today there's no electricity. When darkness falls, Mamou lights a kerosene lantern. Maciré comes home from rehearsal and pulls up a chair despondently: he doesn't like being in the dark.

A tall young man comes out of one of the rooms and greets me in English. "That's our Nigerian tenant," Maciré says. A tenant too! The boy cuts hair at the market. I saw those barber shops during our tour of the city: little wooden booths hung with posters of boxers and black movie stars. I feel sorry for him – coming all the way from Nigeria to end up in these surroundings! But Maciré sees nothing strange about it. The Nigerian is on his way to the Mauritanian coastal town of Nouâdhibou, where he hopes to get to Europe by way of the Canary Islands.

Am I imagining things, or is it noisier in the yard than usual? The children fight; Bintou is sitting next to the tap, crying. Suddenly Mamou jumps up, grabs a piece of wood and gives her oldest daughter a sturdy smack that sends her flapping across the yard. I'm completely astounded by this unexpected outburst, but Kar smiles knowingly. "As soon as the television stops working around here, they beat each other's brains in."

When we make a move to go out, Maciré looks at us in alarm. "Where are you two going?"

Kar shrugs. "For a little walk."

It's pitch black in the street, but Kar says the lights will be on further along. The power station is overloaded – they turn off the electricity in one neighborhood, then the next.

"Shall we see what's on at the Roxy?" I ask. I can hardly imagine there being anything to interest me, but the thought of sitting with Kar in the movie theater where he spent his boyhood evenings suddenly seems quite attractive.

"Sure, if you want to."

They're showing *The Fury* by Brian de Palma. The print is badly damaged: a pale version of Kirk Douglas moves against a background of watery colors, his voice sounding as though it's coming from an indoor swimming pool. I quickly lose track of what's going on, but Kar follows everything. From down below, on the metal benches where the Indians sit, comes the sound of shouting and laughter.

Kirk Douglas' paranormally gifted son makes a woman float weightlessly through the room, the blood dripping from her shoes. Dull red spatters fill the screen. The blue eyes of the luckless boy shoot shimmering rays of light. I think of the *djinn*s Kar saw in the Parisian metro, with eyes you can meet only once. No wonder he loves movies like these!

Before I even realize that the film is coming to an end, the Indians get up. Kar is ready to go too: the bad guy's been shot, so the movie's over. By the time the closing score is playing we're outside, where a strong wind has come up. A few moments later fat raindrops begin to fall, and we race for cover under an awning. "What did I tell you? The Peul have crossed the river and now it's going to rain." Kar waves his arms like a bandleader. "It has to rain hard, that's the only way it will cool off. If the air isn't completely cleared, it will only get hotter." But the downpour stops as suddenly as it came. We walk on through streets steaming with heat.

It's eleven o'clock. If the electricity's been turned on again, Mamou and the neighbors will be watching a dubbed American series or some horrific video. This afternoon Mamou asked me if I'd seen the video of the final hours of Liberian president Samuel Doe. They must be grisly images; Doe was tortured to death by rebels in 1990. While he wept and pleaded, Prince Johnson's guerrilla fighters cut off his ears. That's right, Mamou laughed, she'd seen that part – if I wanted, she could get the tape for me right away.

We pass a *pâtisserie* we hadn't noticed before. "That's new," Kar says. Big fans are turning on the ceiling inside, and there's a patio on the street where people are sitting behind a screen of shrubbery. Kar catches my inquisitive glance. "Do you want to take a look?" He's already crossed the street.

It's scorching hot under the fans, so we end up on the patio. The way Kar pours the beer into our glasses and puts the cap back on the bottle brings our visit to the New Galaxy to mind. But we're in his home town now, and through the open kitchen window I can hear a familiar melody. Leaning back in my chair, I see a man cleaning an oven with a knife in the semi-darkness. He never takes his eyes off his work, just hums softly to himself – he must have seen us come in.

"*Falaye*," I say, "isn't he humming your song *Falaye*?" Abdoulaye was listening to it while he lay on the bed this afternoon. It's the story of a poor young man who leaves his family to seek his fortune and, after countless adventures, returns as a king to his native village.

"That's right, that's *Falaye*." It's such a pleasant, subtle greeting – this place immediately feels blessed.

Earlier in the evening we walked past the Kayes maternity clinic. "That's where Pierrette had Shekna," Kar nodded. The clinic was new then, the square holes in the walls were still filled with air conditioners. I didn't dare ask any further, but now that we're sitting here and he's looking at me almost invitingly – the way he's done before in the last few days when I haven't asked a question for a while – I suddenly take courage.

"No," he says, "Pierrette didn't die here, that was in Bandiagara." Bandiagara is where Amadou Hampâté Bâ was born, the former capital of the Toucouleur kingdom of Macina, gateway to the Dogon – a name that evokes only pleasant associations. "Her brother lived there – she'd taken the children to visit him. She had the baby there."

"And you, where were you?"

"I was in Kayes, I was running my shop, working on the land." Almost forty days after Zévilé was born, they called to say Pierrette was seriously ill. He was more than a thousand kilometers away from her. "When I arrived in Bandiagara, the women were already sitting on the doorstep, crying." Kar stares past me down the quiet street. "I've started to tell you the story of Pierrette," he observes.

"That's right," I say.

He takes a look around him. The customers at the table next to us are getting up; the cook has gone home and the boy who served us is sitting in a chair on the street, waiting to close up. "If I told you all of it, we'd be here for hours."

I nod. Suddenly a deep fatigue has come over me. Is it the beer? Our morning walk out to his father's land, the commotion in the stifling yard, that unreal film of Brian de Palma's – I feel like we've been through an endless day.

"I think it's time to go," Kar says.

There are no stars tonight. I walk next to him carefully, surprised at myself. I've been waiting so long for him to tell me his story – but now that he's about to, it's almost as if I don't want to hear it.

But was he really about to tell me? He keeps putting it off. It's become a game between us. Once I know his story I'll be ready to leave, and both of us are trying to postpone that moment. He won't just give it away, I can tell. I'll have to earn it, even though I don't quite know how.

"One day I'll tell you what happened," Kar says, "but not yet. It will make you cry, and everyone who hears it will cry too." When did he first say that? In the almost literal repetition lies a promise that reassures me.

That night it starts to rain. We all rustle our things together in a panic and run inside. Standing in the doorway, Kar and I look at the water pouring out of the sky. Pans roll across the yard, the branches on the trees whip ominously back and forth, but in the rooms behind us the air is more oppressive than ever. "This kind of wind blows trucks and cars down the street, but stops at your front door," Kar says crossly. Just when I've finally fallen asleep, the roof over the sheepfold next to my window collapses with a crash.

In the morning we survey the damage. The house leaks like a sieve; there are puddles of water everywhere and streams of mud running down the walls – our clothes hanging from the nails are brown and completely soaked. But the sun is shining again and outside everyone is gaping at the remains of the sheepfold.

I'd promised Mamou I would fix breakfast. Above a charcoal burner I do my best to fry an omelet with onions and tomatoes. Abdoulaye hands me whatever I need and watches my every move. He'll make one himself next time, he says. While we're cooking, it starts raining again. Mamou yanks the clothes down off the line and we race under the verandah, where we struggle to find a dry spot. The children come running in with tubs to catch the drips. The only one who seems totally unconcerned is Maciré. He's pulled up a chair and is holding a transistor radio to his ear as he watches me prepare what he calls his 'vitamin breakfast' – a foretaste of what he'll be eating when he gets to Europe. "White people – they know how to cook!"

I feel the rain dripping down my neck and shift my chair around uneasily. "Before you leave for Europe, maybe you should do something about your house," I say.

Maciré throws his arms open wide. "Oh, you'll see, within a few years this will all be taken care of."

"Within a few years!" Kar snorts. "If it goes on like this, tomorrow we'll be floating on our mattresses through the streets of Kayes!"

Kar and I go down to take a look at the bridge, which is lying deep in the water. Car owners and taxi drivers are lined up at the beginning of the vanishing pavement, waiting to wash their cars. The boat that belonged to the French captain Gallieni sunk near here. Children used to bring up spoons, plates and other valuables from the hold, and ironmongers sawed off whatever parts they could use. Later, the wreck could be seen just below water level when the river was down, but now it's disappeared completely under the sand. A similar fate awaits the ferry boat rusting away at the quay.

Kar stares out over the water. "The greatest day of the year used to be the fourteenth of July," he says. "The French celebrated their national holiday by setting up grandstands all along the river. There were people hanging behind motorboats, racing across the water on a little thingamajig." He shows me how it went: arms stretched out in front, leaning back slightly from the waist. "You mean they were waterskiing?" He shrugs. "I don't know what you people call it, but the French were wild about it. Whenever someone fell off, everyone in the stands cheered."

Ducks were let loose in the middle of the river and children swam out to them, yelling – whoever caught one got to take it home. At the dusty crossroads where the extinguished candle now stands, the French hammered poles into the ground. They smeared them with grease and hung presents on a wheel at the top: a bicycle, a doll, a duck, a piece of clothing. Anyone who could reach the top could take what they wanted. The children rubbed themselves with glue at home, so they wouldn't slide back down. "It took a long time before the French figured that one out!"

The warehouses along the quay, where boats like the *Cap Lopez* unloaded their cargo, are deserted now. A rusty iron structure at the slaughterhouse is rattling in the wind. Kar looks at it dejectedly. It was here that they used to tan hides, which were then shipped to Europe. "The white people built up all of this," he says, "and then the blacks ruined it."

The Lebanese shops around the market square were famous. Some of the shopkeepers spoke Bambara better than the people of Kayes themselves. There was a *charcuterie* where they sold slices of meat as thin as paper. One place was popularly referred to as the *Boutique du divorce*, because it had so many nice things men couldn't buy for their wives. "The shop smelled of expensive perfume, and they had beautiful mousseline fabric and sheer stockings. When you walked around in there, you thought you were in heaven!"

The French were expelled by Modibo Keita, but the Lebanese left of their own accord; socialism was bad for business. Russians came in their stead. Everyone in Kayes was astonished: they bought up all the bread at the bakery, as if there wouldn't be any left the next day. They'd buy ten kilos of peanut butter at a time. "The next shipload was a bit more civilized – they'd heard that you don't have to stand in line here to buy food."

They were different from the French. They didn't smarten up their surroundings, never fixed their houses, didn't plant gardens. They didn't even have planters on their balconies like the French, who you always saw puttering around with watering cans. "We felt they hadn't come to stay," Kar says. "And they didn't help us get ahead; the Russians weren't modern, they only sent us old junk."

We spend the next few days wandering endlessly through the streets of Kayes. Kar takes me to a new neighborhood every day. Liberté, Plateau, Khasso – he knows every corner of his home town. In Plateau they used to hold the famous Tour du Plateau cycling race each Sunday; now the asphalt is full of holes. In Khasso there was a beach where the French swam and played *jeu de boules*. You could always earn a little money there: toting coolers, shining shoes – whenever a Frenchman shouted "*Hey, petit!*" they all ran over to him. By the end of the day you'd have a hundred francs in your pocket.

He shows me the house Mai Sangaré built. "Mai isn't stupid like Baaba," he says. "He knows he won't spend the rest of his life in Gabon; he knows that someday they'll throw all the foreigners out of the country, like they always do. Baaba thought his life was somewhere else. Well, he found out when he had to leave the Ivory Coast. He had everything, but now he has nothing, because a man without a house is poor."

Like Bamako, Kayes has a new district called Lafiabougou where buildings are going up rapidly. The courthouse was paid for by the Saudis. The Malians promised them that Islamic law would be practiced, but as soon as they had the money they announced they wouldn't be cutting off any hands. "Moussa Traoré was still in power then. The people of Kayes said: 'Okay, if heads are going to roll, let the first one be Moussa's!' " The building has every convenience, but there's no electricity in this part of town, so the judges and lawyers sit sweating in their little concrete cubicles. The courtroom isn't finished yet, even though the Saudis have already paid more than they ever intended. Kar says the money has been cleverly *detoured.*

Although Kar's memories make me aware of the old colonial aspects of his home town, modern-day Kayes interests me more all the time. It's a bustling city, and when I close my eyes at night all the Sidis, Dras and Diallos in their dusty workshops go filing by. Many of the merchants used to work on the land; they only opened up shop in the seventies, when the big drought came.

Kar walks slowly, and he's always willing to stop when spoken to, even when he's in the middle of a story or when we're almost too late to buy our tickets for the trip home. Some people think I'm Pierrette, others that I'm a new wife he's brought back from Europe. There's a story going around that we're not staying at Maciré's, but at the Hôtel du Rail. One day, when someone shakes my hand and asks if I am *madame*, I hear Kar say I'm a writer from Holland who's doing a book about him.

At first he was reluctant to talk about his lyrics, but now we go looking for someone to translate them. We make an appointment with a young man who writes in both Bambara and French, and buy a notebook for him to work in. When he fails to show up, Kar sputters: "You can't count on Africans. Maybe someone told him he should have asked for money. Maybe he thinks you're going to run off with his work and make a fortune with it back in Europe."

He'd never pursue the matter himself, he knows what people in Kayes are like. But just to show me he's right, we go looking for the boy at his house. He gives some vague excuse about a celebration that suddenly came up. When Kar says he could have at least let us know, the young man flies into a rage: just because Kar is a star, it doesn't mean he can come and scold him in his own house!

"What did I tell you?" Kar laughs triumphantly when we're outside. "Some people don't want to get ahead."

"Why not?"

"Because they don't want to be happy. Some people in Kayes – if you took them to paradise, they'd shout: 'Let me out of here!' They'd rather go to hell!"

When we tell the story to Maciré, he says: "Be glad he never got started. He's the kind who'd claim he wrote all Kar's songs himself, and composed them too!"

After the siesta we sit out in front of the house in lawn chairs. A passing taxi driver sounds the first few notes of *Mali Twist* in recognition. A Malian comedian recently did a parody of Kar's old hit in which he summed up the shortcomings of independence and called on all Malians to leave the country.

The neighbor's boy is poking around with a shovel in the ditch in front of the house – a sour smell reaches us. When he comes closer with his shovel and Kar says something about it, the child shrugs indifferently. Kar jumps up, and before I know what's happening, he's slapped him. I look at him in surprise. "You just hit the neighbor's boy!"

"So what? Did you see what he did? In Bambara we say that someone who doesn't respect his elders insults his own father."

The boy is staring at us from his front door, surrounded by a circle of women. I suffer their angry looks, feeling guilty, but Kar looks straight ahead. "Young people have no more respect for their elders," he says. "Someday they'll pay for it, because a lot of the secrets older people used to pass along are being lost."

Not long ago, a girl climbed aboard a *douroudourouni* in Bamako. She was all dressed up to go out, and turned up her nose at the old man sitting next to her: he stank, she said. Barely had the words crossed her lips when she began shitting her pants. "The passengers almost fainted from the stench, and they begged the old man to call off the curse he'd put on the girl."

"Where did you hear that story?"

"Everyone in Bamako was talking about it!"

"I wouldn't believe something like that unless I saw it myself."

"Yeah, that's probably what the girl in the *douroudourouni* would say, but that didn't keep her from shitting all over the floor!"

Kar tosses an angry glance at the boy. "Once his father would have handed me a stick to beat him with, but these days . . . before you know it they'll drag you down to the police station for slapping a child!"

The evening before we return to Bamako, Kar takes me to the aerodrome, where the people of Kayes always go 'to take the wind'. He's in a lighthearted mood. Walking along the airstrip, he points to the hangar, 'the plane's house', as he calls it. When he starts telling me how neat and clean everything was when the French were around, I imitate Maciré's complaining voice: "Ah no, the whites, they worked!"

Kar laughs. "Do that again!"

I run through Maciré's entire repertoire, from his complaints about the rice he can't digest, because his sensitive stomach can only handle Western food, to his comments about his impending departure for Europe. Kar thinks my imitation is perfect; I have to repeat it again and again until tears of laughter roll down his cheeks.

We drink beer at an open-air café. In the days of Santa Maria, he sometimes performed here for dancing couples who later lay in the grass in the wide surroundings. It's a balmy evening, and

225

the sky turns pink as he eavesdrops for me on the conversation at the next table, where a man has settled down with two pretty women. I look at Kar and realize that the unbending, suspicious man I first met is almost beyond recall – I've seen so many different sides to him since then.

When dusk comes and I remark that it's time for prayer, Kar laughs unconcernedly: "Don't worry. God knows that I love him."

☇☇☇

I've come to know Maciré and Mamou's yard as a world without ritual, but on the evening of our departure everyone suddenly springs into action. A whole crowd accompanies us to the station. Mamou is wearing a bright red dress and a wig, and she's grilled a chicken for us which she carries at arm's length in a plastic bowl. Even the neighbor has come along. The children all carry a piece of our luggage and Kar walks in front like a pasha, empty-handed. At the last moment, Maciré comes running onto the platform. I take a picture of the whole troupe beneath the station clock, prompting him to say: "This is it, I'm off to Europe!"

Kar has spotted a white person in our sleeping car. "Did you see that lily-liver?" he whispers. He barely greets him, and watches tersely as I start a conversation; the suspicious man I first met makes a brief reappearance. But later he invites the boy to eat with us, and urges him to take more food.

We pass the cement factory at Diamou, built by the Russians right after independence. Back then the whole complex was brightly lit at night, but during Moussa Traoré's regime the bosses absconded with the profits. Now it's become a *wouya-wouya* factory where only four dim lamps are burning. "No," Kar says, "when you think about what the Malians have made of their country, you go crazy."

Less than an hour after we pull out of the station, the lights in the train go out and we stop dead on the tracks. Kar stares glumly out the window. "No, Mali, it's not worth it. A lot more *patrons*

will have to bite the dust before anything comes of this place."
We're traveling on the 'weekend train', which leaves Bamako on
Friday night and returns on Monday morning at five. "Weekend
train!" Kar blusters. "If we're lucky, we'll get there by tomorrow
afternoon!"

I sleep fitfully. While the train roars through the night, my
thoughts are haunted by stories about derailments. The wheels
beneath me seem constantly in search of the tracks.

In the morning I find Kar standing at the window in the gang-
way, deep in thought.

"What are you thinking about?"

"About my sheep that's been standing out in the rain. And
about my mangoes – they must be ripe by now."

At Kati, about forty kilometers outside Bamako, the train
makes a long stop while the brakes are checked. Bamako is in a
valley and if the train races on like it did last night, Kar says, we'll
end up in the mayor's office.

He sticks his head out the window as soon as we're rolling
again. "You feel how cool it is here?" When I nod enthusiastically, he glares at me. "But don't you dare . . . !"

〰〰

A surprise awaits me in Bamako: in just a few days, Kar is sched-
uled to play at the Festival des Musiques Métisses in the French
town of Angoulême. He'll be gone for a week, maybe longer.
He's known about it for a while, it turns out. When I comment on
him being so secretive, he says: "Just wait, I'm not gone yet, anything can happen between now and then." After his trips through
England, Switzerland, Canada and the United States, his manager
planned a sixty-concert tour that never panned out. Since then he
only believes things when he sees them with his own eyes.

The first setback has already presented itself. When he went to
pick up his new passport, a civil servant told him he needed a performer's pass. "Performer's pass? Don't you know who I am?"
Kar asked. The official shrugged. He didn't care who he was;

anyone going to France to play music had to have a performer's pass.

At the Ministry of Culture they told him he'd have to wait until next year, because there were no more passes. "Probably all sold to people who knew they stood a better chance of getting into France if they said they were performers," Kar says bitterly. He went back to the passport office and walked straight into the colonel's office. The officer recognized him, and summoned the obstinate official to his office. "This man," he said, pointing to Kar, "served his country before you were even born." The colonel promised him that everything would be arranged by the following day.

That afternoon I hear Kar hammering away in his room. As he tries to split some solid object – a root? – down the middle, he misses and comes out of the room with blood gushing from his thumb. Later I see that he's put half the root in a plastic bag in his suitcase. Now that his mother's no longer around, he has to watch out for himself.

The evening before his departure, we eat dinner with Tanti at a table Kar bought that same day. Fifteen hundred francs – three dollars – is all he paid for it.

"This afternoon Tanti asked me if we were going to get married," Kar says.

"What did you say?"

"That my time hasn't come yet." He's lived alone for more than six years. That's an unusually long time – everyone's amazed by it. But something has kept him from finding a woman to take care of his children. "I've asked my brother Baaba to keep an eye out for me."

"Do you only want a woman to take care of your children?"

"If she loves my children, I'll love her too." In the meantime, though, he's thinking about finding a housekeeper, so his children can move back in with him.

Tanti clears the table. She takes the pan I was planning to scrub and conscientiously scours it clean with sand. Kar has already packed his bags, and there's a pail of warm water on the fire for his shower. Now all he has to do is feed his sheep. I can hardly imagine him flying from this languid world to Europe, and I'm slightly worried on his behalf: are his papers in order, is he sure a car will be waiting to pick him up?

A plane rises into the air in the distance. Kar gazes after it. "Pretty soon they'll pull down the movie screen and roll out the little carts for the aperitif."

"And tomorrow you'll be there."

He smiles. "Seeing is believing."

The day after he returns I find him sitting in his yard, surrounded by family and friends who've come to hear about his trip. I'd secretly expected him to be all aglow from his stay in France, and was even afraid I'd find him a more conceited man, but I notice nothing different about him. He's sitting in his lawn chair in his everyday clothes – short-sleeved shirt, light blue trousers – and he's already commenting on everything. Have I noticed that all the taxis had been painted yellow while he was away, and all the *douroudourounis* green? The government did that. "The next government will probably say: now all taxis have to be red!"

That morning he'd bought a white rooster. It looked so big at the market, but when he got home he discovered it was a lot smaller than his chickens. They walk all over it, and Kar watches ruefully. "If you heard what I paid for that bird, it would bring tears to your eyes."

When his brother Baaba's son gets up to leave, Kar slips into his room and comes back with two shirts that he brought back from France. He gives me a shawl with RFI, Radio France Internationale, printed on it, a copy of the French magazine *Revue Noire* and his new CD. "Don't tell anyone I gave you this," he says, "it just came out – I could only get my hands on two of them." The CD is called *Les Enfants de Pierrette*, named for the song in which he sings about his children's sorrow at their mother's death. It was recorded at a studio in Bamako, and several

Malian musicians, including Ali Farka Touré, played on it. "When Farka heard the title song, he shook his head. 'How can you sing about sad things like that?' he asked. I said: 'Why not? It all happened.' "

He performed twice in Angoulême. The promoters were so enthusiastic that they're planning to invite him back next year. After every show he was overwhelmed with flowers – his hotel room was full of them. "White people!" he says. "Flowers! What a waste of money! I didn't know what to do with them, I couldn't even take them with me. Couldn't they have come up with something better? Something I could give my children?"

He took a lot of pictures, but on the flight back he started talking to a French missionary who lives in the Dogon and was distracted when he left the plane. At home he discovered that he'd lost his camera. It had been in his coat pocket, along with a full roll of film.

"Who says it's gone? If you left it in the plane, they'll keep it for you."

"No, forget it, all that fuss. What's gone is gone. No use chasing after it." His fatalism amazes me. One call to the airline and he'd find out what happened to it. But he seems so determined, I don't insist.

Around noon everyone goes their own way, and we remain alone in the yard. I flip through *Revue Noire* to see what they say about him.

"I give you my only extra copy and you're not even pleased with it," Kar says.

I look up in surprise. "Of course I'm pleased with it."

"No, you act like it's only normal that I give it to you, while there are so many other candidates!" He sits back in his chair, staring past me at the chickens trying to corner the pint-sized rooster. I want to make a retort, but keep myself in check – he acts contrary so often, it usually blows over. I look at the CD and see that the lyrics haven't been translated. "We could work on that together in the next few days," I suggest.

Kar shrugs.

"Couldn't we?"

"You and your lyrics – what's it to you?!"

"But . . . we started doing that in Kayes, why shouldn't we finish it?"

Again he shrugs. "We'll see."

"I went to the radio station," I say after a while.

"Oh yeah?"

"They made me a copy of your earliest hits."

"You should have let me arrange that! Why didn't you wait till I was back?"

"I didn't want to bother you, I thought it was better for me to . . ."

"I bet they asked you for money."

"That's right, a little, for the tape, but that seemed reasonable . . ."

"Reasonable, reasonable! Thieves is what they are. I warned you, but you never listen, you always have to . . ." Suddenly he falls silent. "Forget it."

I sit across from him, crushed. He's been away for only ten days, but the trust built up so painstakingly in the weeks before his departure is gone completely. "Why didn't you call Baaba's shop to find out if I was back?" he says. "Why did you wait until other people told you?"

"Baaba's shop?" I'd called there once, in the very beginning. The man who picked up the phone only spoke Bambara. I heard voices, laughter, in the background. Baaba wasn't there, neither was Kar. "I didn't want to disturb him," I say hesitantly.

"You wouldn't have disturbed him. What could be more normal than calling my brother to ask if I'm back? But you have to play the little shrewd one, you have to find out the sneaky way. I don't like that."

I'm too hurt to reply. I was pleased to see him, anxious to hear his stories about France, but now . . .

"I won't be around for the next few days," he says abruptly.

"Are you leaving again?"

"Yeah, I have to go somewhere. Not for long, just a couple of days."

I know I shouldn't pry, but I can't help it. "Where are you going?"

He waves his hand vaguely. "To visit someone. Close to Ségou."

Neither of us says a word for a long time. "Everyone has a right to his own business," I say finally, but my heart has sunk to the soles of my feet. "When do you leave?"

"I don't know. As soon as possible. Maybe tonight."

After we've eaten, we walk through the center of Bamako in the glowing heat of the sun, in search of a friend of Baaba's who operates a bus Kar may be able to take. I should leave, but I can't bring myself to do it. Disappointed and full of dark premonitions, I walk along beside him. Why is he in such a hurry to leave, why won't he tell me where he's going? Did he borrow money from somebody he has to pay back, or is he going to see a marabout? But when Kar runs into an acquaintance, I notice he's assumed his jovial pose again. He stops at a shop and asks about the price of a bike for Tanti. The salesman looks at him questioningly and asks: "Is that you, Kar Kar?" Laughing, he says: "No, it's a picture of Kar Kar!"

After a long search we finally run into Baaba's friend. The bus is leaving this evening at seven. I hear Kar reserve a seat. Then we stand facing each other without a word. The hubbub around us reminds me of our departure for Kayes, and sadness wells up in me. If I let him go now, it occurs to me, I'll lose him.

"See you in a few days?" Kar puts out his hand. "I have to go back to the house to get my things," he says impatiently.

"Why don't you take me with you?"

He looks at me in surprise. "This isn't the train to Kayes! This is a *wouya-wouya* bus, and traveling at night takes twice as long as during the day. Besides – I know when I'm leaving, but not when I'm coming back; I might get stuck somewhere if the rains come."

"What do I care? In Zaïre it sometimes took me two days to

cover a hundred kilometers!" I see him hesitate. "Maybe you don't want me to go along."

"No, no, it's not that. It's just that a white person isn't used to traveling like this, you don't know what you'd be getting into."

I know all too well. White people don't drive into the Malian interior after dark: the roads are full of suicide jockeys who keep themselves going with speed and other drugs. But if Kar isn't afraid, why should I be?

He looks at me skeptically. "Are you sure you want to come?"

I nod. "I don't have to go all the way. You can leave me somewhere when you need to arrange your business."

"Can you be at the bus station at a quarter to seven?" I breathe a deep sigh of relief. "But it won't be an easy trip, so don't say I didn't warn you!"

✵✵✵

He's sitting on a wooden bench at the bus station, a black RFI backpack on his lap. "White people aren't so dumb," he says. "This backpack looks small, but you can fit everything into it!" There's even room for the two fans he just bought, he notes contentedly.

The bus has arrived: a rickety junk-heap that was once yellow but bears the scars of years of bad maintenance. The driver is nowhere to be found. While other buses roar up onto the square, the passengers wait passively beside their baggage amid clouds of exhaust. After fifteen minutes I already feel completely filthy. Kar, who took the TGV from Angoulême to Paris only a few days ago, sighs: "Africa is backward. After thirty-five years of independence we could be grown-up, but we're still little children."

A *douroudourouni* with a screaming ambulance siren races past. "A siren!" Kar sputters. "You'd never have thought of doing that in the days before democracy. They'd have thrown you in prison! But these days everyone thinks they can do whatever they like."

The bus from Mopti pulls in, causing a wave of commotion;

cholera broke out there last week and new cases are being reported every day. When a passenger steps down from the bus carrying a four-liter bottle of water, someone shouts in horror: "Is that from Mopti? You'll get cholera straightaway!" The man glares at the heckler. "We've been on the road for three days, if there was any cholera in here it's gone by now! Watch this!" Amid laughter from his fellow-passengers, the man raises the jug to his lips, then passes it around demonstratively.

A shoe-shine boy has been hanging around us for a while. Kar shakes him off irritatedly. "What do I need with a shoe-shine? They'd just get dusty again right away in this damned country." The man next to him glances affrontedly at Kar. Cursing your country is something you don't do here, especially not when there's a white person around. Then the man does a double-take. "Kar Kar?" He's from Nioro – it turns out they know each other.

"Did you see how shocked he was?" Kar laughs when the man's gone. "But when he saw who I was, he shut up real quick – he knows what I've done for my country. I'd say the same thing to the president; I was someone back when he was still playing in the street."

I sit beside him and keep quiet. His ornery behavior this afternoon still gnaws at me, but the excitement of the trip has gained the upper hand. I'll have to swallow a lot more dust before he hears me complain.

As soon as the doors of the bus open, the crowd shoves its way in. It's a Chinese bus, clearly made for people smaller than we are, but the passengers are packed in anyway. Kar and I end up sharing a single broken folding chair in the aisle. Some of the passengers start complaining that they paid for a whole seat, not half of one. But everyone wants to leave tonight, so after a bitter struggle we all snuggle up together fraternally.

Kar knows the driver and his assistants and gives them a loud dressing-down. The steering wheel of the bus is so hard to turn that the driver can barely maneuver through the busy traffic. "Couldn't you have taken a look at that before we left? Not one of you is interested in taking care of this bus. All you people think about is making as much money as you can!" It's good to see him making such a fuss: this is the Kar I know. "Now I understand why Baaba's friend had three buses, then two, and now only one," he says. "This one will break down too before you know it, and what will he do then?"

We stop for fuel on the other side of the Niger and five more passengers wriggle their way in. They crawl over us, heading for the full rows of seats behind us. Kar leaves the bus for a moment, and acts disgruntled when he comes back: why was I talking to the passenger on my left, do I know him or something? I shouldn't talk to people he hasn't introduced me to – this whole bus is full of riffraff. They all go to the weekly market in Niono to arrange their affairs, then come back that evening on the same bus.

The driver is a scrawny young man who looks especially puny behind the big, stiff wheel. Out of the darkness come the headlights of heavy trucks, tearing by so fast that we're forced off the road again and again. The six co-drivers – all of whom have surrendered their seats to passengers – are standing around him like supporters at a soccer match, and breathe sighs of relief whenever he succeeds in avoiding another truck. I begin to realize what the whites in Bamako were talking about, and wonder whether those of us in the aisle up front have any chance of surviving if we're hit by one of those juggernauts. Our driver's predicament hasn't escaped Kar either. "He was dead before he even started this trip!"

Around two o'clock we stop at a village that moves to the rhythm of nocturnal traffic. Women are sitting behind huge pans of meat and rice, and the subdued light of oil lamps illuminates display cases of peanuts, cigarettes and sticky sweets. Nescafé with sweetened milk is served at long wooden tables. A truck driver who's just stopped asks for a *café noir*. "Take a good look at this," Kar says. The man behind the table tosses two tablespoons of Nescafé into a little hot water and adds a spoonful of sugar. The driver knocks it back at a single go. Kar watches him from the corner of his eye. "Another twenty-five franc pill and he'll be vibrating all night." I see that the men at the coffee stand are indeed buzzing around quite speedily. Kar says the pills come from Nigeria – you can buy them in all shapes and sizes.

Even the *talibés* – children from the Koran school sent out by their marabout to beg – work here at night. Empty tomato cans hung around their necks, they walk past the squatting diners, reciting verses from the Koran in high, piercing voices. Some of our fellow passengers are napping in the sand along the road and they get up groaning when the bus signals that it's about to leave. As soon as they're inside they fall asleep again, and I doze off as well, despite the chattering of the co-drivers echoing in my head.

We pass Ségou and arrive at a little past five in Markala, where Kar asks the driver to stop. The marketplace is still shrouded in darkness, and Kar walks out in front of me to a gas station where a neon light is burning. "We'll have to wait a bit, until it gets light," he says. "Then we'll find a car going our way."

He pulls a sheet out of his pack and spreads it on the concrete slab next to the building. Just when we've collapsed in exhaustion next to our baggage, a watchman comes over to say we can't sleep here. Kar meekly refolds his sheet. "He probably thought we were tramps!" he sniggers once we've found a bench on the market square across the street. "He may not even have a chair of his own to sit on at home, and I could probably buy his father's house, but to him we're tramps. That's the stranger's lot: no one cares about you." He's bent over, his backpack on his lap. "One of the songs on my new CD is about that. *Maybe you own villas, maybe you were born with a silver spoon in your mouth, but no one cares where the stranger's from.*"

"When did you write that?"

He shrugs his shoulders in annoyance. "What does it matter?" But a little later he tells me anyway. It must have been in the early nineties, when he was living in Paris. That was the first time it became clear to him. "But, as you can see, you don't have to travel that far, it can happen to you in Markala as well! Even though there's a Bambara proverb that says: 'Strangers and pregnant women deserve to be honored'. You don't know who a stranger is in his own country – maybe he's a prince – and the woman may be carrying a king's child."

The market slowly comes to life. A boy who was sleeping on the ground opens his stand and puts water on to boil for coffee. A woman is fanning a charcoal fire. Soon the aroma of *beignets* wafts our way.

"In Angoulême we ate in a big cafeteria," Kar says. "All the musicians sat together – when we had finished we made music with our knives and forks." The first time he came on stage, the announcer introduced him as 'the John Lee Hooker of Mali', so that's what everyone called him from then on. One afternoon he saw a man sitting a few tables down who he'd spent time with when he was in America. Kar walked over to him excitedly. The man was talking to someone else; he saw Kar, nodded briefly and went on talking. As soon as he was finished, Kar went back to him. "Don't you remember me?"

"Sure I do," the man said. "You're Boubacar Traoré." And that was it. The man had been wild about his music; he'd promised to do all he could to bring him back to America, but once Kar was back in Bamako he never heard from him again. What about the letters he'd written? Kar asked. The man claimed he'd never received them. When someone else came and stood at the table, the American turned to him and Kar walked away, offended.

I can picture it easily. The American impresario, in search of new talent, being approached by a Malian singer he'd brought to the States years ago. A man like that operates at a pace Kar can't possibly imagine. "A typical American impresario," I reassure him; "one day he's enthusiastic about one thing, the next day it's something else."

"No, you don't get it. It was as though he barely recognized me. But in America we were the best of friends!"

"That's how it goes in that world, I'm afraid."

"So you think it's normal – you wouldn't be shocked if something like that happened to you!" He stares at me, puzzled. I've made a mistake, I realize, but I don't really know how I could have avoided it without being hypocritical. I can imagine how he

237

felt, the proud man from Kayes getting up from his table twice to say hello to a man who barely recognizes him. But I can imagine the American's reaction just as easily.

"Let's stop talking about it," Kar says, "I get angry just thinking about it. You're the first person I've told, but I should have kept my mouth shut. You don't understand anyway." He sits beside me, closed and sullen: a man alone with his thoughts. Yesterday's uneasiness has settled between us again, and I blame myself for not letting him have his say. If I'd acted just as shocked as he was, I sense, he would have told me more. But what, exactly?

We drink coffee, eat *beignets* and let the morning rush roll past us. Our sleepless night in the dilapidated bus has left us both exhausted, and despite our bickering Kar is as attentive as can be. He keeps asking if I'm not too tired, and goes looking for water so I can at least wash my face.

While we're waiting for a car at the taxi stand, a pick-up truck drives by with three enormous black cows in the back. "He's on his way to Bamako. Must be a rich businessman who's going to make a sacrifice," Kar says with an appraising look. Black cows are the best offerings.

A little later we climb into a *bâchée* – a pick-up with wooden benches under a cloth canopy. I hear Kar mention the name Sansanding, a village on the Niger I know from the stories of Hampâté Bâ. At the beginning of this century, it was the scene of the reign of terror of Mademba Sy, a postman who was crowned king by the French and went down in history under the nickname 'Pharaoh of the Niger'.

We travel on amid passengers with chickens, sheep and bags of rice. The driver stops to buy mangoes, then makes a huge detour to pick up another passenger. "I think he's going by way of Mauritania," Kar notes dryly. "Whatever he's up to, he's in no hurry. If he gets there within two days he'll be pleased. After all, the road is his home."

He starts talking to a farmer who's going out to work his land. "He's telling me about a village chief around here," he says after a while, laughing. "A long time ago, a marabout told him he had to leave his village every morning and every evening: he's not allowed to see the sun come up or go down there. If he sleeps in even once, he'll die that same year. Imagine, what a life! Especially in the rainy season, when he has to go out the door no matter what!"

❖❖❖

The sun is beating down on us by the time we get out of the *bâchée*. Pulling on our packs, we start down the deserted sand path towards the village, a long way from the main road. Kar glances at me out of the corner of his eye. "Still holding up?" I nod. "We look like tourists," he laughs. As it turns out, he has no idea where the person we're going to see lives.

"So you've never met him before?"

"Oh sure, but this is the first time I've ever visited him here." He doesn't even know if the man's in Sansanding. "We'll find out soon enough!"

At the village entrance he asks for directions to the *medersa* – the Koran school. A young man walks along with us. It's a big village, with several mosques towering above the clay houses. Our guide avoids the center, I notice, leading us along the edges of Sansanding as though trying to shield us from prying eyes. Kar still hasn't said anything about our destination, but I take it we're on our way to a marabout. Every influential teacher has his own Koran school.

At the *medersa* they tell us the marabout just left for home. A little later we walk into a big, neatly swept courtyard surrounded by countless doors. Our guide leads us to a section of the yard roofed with reeds, where two men are waiting. Someone brings us water to drink and rolls out a plastic mat. "Go ahead, lie down," Kar says when he sees me hesitating. "They know we've had a long trip." The men look on in silence. It's unusual to see a white person around here, and I'm grateful that Kar never seemed to consider leaving me behind somewhere.

The courtyard is a hive of activity. Women are sweeping the dirt with whisk brooms, and youthful disciples of the marabout are busy building a patio. But the noisiness is missing: no blaring radio, no laughter or shouting. It's as though I've walked into the hermitage at Achel, the Trappist abbey my brother and I used to cycle to in summer when we'd sold another pack of mission cards for Father Angelus. There'd be monks working everywhere, but the only sound would be that of the refectory bells. The monks fed us milk and shortbread cookies, and we could choose something from their shop as a reward for the cards we'd sold: a gilded cross with rhinestones, a children's book or a little porcelain angel. Sometimes Father Angelus would take us to the woods behind the abbey, where a little brook flowed that had the same sour smell as the Dommel in Neerpelt. Resting my head on my backpack, I'm asleep before I know it.

When I wake up, Kar is leaning on one elbow, looking out over the yard. The two men have disappeared. The marabout is helping someone else; Kar hasn't seen him yet, but the man knows he's here.

"You see this yard?" he whispers. "It's the size of Bamako!" He knew this marabout was wealthy, because he comes to the capital for consultations with important businessmen and politicians. It's almost impossible to see him there, that's how busy he is.

"*Salam aleikum!*" A man in a sky-blue *boubou* comes striding towards us. I don't know exactly what I was expecting, but he looks pretty worldly for a marabout. He's about thirty-five, short and stocky, with an open, good-humored face. He shakes my hand – something many pious Muslims refuse to do – and apologizes for his shaky French. We must be very tired after our long trip. Tonight we'll be his guests; he'll have his wife arrange everything for us. He instructs a little boy to bring me a bucket of water, and waves for Kar to follow him.

When I come out of the shower, mattresses with clean sheets are lying on the other side of the yard, and the marabout's wife is busy cooking. She prepares the food in huge pans above different fires, and later she'll send it in smaller pans to all the corners of the yard. Kar's conclave with the marabout doesn't take long. The man has other things to take care of, Kar tells me after he's had his shower, but he's promised Kar he'll go to work for him this evening.

We've come all the way from Bamako, so no one finds it strange when we fall asleep again after the meal and spend the rest of the afternoon lazing in the shade of the mango tree. Meanwhile, the marabout goes to the Koran school and is brought home later by a singing crowd of *talibés*.

Kar starts talking about the festival in Angoulême again. Before I know it, the American impresario is back with us. He tells the whole story all over again, as if I hadn't understood him this morning. In America they were the best of friends, but when he saw him in the cafeteria . . .

"Who knows how many musicians he's seen since then!"

"So you'd do the same thing?"

"No, that's not what I mean, but an American impresario . . ."

"So if I run into you in Amsterdam someday, you'll just greet me and nothing else?! Or maybe you'll say: 'Hello, Kar, how are you doing?', then walk away!"

"No, I wouldn't do that, but . . ."

Kar shakes his head in despair. "How can I believe you, if you say that American was right? Why wouldn't you do the same thing?"

I could kick myself for interrupting him again. Why don't I let him talk, why am I so impatient? This way I'll never find out what's bothering him. But since I've been here, my defiance only seems to have grown. He's paranoid, I think spitefully.

Kar lights a cigarette and looks away from me, towards the tree where the marabout has settled in the shade with his students: he's reading to them from a notebook in his lap while two *talibés* fan him. Sometimes he tells them a story or asks a question, which starts his disciples chattering all at once. I think of good-natured Father Angelus in his white habit who took us to his favorite spot at the waterside. What did he talk about? He always made us forget the stench of the water, which caused us to gag at home.

It's a cheerful lesson, with lots of hearty laughter. I've seen Koran classes that were quite different: some marabouts deal out blows left and right during their lessons. I'm relieved that Kar has come to such a worldly man for advice, and not to a marabout who mumbles through his beard in a room full of cat's claws and other occult objects for making *gris-gris*.

"I'll tell you something else," Kar says, "maybe then you'll understand what I mean." A few years ago, a Malian who'd been in contact with Kar's record company in England announced on the radio that Boubacar Traoré was requested to report for a tour of Canada and the United States. "That man did me a lot of harm."

"What do you mean?"

"No one asked him to do that – I'd already received faxes about the tour. I arranged my own affairs quietly, but he shot off his mouth all over Mali! People thought I was going to earn tons of money, and that made them jealous. You don't know what *griots* here are like. They can't stand it when someone else is successful, and they can ruin everything for you." Traditionally, they're the only musicians in the country – they live from singing the praises of noble families. Singers like Kar who don't belong to the caste of *griots* are feared competitors. "When you meet them they're all sweetness and light, but once your back is turned . . ."

His tour of Canada and the United States was a success, and he came home with stacks of concert reviews and calling cards from agents, radio people and journalists. They were all going to write to him, a new tour was in the making. "And then . . . silence. Total silence. No letters, no faxes, nothing. My own letters never got a reply. It was like someone had seen to it that my name was erased from everyone's memory." He sighs. "I did get one letter: my agent had moved to Brazil, so unfortunately my new tour had been canceled."

How often things must go like that, I reflect; how often plans are made during a successful tour that don't work out. Someone goes bankrupt, someone else decides to put their money into a different project. Kar was almost fifty when he entered that uncharted world: a man with his own views on how things work. I finally understand why he was so shaken by his encounter with the American. It was the first time he'd run into someone from that period, and his worst fears were confirmed: something had happened to make that man barely remember his existence.

"Europeans don't know how Africans work against each other," he says. "But I've had experience. That's why I try to arrange my affairs quietly, that's why I say as little as possible about what I'm doing. The more they know about you, the more harm they can cause. If you only knew what I've been through . . . no man could survive that, but I did. Since then, I can't trust anyone." He tosses me a brief, almost apologetic glance. "Not even you."

"Why don't you tell me about what happened?" I say waveringly. "Maybe it would help me understand."

Kar shakes his head. "I've been trying to tell you since this morning about how Africans work against each other, but you just look at me like I'm stupid. If you can't even understand that, how could you ever get the rest?"

The marabout's lesson is over. Kar sends a boy out to buy two cigarettes. "You have no idea," he says, suddenly calmer. "They can even make the two of us fight. Nothing's easier than that."

When no reply came to his letters, an old friend told him about a marabout from Sansanding who was visiting Bamako. "There are plenty of *wouya-wouya* marabouts in Mali, but this one has a good reputation. He went to work for me, but it was too late; the damage was done. Yet I knew that one day I'd get another chance. This time I've come earlier to ask for protection."

The marabout's wife has prepared a third bed, on which a young man is resting. He teaches at the *medersa*. When Kar and I get up to go for a walk, he offers to come with us.

Kar makes straight for the Niger: when you arrive in a new place, he says, you have to know how the river runs. Sansanding lies slumbering peacefully in the late afternoon sun, but while we're walking down by the river, the teacher informs us that things aren't as peaceful as they might seem. Our host is apparently at the center of a bitter power struggle between several marabouts. For years he received financial support from Kuwait, so he could build a mosque and send students to Kuwait on grants. That made people jealous. Since the Gulf War, his financial backing has dried up. The teacher came with us to make sure we didn't walk through the center of the village; if the villagers see that the marabout has visitors, they're bound to start speculating about a new sponsor.

Kar nods gravely. Now he understands why our guide this morning – one of the marabout's acquaintances – took such a detour. "In a village close to here, things are a lot worse," the teacher says. "There's so much strife, they have eight separate mosques!"

Kar has picked up something from the river bank. He looks at it carefully. It's a dried-out toad. It's as flat as a pancake, but the skin is completely intact and the head and legs are still on it. "See that? It hasn't decomposed at all, no ant has even touched it." He turns the dried carcass around and around. "They're magic animals. Did you know that a snake's poison originally comes from a toad?" He tosses it into the river. "So, another couple of weeks and it'll be swimming again!"

I gasp for breath. "You're kidding!"

"Oh no, I'm not! It's amazing, but true. I told you it was a magic animal, didn't I?"

Biology was never my best subject, but a dead toad coming back to life . . . Kar went to school for five years. Didn't he have biology lessons? Or did his father's lessons make a more lasting impression? We watch the carcass float away. "Why didn't we take it with us?" I ask. "Then we could have seen if it was really true." Kar only laughs – he doesn't need that kind of proof.

Everyone in the marabout's yard is sunk in evening prayer. Since the start of the controversy surrounding his person, the teacher told us, the marabout no longer prays at the mosque. Kar doesn't join the rest, as the marabout belongs to a brotherhood with different customs. Instead, he rolls out his rug under the mango tree. After prayers, the disciples raise their voices in song and go on for almost an hour. We listen to them in silence. Kar looks at me with a little laugh: "See what I mean?"

In the morning, the marabout calls Kar to him. He comes back with a packet of herbs which he stuffs into his RFI backpack. A *talibé* brings him a slip of paper which he copies carefully and puts in his wallet. We're finished. The marabout has reserved seats for us in the *taxi-brousse* to Markala. One of his disciples walks with us to make sure we really leave.

A few days after our visit to Sansanding, as I'm walking up the hill in Lafiabougou, a man in a green *boubou* and white skullcap catches up with me. "*Anitjé!*" He walks along beside me, laughing, a rug tucked under his arm. Obviously, he's just come back from the mosque. It's Kar! "Haven't you ever seen me like this? This is what I wear on Friday!"

He changes at the house. Only when he's put on his checkered cap is he really himself again. I remember the video of his first television performance in 1987, with him wearing a blue knitted Peul cap, a weird thing he'd bought specially for the occasion; apparently, even Pierrette had commented on it. In Paris he bought himself the checkered cap. He wore it when a British photographer took promotional photos for his tour, and since then no one recognizes him without it.

As he's pulling some feed for the sheep down off the roof, I see he's wearing a leather thong around his upper arm – a broader version of the *gris-gris* around his thighs. In the next few days I notice more signs of our visit to the marabout. After prayers he rubs himself with transparent ointment from a big bottle, and the penetrating odor of burning grass occasionally hangs in his room. We don't talk about these things, but he doesn't hide them from me either. Looking for my bag one afternoon, I walk into his room and find him bent over the incense burner, into which he's sprinkled some herbs. I turn to leave, but he gestures for me to stay and points to where I left my bag.

"That stuff stinks," I say when he comes outside.

"You think so?" He goes back inside, takes the atomizer with eau de toilette from next to his bed and sprays himself all over. "That better?"

The ease with which he accommodates all these things amuses me. It isn't completely foreign either, I've seen it before. My grandmother never went to sleep without kissing the relic she kept on her night stand – a thread from the dress of Saint Theresa on a red velvet cushion. She had a glass statuette of the Virgin on her dressing table, filled with holy water from Lourdes. Each morning she'd unscrew the light blue crown from Mary's head, take some water from the bottle and make the sign of the cross with it. Whenever she'd lost something, she'd walk through the house with the little statue of Anthony of Padua – the patron saint of lost things. As soon as she'd found it, I had to cycle to the church to toss a franc into the offertory box.

Something V. S. Naipaul said keeps pounding away in my head: "They're not like us, they believe in magic." I heard those words at the time with a certain skepticism, but now they're almost reassuring.

For Kar, I notice, the bond between us has become closer since our trip to Sansanding. He hadn't expected a European to be able to make a difficult journey like that. To think that I put up with all those trials for his sake! "Now I can't be angry at you anymore," he says. "Because now you not only know my family and my home town, you've even met my marabout!"

Meanwhile, his CD *Les Enfants de Pierrette* has been released in Mali, and the co-producer – the Centre Culturel Français in Bamako – has arranged for Malian television to make a video clip. The producers are hurried, self-important young men, but Kar jokes with them and treats them like little scamps. They've chosen the number he wrote about the time he spent as a farmer, and take him to the plots of land along the Route de Koulikoro, where they stand him in a field with his guitar against a backdrop of reed huts. *That's how people are. When I was rich, I had friends. But when I put my hand to the plow, they left me, one by one.* While his melancholy voice flows over the fields, tears come to my eyes. Snatches of conversation drift through my mind. *What I've been through . . . If anyone had told me then I would ever sing again . . . I thank God for letting me keep my voice . . .* So many things have conspired against his being here at all, but there he stands, as if this is what he's been doing all his life.

He showed me a photo from when he still had a shop in Kayes. A thin, unobtrusive man with a little mustache standing amid jars of lotion, cheap perfume, children's underwear and other dry goods. I never would have recognized him. There's no trace of the glowing self-confidence of his younger years, nor of the charm and brashness that make him stand out in any crowd these days. It's as though, in the middle of his life, he had moved into his own shadow.

What was wrong with him then? And why did Pierrette leave him in Kayes not long afterwards? She didn't like Bandiagara, her brother Mamadou told me once. Her little sister had died there at the age of five. Everyone claimed that the Dogon had devoured her, because she was so pretty. So why did Pierrette go there, especially when she was pregnant? She'd been in Bandiagara for four months when she had Zévilé. It was a bush town, with far fewer facilities than Kayes. Why did she stay there so long? "Other people have wondered the same thing," Kar said when I asked him about it once. But he didn't give me an answer.

While he's out there singing in the field, the drama of his life bears down on me again. Whatever happened, it happened in Kayes – he's let that filter through on a few occasions. That's why his children didn't stay there after Pierrette died; that's why he left Kayes himself, and why Abdoulaye will be coming to Bamako sometime soon.

"Could you sit down over there?" The director has placed a stool in front of a hut, and Kar willingly runs through the whole thing again. Life may have offered him little comfort, but in his music he's completely at home. The guitar has no secrets for him; once he picks it up, he has a new song the same evening. It's a gift from God, he says. First he hears the melody – the words follow of their own accord.

A few days later the clip is on television. When I comment that at least he didn't have to pay for it this time, he says: "I didn't, but you better believe the Centre Culturel Français did. I know these people!"

His songs are often on the radio now, and the commercial Klédou station even plays an hour of his music, non-stop. A lot of the neighbors have bought his new tape, and they turn their ghetto blasters all the way up when he comes riding up the hill. The sound of "Kar Kar, *ça va?*" has become louder and more frequent.

Kar lets it all roll over him. On his last album, he sang: *I've had success, I was known in east and west. But today's children don't know me. When you've got gold, everyone knows you. When you've got nothing, not even your family does.* "You'll see," he says. "In the next few weeks it will suddenly turn out that more and more people know me!"

That weekend he gives a concert in Bamako with other Malian musicians. During the break, I watch from a distance as he stands at the bar. He shakes hands, talks, laughs, has his picture taken with a fan. But as soon as his colleagues start talking together, he looks away over their heads, absent-mindedly. When he sees me, his eyes light up and he waves for me to come over. We lean on the bar together and look at the crowd milling around us. It's one of those moments when I feel that, despite our 'misunderstand- ings', as he calls them, Kar trusts me more than many others. Although he occasionally says our friendship will end in a fight, he says other things as well. His children will never forget me, he said yesterday. Even after he's dead, they'll talk about me.

After the concert he's nowhere to be found. I look around for his scooter at the entrance. Gone. Did he have an appointment, or has he gone home? What would it be like to be alone after all this commotion? I decide to go after him. When the taxi stops in front of his house, I see a candle burning in his room. He's sitting in the yard, in his boxer shorts, listening to the radio. He's glad I came, that I left the reception down there to be with him.

"You should have stuck around for a while," I say. "The minister of culture was there too."

"The minister of culture – what's he mean to me?! I wouldn't care if his head was studded with diamonds! All I have to say to him is that I've been waiting for years to receive a decoration."

It's late by the time he brings me to the bottom of the hill. At night the taxis charge more – I'm braced for the scene Kar's going to make. But the cabby asks for only a thousand francs. Relieved, I climb in. The driver sits smiling shyly the whole way. Then he musters his courage and asks: "So you know our Kar Kar?" He was only a baby when Kar had his first hits. "But when my father saw him on television recently, he amazed us all by getting up and dancing around the living room!"

I'd like to go to Bandiagara. Kar says he would too; it's been years since he visited Pierrette's grave. But there's nothing to indicate that he's really planning to go. He's busy putting the money he's earned from his music this month into his house. Five new rooms are under construction. The workers have laid neat rows of stones in the yard; women come up the hill every evening, balancing big plastic tubs of water Kar uses to sprinkle on the stones.

He's bought another sheep – a ewe, heavily pregnant and in need of protection from the ram that's been alone too long. The charge of dynamite in the well has produced a measly little stream of water. "Don't you worry," Kar says when he sees me looking skeptically into the depths, "it's still full of grit from the explosion – before long, you'll see!" It's the best water in the world, he claims, and there's already life down there: a mouse has fallen in and is paddling desperately back and forth.

Suddenly, one day, he has a housekeeper working for him. The little room where the chickens were kept has been painted: now it's the storeroom where she keeps the pans and the food, and where she sleeps in the afternoon with her little daughter on a cloth spread out on the ground.

Then the vacation starts and Kar's oldest son, Sambou, a school teacher in the west of the country, comes home. He has come by way of Kayes and brought Abdoulaye with him, who reports excitedly on the big storm they had there.

"You'll never guess what happened," Kar says.

"What?"

"The rooms where Pierrette and I lived with the children have caved in." He's heard the news without visible emotion. "Just wait, before long the rest of the house will fall on their heads as well!"

Abdoulaye rides his new bike down the hill to visit his sisters and gets a flat tire right away. In Kayes he was a thoughtful boy who tried to bring some order to Mamou's chaotic courtyard. Every morning he pulled the sheep out into the street by one leg to drive them to his grandfather's land. But now that he senses the regularity which reigns in his father's yard, he suddenly becomes a child again. In the morning he sneaks off before Kar can ask where he's going, and before long his bicycle is rattling in disrepair and his new soccer ball is flat. He's acquired the tough walk of the little ragamuffins of Lafiabougou – bouncy step, shoulders hunched, chin out – quite readily as well. "He and I are going to have a little run-in pretty soon," Kar predicts.

It doesn't take long. When Abdoulaye loses the keys to his room while he's out bicycling, Kar scolds him in front of his new friends and slaps him hard. Crying, he hides his face in his hands and his friends slink off.

"Don't be so hard on him," I protest, "he's such a sweet boy!"

"Such a sweet boy! Losing his keys!" He watches mournfully as one of the workers pounds a huge hole in the wall with hammer and chisel, until the door jumps its bolt.

But the incident is soon forgotten. The next afternoon I see Abdoulaye and his friends along the road, sitting around a big pan full of meat. They laugh when I ask what's in it. "Cat," Abdoulaye says. "Two cats." He points to the rocks up the hill where stray cats always wander, and gives me a heartbreaking rendition of how the animals hissed and meowed when the boys went after them with their sticks. He praises the taste of the thighs, and slaps his own rear end to make his meaning clear.

I go on my way, slightly repulsed. But Kar laughs when I tell him about it. Abdoulaye eats rats, lizards, birds, mice, everything! "They actually did that pretty fast," he says admiringly. "About two hours ago he came to say they'd seen a couple of cats up in the rocks, and now they're already eating them!"

When evening comes we flee the heat of the courtyard and move to the vacant lot across the street. The toads are croaking, which Kar says is a sign of rain. He points to the new streetlights along the asphalt road down below us: a dotted yellow line linking Lafiabougou with the center of Bamako. At least this government does something for its citizens – you couldn't say that about the old regime. "Moussa Traoré was only interested in power. He said: 'Do what you like, as long as you don't elbow in on me.' If someone got rich in his day, you knew he had to be a thief."

Sambou usually goes to drink tea with his friends after he's eaten, but this evening he stays home. We talk about Kassama, his remote teaching post south of Kayes. He lives in a hut with no modern conveniences. Kassama is less than two hundred kilometers from Kayes, but the road is so bad and transportation so rare that it sometimes takes a week to get there during the rainy season.

The whole area around Kassama is in the grip of gold fever. A lot of teachers have quit their jobs, and the fields in the surrounding countryside are deserted as well. Sambou didn't have any trouble acquiring the plot where he grows corn. "My son can survive anywhere," Kar says proudly. "He lived out in the bush when he was little, and I always took him along when I worked on the land."

The elders in Kassama have warned the young people: the earth is full of *djinns* who should not be disturbed. But the gold diggers won't listen, and simply go to other towns to avoid their elders. Sometimes they work for ages without finding a thing; then, to placate the *djinns*, they decide to sacrifice someone. "If you're the one they choose, that's it," Sambou says. "Even if someone warns you and you stay out of the mine for a long time, you can't escape: as soon as you take your chances again, the sandpit you're working in will cave in and you'll be buried alive." So many people have disappeared in the mines through the years. Parents always beg him to keep their children at school, because students are the favorite victims.

"More than other people?"

Sambou laughs. "Ah, yes, the devils like the students too much!"

Gold diggers are the devil's partners, the elders of Kassama say. A miner who wants to become rich and build a home will never find anything. The only ones who stand a chance are those determined to waste their money on women and gambling.

Kar confirms Sambou's stories; he knows them from when he worked as technical agent in the bush south of Kayes. Not only is there gold in those parts, but there are diamonds too. He saw a boy on television not long ago who had been looking for a rock for his slingshot and found a diamond worth millions. There used to be places where the veins of gold lay right along the road, but no one dared to take it because it brought bad luck. But now that freebooters from Burkina Faso, Guinea and other neighboring countries have come to the area and the gold factory is being built at Sadiola, no one listens to the old people's warnings anymore.

"The ones building the factory in Sadiola – are they working with the devil too?" I ask.

"No, they work with machines," Sambou says. "Everyone knows devils are afraid of machines!"

According to Kar, there used to be a lot of *djinns* in the center of Kayes as well. Sometimes you'd hear an invisible horse galloping through the streets at night, a hen with a whole group of chicks would flap past you, or there would be this strange woman standing there, asking you for a cigarette. But the cars, trucks and heavy machinery chased the *djinn*s off into the bush.

It's dark in the courtyard. The only light comes from the glowing embers in the charcoal burner Sambou uses to make tea, and from the flashlight which Kar restlessly switches on and off to find something in his room, or to set something aright in the yard.

I'm surprised that father and son are in such agreement about the *djinn*s around Kayes. Sambou went to art school, so I would have expected more skepticism from him. But the local customs and the stories of Kassama have colored his thinking. There's a protected forest there, he says. Anyone who dares to gather wood in it finds that he can't get the bundle of wood off his head when he gets home. Only when he brings it back to the forest will it come loose.

At first Sambou was rather put off by the people of Kassama. He'd be talking with someone in front of their hut when suddenly they'd walk away, scoop up a fresh cow pat and toss it in a special clay pot. Just like that, with their bare hands! In the beginning he watched in horror, but he's gotten used to it. The people use the manure to patch their huts before the rains come.

The inhabitants of Kassama are Christians, but Christianity hasn't taken a firm hold. "When you're looking for gold, you don't have time to pray." A white missionary who lives in the middle of the village has a picture of Jesus which Sambou can't stop looking at. "If you watch carefully, you see him close his eyes and open them again!" It fascinates him, but at the same time he finds it frightening.

"That's an optical illusion!" I say. I try to explain it, but he doesn't understand. I remember the dried toad Kar picked up and threw into the water. That Kar never studied biology is one thing, but how can Sambou have gone to art school without having heard of optical illusions?

It doesn't have much to do with education, I reflect. I've seen it so often, I should know better. Zaïrian students who'd been to the diamond fields were also full of stories about subterranean spirits who tried to pull you underground. Everything they'd learned at the university seemed to go up in smoke as soon as they were surrounded by the stories of their forefathers. Those tales were much more powerful, and elicited much greater fear.

As a child Sambou often went with his grandfather to his land behind the aerodrome. The tree where you couldn't fall asleep because of the *djinn*, the termites with their magic powers – he grew up with the same stories that Kar did. When he sees something he doesn't understand, he searches for a magical explanation. That makes white people's technology every bit as wondrous as the sorcery of his ancestors. "The only thing left for the whites to invent, after the telephone and the fax, is a machine that lets them summon each other up in the flesh," Kar says. He thinks that will happen before long: in American movies, they've been doing it for years.

Sambou, too, believes in the limitless powers of technology. Every Malian would like to go to the World Cup soccer matches, he says. But a friend of his told him you don't have to go all the way to France because you can see every match live at the Modibo Keita stadium in Bamako.

"By satellite?" I ask.

"No, you sit in the stands and you see them playing on the field, just like you were in France!"

"How do they do that?"

"I'm not exactly sure," Sambou says, "but I think they use laser beams."

Shekna, Sambou's younger brother who's attending the police academy in Bamako, spends the night in Lafiabougou from time to time. Tanti visits more often, and every Sunday Kar's eldest daughter, Mantjini, comes to cook; it's starting to look like a real family up there on the hill. Zévilé, the youngest, is the only one who rarely comes by. She's a different child, Kar says, you can tell she wasn't raised by Pierrette. All his children are discreet and tactful, even Tanti, who was only four when her mother died.

They know how to keep a secret, and never ask him for a thing. But Zévilé is a motormouth, and is always begging for presents.

That Sunday, Kar's brother Baaba comes to visit. He stays all day, seemingly without much to say. Shekna left early for the Modibo Keita stadium, where he's working as security during the Mali–Ghana soccer match. Kar waters his trees, his plants and his stones; Baaba and Sambou talk about the horse races. After we've eaten, Baaba and Sambou listen to the match on the radio while Kar takes a siesta in his room. The heat in the courtyard is paralyzing. I stare at the hill where Abdoulaye grazes the sheep. It must be cool up there under the mango trees. But it's absurd to imagine I could get anyone to go with me.

I feel the Sunday-afternoon lethargy of my childhood chafing at me. Why am I sitting here, what am I doing for God's sake? *You're in too much of a hurry* – how often has Kar accused me of that. Me, the slowpoke! If I do give in to his rhythm, what do I get for it? This? The story he was going to tell me – I know I'll never hear it in this yard. We have to get away from this deceptive calm. We'll have to go to Bandiagara.

By the time Kar wakes up I'm bristling with defiance. "We could at least take a walk," I say. He grins at Baaba: "Did you hear that? Her royal highness wants to take a walk!" But on the way back from taking Baaba to the *douroudourouni*, he passes his house without a word, then looks over his shoulder with a laugh. "You wanted to go up the hill, didn't you?" He knows that Europeans like to take walks, he says – everyone in Paris went out strolling on a Sunday.

A mild wind is blowing up here on the hill. Seated on a rock, we look down on the city. Far below us lies the Niger – a thin, light blue stripe. "It hasn't been raining enough," Kar says with concern. "To think that some years the Niger leaves its banks and floods all the houses in the surroundings!" As soon as it starts raining in Lafiabougou, the streets are deserted; the people have no raincoats, no shoes either. They wait until it stops, then plod around through the mud in plastic slippers.

When I mention Bandiagara, Kar looks at me in annoyance.

"You're always wanting to go somewhere! Can't you ever just stay quietly in one spot?"

"Wouldn't Sambou come with me?"

Kar thinks about it. "He could do, it's actually not such a bad idea. Sambou doesn't have anything to do anyway, and he hasn't been to his mother's grave for years." While he's talking, he keeps a close eye on his house below. The ram has climbed up on a wall and is looking out into the street, where an old lady is being tormented by a group of boys. "*Tsjatso! Tsjatso!*" Piebald – the television sketch may have been banned, but the insult is still alive. When the woman starts after them, the boys shriek and scatter in all directions. As soon as she turns around, however, they begin all over again.

An orange scooter comes cruising up the hill. Past the foundry, it turns left into Kar's yard. A few moments later we see a little figure standing in the doorway, waving to us. "If it isn't my brother-in-law Mamadou." Kar helps me stand up. "Come on. Let's hear what he has to say."

━━━

My suggestion about going to Bandiagara with Sambou turns out to have been a master stroke. "When were you thinking of going?" Kar asks one day. He doesn't mention Sambou – he's obviously thinking about accompanying me himself. The work on his house has stopped for the time being, and now that he's got a housekeeper his children can get along without him for a while.

This time we leave from the big bus station across the Niger. The head of the bus line recognizes Kar and gives us two free tickets to Mopti. When the doors open, our names are called first. "Some people know how to do things," Kar says as we install ourselves in the middle of the bus. "After what I've done for my country, I should really travel for free all the time."

He's brought his water cooler, which had been standing in a corner of his room since we came back from Kayes. The spigot was clogged, but yesterday he took it apart and checked it, rinsed out the cooler, cleaned the filter and washed off the outside, so now it's spick-and-span. He sets it carefully on the floor between his feet.

We're traveling under a lucky star. Did I notice how busy it was at the bus station? That's because it's the seventh day of the lunar month – an ideal time to make a trip. But that doesn't keep us from stalling fifteen kilometers this side of Ségou. Four co-drivers crawl under the bus, to no avail. The driver announces that we'll have to wait until an empty bus from Ségou comes to pick us up.

Everyone climbs out. I take my RFI scarf out of my bag, and Kar makes a bed of leaves on which he stretches out comfortably. "Our ancestors traveled by donkey all the way to Ghana to buy cola nuts," he says. "They never had any trouble. The problems began when we started going by bus and car." Some of the passengers have sought the shade of a tree; others have disappeared into the woods or are taking a stroll. If there were Moors in the bus, Kar says, they'd be making tea.

Just before two o'clock we arrive in Ségou. Kar has his cooler with him and gestures to a woman selling iced water. Before I know it, he's laying down the law again. She's asked for a hundred francs instead of ten – what does she think, that's he's Nigerian or Gabonese?! He makes such a scene that the woman slinks off under the accusing looks of our fellow passengers. "So," Kar says contentedly, "she'll think twice before she tries that again."

A little newsboy has been staring wide-eyed at him the whole time. Shyly, he asks when Kar's new tape will be coming out. Kar laughs and puts his arm around him, and for the next fifteen minutes we have a faithful servant who finds a table for us on the restaurant's patio, brings us iced water and food, and finally carries Kar's cooler to the bus, beaming with pride.

After Ségou we take the road that leads to Bandiagara. He made this same journey six years ago: a thin shopkeeper from Kayes, exhausted by the long train trip, full of dreadful premonitions about the misfortune that lay ahead. He had almost no

257

money in his pocket, because business was going so poorly – a detail I gleaned from Pierrette's brother Mamadou, who raced down to the bus station in Bamako to bring him a little money.

But Kar's thoughts aren't occupied by the past. He's the same cheerful, excited companion he always is when traveling, and he lets everyone in on his whims. We stop at a village where they sell colorful baskets. When the driver buys a wicker airplane dangling from a tree, Kar shouts: "Hey, driver! Why don't we all hop in that plane – we'd get there a lot faster!" He translates what the men in front of us are saying about the cholera epidemic in Mopti, laughs at the fat woman who tells so many tall tales that everyone calls her a *griotte*. He peers at her out of the corner of his eye. "Women like that . . . all you have to do is touch them and they start shrieking. To say nothing of . . ." He wishes he could translate what she's saying, only she's speaking Soninké. Poular, Songhai – a few of the languages spoken in this bus are foreign to him.

At every stop we're overrun by women selling plastic bags of *karité* fruit. Everyone eats themselves silly on this soft, green fruit of the shea butter tree; before long the floor is covered with rinds and a rancid odor fills the bus. When Kar offers me one, I refuse politely. Ever since I ordered a helping of *karité* ice cream, I can summon up the bitter taste of the sticky fruit's flesh at will. But Kar buys a whole load of them and goes through two bags in no time. He says *karité* fruit is good protection against ninety-nine different illnesses.

The ploughed fields along the road are chapped with drought. Kar didn't know things were this bad all over the country. "If you've never seen what drought is, you can't imagine it," he says. He lived in Nioro during the great drought of the early seventies. Moors on camels crossed the border by the hundreds, people walked around with their stomachs swollen from hunger. Trucks arrived from Dakar three times a day with bags of food. 'Red sorghum' they called it. It came from the United States – rumor had it that this was what Americans fed their cattle.

At San, Kar stumbles out of the bus: he has a stomach ache

from all the *karité* fruit, and he's dying of thirst. We drink cola at a little stand at the market. He seems to know his way around town. "That's because I used to live here," he says.

"You lived here too?!"

He points to a tree on the square: that's where they hung the posters to announce his concerts. It was in 1965 – he'd gone out to seek his fortune, just like Baaba. He brought dried fish to what was then Upper Volta and came back with jeans and second-hand clothes. Once, when business was going poorly, he sold his electric guitar – the one his brother Kalilou gave him before leaving for Cuba. He sold it to the young people's association in San, and sent the money home.

As the bus pulls away, Kar looks out the window and says: "There was a woman here who I'll never forget." He and a friend lived on the first floor of a building that looked out onto a big courtyard. One day he was standing on the balcony and saw her down there. She was tall and thin, with the dull, fair tint of the Peul that Malians call 'red'. *Fanta rouge* – she was known throughout San for her beauty. But she rarely left the house; her husband was wildly jealous.

The next time he leaned over his balcony, he had the feeling she'd noticed him. He was no stranger in town; he gave a concert almost every weekend and his songs were on the radio all the time. Not long afterwards, when he saw her at the market, she smiled.

He didn't dare approach her for fear of her husband, but he increasingly went out on the balcony to look at her. All the women in San lay at his feet, but down there was one who was as desirable as she was unreachable. He didn't quite know how it happened, they'd never spoken a word to each other, but after a while he felt that something had started between them. One time, when he was on his balcony again, she stepped into the open-roofed shower with a bucket of water. Women were cooking in the yard, children were playing in the sand. None of them saw what he saw: without taking her eyes off him, she slowly undressed.

The sun is going down over the dry fields and Kar looks silently out the window. "I don't think I've ever desired anyone so badly in my life. She seemed to understand me, she knew exactly what I wanted." While she was standing there, she began caressing herself. It was as if his hands were gliding over her body, and she gave him everything.

She drove him absolutely crazy – he felt like he'd been to bed with her before he'd even shaken her hand. His roommate knew about it, and when they were walking through town one day and almost ran into her at the corner, he slipped away discreetly. Kar shook her hand. He knew her husband didn't let her go outside very often, he said, but did she know the club where he was playing? Above it was a room where he would like to spend a few hours alone with her sometime. The words were out before he knew it – he had to be quick, anyone who saw them standing together on this corner could pass the information along.

There was nothing she'd like more, she said, but there was one problem . . . "My husband has had me fixed," she blurted out.

Kar sighs. "I was crippled with misery. On the way home my friend had to help me along, that's how broken up I was. Her husband had her fixed!" He looks at me. "Do you know what that means?"

"I can imagine," I say cautiously.

"When a woman has been fixed, her lover can become impotent or incurably ill, or she can come down with something herself. In any case . . . a man who hears that is completely demoralized, from one moment to the next."

He's been sitting there, talking, completely lost in his story. "*Fanta rouge* is what they called her," he says dreamily. "Oh, it's great to be young. I learned a lot back then. That's because I was always on the move – not like the young people today who sit in front of the television and don't go anywhere. They think they know everything, but they don't know a thing."

As it grows dark, the bus stops more often to drop off passengers, causing Kar to comment that we're becoming a *douroudourouni*. We don't have to go all the way to Mopti, he

says, we could get out at Sévaré and take a car to Bandiagara.
"Unless of course you want to spend the night in Mopti . . ."

"Oh no," I say. Mopti is one of Mali's tourist attractions –
brightly colored canoes on the Niger, clay mosques, a market
with a vast array of fabrics. It's only twelve kilometers from
Sévaré, and at any other time I wouldn't hesitate for a moment.
But now . . .

We arrive in Sévaré around ten. Half an hour later we're on our
way to Bandiagara in a beat-up Peugeot station wagon rattling
with bottles of soft drinks and beer. The driver will go on tomorrow morning to Sanga, the heart of the Dogon, to bring supplies
to a hotel. Kar says we're going with him. "That's what you
wanted, isn't it?" he laughs when he sees my startled expression.
"You Europeans are always talking about the Dogon. This is my
chance to see them too."

The windows of the Peugeot won't close, and red dust blows
into the car. I wrap the white RFI scarf around my face, so Kar
calls me 'nurse'. As the car races through the night, we fall
asleep. The cooler next to us falls over, but we only notice it when
we wake up to find a young man sticking his head through the
open window.

"Where are you going?"

"To Bandiagara," I say, still drowsy.

He yanks open the door. "*Eh bien, voilà!*" It's past midnight,
but three young men are following us, saying something about
'guide', 'Dogon country', 'Sanga' and 'cheap'. Kar is too tired to
object, he stumbles along like a sleepwalker to the clay house of
Pierrette's brother Barou, where he once found the women crying. He takes our bags from the young men, mumbles a good
night and leads me into the moonlit yard.

We've arrived unannounced, but that's no problem in a remote
place like Bandiagara. After some confused rummaging about,
Barou is wide awake. He fetches a couple of chairs while his wife

Anta arranges mattresses and sheets. The children, who sleep in the courtyard, roll over restlessly and the sheep in the corner start moving as well. It's windy and one of the children coughs deeply. He's lying completely uncovered, I notice, but no one seems concerned.

"They take life as it comes out there in the country," Barou's brother Mamadou said to me before we left. After Zévilé was born, Pierrette was very weak and kept bleeding, but it never occurred to Barou to notify the family; or maybe he just didn't have enough money to call. It was unthinkable in the city, but it happened often enough in the countryside, especially when you had to live off a teacher's salary. Mamadou thought it was high time Barou visited Bamako; he was slowly turning into a bush sheep out there in Bandiagara.

"What do you think of Barou – he looks like a Peul, doesn't he?" Kar asks. "And he's not even wearing his knitted cap. Wait till tomorrow, then you'll see!"

Barou laughs. He's the dependable type, just like Mamadou said. Their father came from Bandiagara. After he died, Barou – as the eldest – felt obliged to move into the family home, even though he knew no more about Bandiagara than his brothers and sisters. He's been here for fifteen years now. On the few occasions he's been to the capital, he's felt miserable. His life is divided between his home, the school and the mosque: he doesn't need anything more. Bandiagara has no electricity – some people own a generator or a television that works on batteries. There's a courtyard near his house where everyone goes to watch television, but he doesn't even know where it is.

Anta has brought a pail of water to the shower and waves to me that I can go in. While I stand pouring cups of water over myself in the soft light of the moon, I suddenly realize that the wall facing the street is so low that I'm standing half-naked in the middle of the village. I think of the young men who walked us to the door, and am thankful that I haven't come here as a tourist, that I belong with the people sitting out there in the courtyard.

Early the next morning, Kar pulls out his wallet and sends Barou to buy Nescafé. He comes back with two little packets. "What are we supposed to do with those!" Kar shouts, forgetting that he presented me with just such a packet when I first visited him. "You should have bought a *can*!"

"A can! But that costs six hundred francs!" Barou sputters.

"Exactly! That's what we need!"

While Barou, in his faded *boubou* and knitted cap, waits for the sorghum porridge with curdled milk his wife is fixing, Kar announces that we're going to the Dogon. Barou looks at us in astonishment. "To Sanga? Today?"

"That's right, we're off for some tourism. And you need to get away too – everyone in Bamako is worried about you. Mamadou says you're turning into a bushman."

Barou shrugs diffidently. "No, that's not my kind of thing, I'll just stay here."

"People come from all over the world to see the Dogon, but you live forty kilometers away and you've never been there!"

"But what would I . . ."

Kar shakes his head and laughs. "He that travels far, knows much. What do you teach the children at that school, anyway? Come on, it's vacation time, we're going out for the day!"

Anta has placed a calabash full of steaming sorghum porridge in front of us and Barou hands me a wooden spoon. *Crème* is what he fondly calls this dish. Thanks to the Peul there's never a shortage of milk around here, he says, patting his round belly. His children are sitting around their mother, eating. He used to have eight of them, but there are only five left. Did I notice the scars on his little daughter's head? She's the one twin Anta saved from a fire in the children's room last year.

"That little one is a sorceress," Kar says. "She ate up her twin sister!" I'm shocked by his remark, but he and Barou laugh. Only Anta looks a bit glum. Later Kar tells me that Anta claims she was at home when the fire broke out. So why didn't she hear the children crying? According to him, that's impossible in a little yard like theirs. Maybe she left incense burning when she went to the market, and came back to find the room in flames. After that, of course, she'd never dare to admit that she left her children alone.

The *wouya-wouya* Peugeot that brought us to town last night stops in front of the house. Barou gets up hesitantly. Kar is older than he is – it would be hard for him to refuse, but he's not particularly enthusiastic. "Take a look at Barou," says Kar after seating himself in the front of the car. He turns laughingly and looks at the skinny, worried little figure on the worn backseat. "Barou, *chef de famille!*"

Clay houses, sand roads down which men are driving cattle and sheep – if I didn't know Bandiagara from Amadou Hampâté Bâ's books as a lively town with a rich past, I'd think we had ended up in some forsaken corner of the world. Kar points to a yellowish building. "That's where the Italian nuns live." They took care of Zévilé when Pierrette was too weak to breast-feed her; they were the ones who gave Pierrette the medicine he found in her room after she died. "Forty packets of milk they gave me when I took Zévilé back to Bamako. Forty packets, imagine that, and all for free!" Mamadou also told me about all the milk from the nuns. If it wasn't for that, Zévilé might not have made it.

No money to make a phone call, buy medicine or milk – until now I hadn't really appreciated just how poor they were back then. Kar gave the left-over medicine back to the nuns. It was worth more than thirty thousand francs.

My empathy for Pierrette is growing. Her death brought so much sorrow, but wasn't it caused by neglect? Kar teases Barou about his foolishness and naiveté, yet he was the one who let his own wife die in Barou's house! But Kar obviously holds no grudge against him, and doesn't seem to hold him responsible for her death in any way.

In Bamako I had met a French doctor who'd studied the incidence of childbirth-related deaths in the Malian interior. Becoming a midwife in a maternity ward was a status symbol here, he said; you didn't have to be competent at all. The women rarely received check-ups during pregnancy, and many of them died of severe bleeding after giving birth, something that could be prevented with a bit of know-how. When I told Kar about it and asked if that was what had happened to Pierrette, he said absently: "No, with Pierrette – that was something different."

And Pierrette herself? Did she feel death approaching? Why didn't she try to get hold of her husband? "Pierrette was very religious," Mamadou said. "When she felt her strength going . . . maybe she thought it was God's will."

But, as is often the case, there are different versions. When I ask Barou in an unguarded moment if Pierrette knew she was going to die, he says: "No. Maybe in the last few days, but before that . . . she was a little weak, but otherwise everything was okay. She was almost past the forty critical days after the birth, when suddenly she got this terrible pain in her stomach. Two days later she was dead." It's like the story of the twins in the burning room: they've adapted it to suit themselves.

Mamadou had been surprised when he suddenly found Pierrette at his door, on her way to Bandiagara with Mantjini, Abdoulaye and Tanti – Sambou and Shekna were already studying in Bamako. "Why are you going to Bandiagara now?" he'd asked. "The school year's just started!" Things weren't going well in Kayes, she told him, they had no money – she hoped that she and the children would be able to relax in Bandiagara. He didn't know she was pregnant again.

Something else was bothering her, but he didn't find out what it was. Pierrette wasn't the kind to burden other people with her problems. At the bus station, she cried. *Take care of my children, Kar will try to go to France*. He'd barely paid any attention to those words at the time, they only came back to him later. "It was as if she knew she was going to meet her fate," he said with the same resignation with which everyone speaks of her death.

"Why did you let her go?" I asked. "Why didn't you try to get her to stay in Bamako?"

"But how was she supposed to get along here? I was still single.

265

I'd just started working, and was living in a room somewhere – I had nothing to offer her." Life in Bamako was expensive, he said. In Bandiagara Pierrette wouldn't have to pay rent, and there was always milk and meat for the children.

We've driven into a rocky area and Barou looks around wide-eyed. The wiry little Dogon women he sees at the market in Bandiagara are walking around here. The tomatoes they sell are the biggest in all of Mali. Do they come all this way with those heavy baskets on their heads, and do they have to walk all the way back in the evening? He can't get over it.

As it turns out, our dilapidated Peugeot belongs to the Hôtel Femme Dogon, one of two hotels in Sanga, and before we know it we've been incorporated in the local tourist industry. We can take the same car back to Bandiagara later on, the driver says. That means we have just enough time for a '*petit tour*' of the Dogon village of Banani.

The bottle of water we buy in the hotel restaurant costs a thousand francs. Barou looks at us in shock. A poster on the wall says *Coca-Cola un jour, Coca-Cola toujours.* Paying for soft drinks is one thing, but for water? Kar laughs and pats him on the shoulder. "That's right, Barou, we're tourists now!" Our guide is costing us four times that much, but we don't tell him that.

We climb along a rocky path that becomes narrower as we go. The sun beats down mercilessly, and soon beads of sweat are standing out on Barou's forehead. "Where are we going, if I'm allowed to ask?" The guide points to some unspecified spot on the horizon. "That far?" His rest stops become more frequent. Dogon with wood and sacks of flour balanced on their heads pass us at a brisk pace. "Did you see that?!"

There are the famous dwellings carved into a steep rock wall by the Tellem in a distant past. They lived from hunting and gathering wild fruit they found in the forest. When the Dogon – who were farmers – began cutting down the forests, they moved away. Now only the *hogon*, the village elder, lives in the rock wall, and the dead are hauled up on ropes made of bark.

We stand looking at the honeycombed rock. "To think that

people crawl in through those openings," Kar says, impressed. "They look barely big enough for a bird!" The guide points to where the *hogon* lives. As soon as he's chosen, the people hoist him up there and he never comes down again. We try to find signs of life, but can't. Everything that happens here is hidden from view, the guide says; the *hogon* lives in complete isolation. Only the village elders visit him sometimes for counsel.

"But what does he eat," Kar asks, "and how does he wash himself?"

"A girl from the village cooks for him," the guide tells us, "and every morning he's licked clean by a snake. The day the snake doesn't show up, he knows he's going to die."

My ears are ringing in disbelief, but Kar and Barou nod sagely. You can expect anything to happen to people who live in bird's nests. "You should write that down," Kar says to me. "Now that's really interesting information."

Below us lies Banani, a pretty village with tiny houses and clay granaries with pointed reed roofs. "Ah no, God did his job!" Kar sighs. "I've heard a lot about the Dogon, but you have to see this to believe it."

Barou has discovered a little tourist market down there, with about fifteen white people standing around. They've been here for the last week, the guide says – they've come to live with the Dogon for a while. "How did they get there?" Barou wants to know. "I don't see any road where a car could . . ."

"On foot, of course," the guide says. "You'll see, we're going down there ourselves." All the way down! Barou looks at us accusingly. If he'd known that . . . "Aren't you tired?" he asks me, sounding hopeful. When I shake my head, he says: "Whites love to suffer."

The village reminds me of the open-air museum where my parents took me as a child, where imitation farmers in blue smocks warmed their hands at the hearths in eighteenth-century farmhouses. Here men are weaving ropes of bark under a lean-to, while a little further along a typical Dogon dish is simmering over a fire. From the *maison des règles*, where women go when they're menstruating, two girls look at us miserably. They spend five days in total isolation, the guide explains. I'm ashamed to stare into their lives like this, but Barou and Kar view the scene with interest.

On the way back to Bandiagara we see two masked men in colorful garb running through the orchards of shea trees. I suspect for a moment that we're being treated to a free encore to our *petit tour*, but the driver assures us they're authentic. The men are charged with protecting the orchards, because at this time of the year people not only steal the fruit, but take wood as well. Kar nods approvingly: they're like forest rangers.

Barou is relieved when we get home, where Anta is sitting in the gallery sorting peanuts with some of her neighbors. He falls asleep on a mattress amid their talking and laughter. Later, when one of his fellow teachers comes by, Barou gives him a detailed description of the wondrous things he's seen. The Dogon have a hard life – that's one thing he's sure of. All that climbing along narrow, rocky paths – it's not his cup of tea. And they have to walk so far to get to their land!

"Hasn't it rained there either?" his colleague asks.

Barou shakes his head. "No, it's dry as a bone."

"You people should lay the old man out in the sun for a while, that would make it rain," the colleague laughs, pointing to one of the rooms at the side of the house. It's the first time I hear that someone else is living here. It turns out he's a distant uncle of Barou's, as old as the hills, whose children lead busy lives in Bamako. They don't visit often, and recently he's started begging Barou to take him to the capital, so he can see his children. "And he can't even go to the toilet by himself!"

Later that afternoon, Barou suddenly appears in the doorway with the old man. "The monster has risen!" he cackles as he pushes him along towards the toilet like a walking doll. I'm stunned by his disrespectful remark, but Kar and Anta roar with laughter.

"You know what he does?" Kar says when he's recovered from the hilarity. "He washes him. There aren't many people who'd do that," he says admiringly. "God will reward him."

When evening comes, Kar still hasn't been to Pierrette's grave. Is he waiting to go alone? Or is one day in the week better than the others, the way the leaves of the medicinal plant in his yard are best plucked on Thursday, and alms given on Friday? I don't ask him about it – I'll find out when the time has come.

A pleasant calm has settled between us in the last few days. The time when every word, every gesture could give rise to a storm of misunderstandings seems past. The Kayes-effect has taken hold: here in Bandiagara we're well-traveled urbanites, and Barou's gullibility, like Maciré's laxity, drives us together. Barou thinks only the best of people, Kar says – even when they kick him in the pants.

"Where did you say they have television around here?" Kar asks after dinner. The music program that often airs his video clip is on this evening. Barou sends one of the boys from the neighborhood along with us.

We end up in a courtyard where about fifty people are sitting in front of a television set. Kar looks at the screen in amazement. "This is what was on a couple of days ago," he says. As we discover, they can't get Malian television in Bandiagara: every morning a videotape of the previous evening's broadcasts is sent from Ségou to Mopti, from where copies are made and distributed in all directions. But Mopti has a peculiar copying policy: if there's a program they don't like, they just replace it with something of their own choosing. That's how, under the waxing moon of Bandiagara, we end up watching a badly damaged episode of the German detective series 'Derrick'.

***

"Take it easy, you don't have to come along," Kar says the next morning when Barou gets ready to accompany us on a walk through Bandiagara. But Barou won't hear of it: today it's his turn to be our guide. He's still a little stiff from our legendary hike through the Dogon, but he applies himself enthusiastically to the task. Every few steps he pulls us into a house or stops to greet someone, because he can't walk through Bandiagara with a clear conscience if he hasn't introduced us to the village chief, the marabout, the school principal, Anta's family and his own. The respectable old men in flowing *boubous* who sit together in their front rooms – their eyeglasses may be stuck together with tape and rubber bands, the mattresses they sit on may be dirty and worn, yet they radiate wisdom and dignity.

Barou introduces Kar everywhere we go as the widower of his sister Pierrette, who died in Bandiagara. Most of them remember the tragedy, and the women in particular react emotionally. They raise their hands to their foreheads, call on God, grab hold of Kar and ask if the baby survived. When Kar tells them that Zévilé is now in the first grade of elementary school, they cry, "*Alhamdu lillah*, God be praised," and ask about his other children.

Kar doesn't like formalities; he scolds Barou the whole way from one house to the next, but he still follows him meekly and accepts the belated condolences, nodding, his head bowed.

Barou's ancestors were followers of El Hadj Omar Tall, the Toucouleur conqueror whose Muslim army swept into the country in the last century from what is now Senegal. After his death, they followed his nephew Tidjani Tall to Bandiagara, where he established the capital of a Toucouleur empire. Barou takes us to the old palace of Aguibou, the son of Tidjani Tall. Only the clay façade of the walled domain is still standing, but there are plans to restore it. Last year the minister of culture laid the cornerstone. "That was the last we heard of it," Barou says regretfully.

"I'm sure it was," Kar says. "They're much better at spending money down in the capital."

Posters have been taped to all the shop doors, warning against cholera and exhorting people to keep their toilets clean. Looking like a fallen angel in his faded *boubou*, Barou flaps by them blithely, on his way to the next attraction.

We stop beside what's usually a river in the rainy season. Women have dug holes in the sand with their bare hands, leaving little puddles of water in which they wash their clothes. People forced to eke water from a dry riverbed – it's a sad sight.

The fancier neighborhood in Bandiagara is called the *quartier millionaire*. "Who lives here?" I ask. *"Oh, les gens des projets,"* Barou says. People who work on development projects – it's a class spoken of with increasing respect in the African interior. "What kind of projects are they?"

Barou laughs. "Just a minute, I'll show you!" Earlier this morning he gave us a tour of his school, a rickety cluster of buildings with iron shutters instead of windows. When it rains, they close the shutters, so the children sit in the dark and lessons come to a stop. Fortunately, when the principal was studying in Switzerland he made friends with a few good-hearted people who send him school supplies and second-hand clothes each year. None of the pupils would have a notebook otherwise, and none of the teachers would have trousers to wear: when the clothes arrive, the teaching staff naturally gets first pick.

Barou takes us to the building that will soon house the Regional Inspectorate of Schools. He walks through the gateway reverently, points to the monumental generator in the courtyard, leads us through echoing corridors while he opens the doors onto one empty room after another.

It's a German project. The director has built a villa for himself in the *quartier millionaire*, but he's never there – he's too busy shuttling back and forth between Mali and Germany.

"Uh oh," Kar says when Barou opens the door to the conference room, where a huge dusty table stands waiting for the gentlemen of the board, "these fellows are going to get away with a lot of money. Won't that make people jealous! It'll take all the marabouts in Bandiagara and surroundings to protect them."

Kar and I snigger as we wander through this factory of good intentions, but nothing can curb Barou's appreciation. Isn't this a beautiful building? All the offices are air conditioned! He wants to fetch a key from the watchman to show us another empty room, but Kar throws an arm around his narrow shoulders and says: "Enough's enough, Barou! We've seen it all!" He winks at me. "Barou! He'd make a detour for some fly speck, to show us a

271

tomato growing somewhere! He thinks we're as impressed as he is, that we've never seen the inside of an airplane!"

On the way back to the house, Kar and Barou talk about a man from Bandiagara who made a fortune in the Ivory Coast. His name was Tembely, and he became so rich and influential that his friends even included President Houphouët Boigny. One day he decided to build a villa in Abidjan that would make everyone sit up and take notice. When it was finished, he threw a big party and invited all his friends. His guests walked through the house as if it was a museum, admiring the marble floors, the crystal chandeliers, the architectural novelties, the paintings on the walls. "Well, what do you think?" Tembely asked at the end of the evening, when just a few close friends – including the president – were still around. They all expressed their approval, except for Houphouët Boigny.

Somewhat intimidated, Tembely finally asked if the president had any comments. "It's a fine house," Houphouët Boigny said. "There's only one thing wrong with it."

"What?!" everyone shouted, amazed and indignant. "What's that?"

The president was silent for a moment, as though deep in thought. "The foundations are no good."

"What do you mean?" the architect protested. "There's nothing wrong with the foundations – the ground is excellent, it was all inspected beforehand."

"That's not what I mean," the president said. He turned calmly to Tembely. "This house is built on the wrong soil. Can you take it with you when you go home? No. You shouldn't have built it here, you should have built it in Mali."

It's Kar who tells the story – precisely as though he'd witnessed the conversation. There's a strange intensity in his voice that catches my attention. "What happened then?"

"That same week, Tembely sent two trucks full of medicine to Bandiagara, and not long afterwards he began building a villa here." When it was finished, people came from all over to see it. "More luxurious houses have been built in Mali since then, but in the seventies it was the most beautiful villa in the whole country. They talked about it even in Kayes!"

After the siesta, Barou takes us there. We peer in at the grounds through the blue iron fencing. It's a fifties-style villa, a villa from a Jacques Tati movie, full of gadgets and frills. There are lampposts around the blue-painted ponds in the garden, and the glass chandeliers hanging in the portico tinkle in the wind. "The whole place used to be lit up at night," Barou says in a whisper. Tembely wasn't here very often, but when he did arrive the people of Bandiagara would wait for him at the entrance to town and bring him in triumphal procession to his home. He threw brilliant parties, blocked off whole streets so the best horsemen in the surroundings could perform the most unbelievable stunts. In the zoo behind his house he kept giant turtles and rare birds from the Ivory Coast.

But now Tembely's money, like that of Kar's brother Baaba, has *spoiled*, and his house is in miserable shape. The chandeliers in the gallery hang crookedly, the ponds are empty and not a single animal has survived. Tembely lives in Bamako nowadays, and hasn't been back here in years. Barou thinks he may even have sold his generator.

"Come on, let's go," says Kar, who's had enough of staring through the fence like a ragamuffin.

"No, no," Barou says hurriedly, "not yet. We haven't seen it from the inside!"

A watchman lives with his wife and children at the rear of the estate, in the former servants' quarters. The contrast with the front of the house is startling. We walk into an African courtyard: amid scratching chickens and rummaging sheep, a woman is cooking over a fire. The watchman takes a key ring from the wall and walks silently out in front of us to the kitchen door. He leads us from room to room, occasionally drawing our attention to a detail we'd otherwise have missed. Tembely has two wives, he tells us as he opens the door to the spacious bedroom. His master slept with one of them in here, while the other spent the night in the adjoining room.

I stand in the bedroom, feeling a bit conspicuous. There are holes in the mattress where the kapok pokes through indecorously. But Barou walks around completely at ease; it's obviously not his first visit to this museum of broken dreams. There used to be a portrait of Tembely hanging in the hall, he says; the watchman must have moved it.

Kar didn't want to come inside at first – he doesn't like sticking his nose into other people's affairs. But he looks around in amazement too. In the darkened parlor where gold leaf is peeling off the gaudy scrollwork of dusty Italian furniture, he shakes his head. "Money is bad," he says. "I saw it with Baaba – it attracts only the wrong things."

"What will happen to this place?" To me it seems unlikely that anyone will ever live here, that Tembely will ever sleep on that ruined mattress again. But Kar says everything is still in perfect shape – it just needs a bit of cleaning and dusting. "The important thing is that Tembely built it. If things go badly for him in Bamako, he knows where he can go. If Baaba had thought of that back in his glory days, he wouldn't be living in rented rooms!"

That night I dream that someone is hitting me in the face with an icy hand. I sit up with a start: it's raining! We all pull our mattresses under the verandah; within a few minutes the yard has become a mire. When I get up later to go to the toilet, I slip and fall in the mud.

"What's going on there?" Kar calls out in alarm.

"Oh nothing," I say, knowing how much he hates it when people are clumsy. I take the plastic pitcher under the tree and rinse the mud off my legs. But Barou saw it all. "She took a dive. And a real doozy at that!"

To my surprise, Kar laughs. "That's nothing," he says, "Pierrette slipped one night – she was completely covered with mud!" Barou lived in Kayes at the time. Pierrette had bruises all over, he remembers, but for days afterwards they couldn't stop laughing when they thought about it.

When I'm back in bed again, the laughter remains in the air for a while. I'm pleasantly surprised at the way they've summoned up Pierrette. It's as if she's with us tonight, as if the way that leads to her has finally been made smooth.

⁊⁊⁊

It's Sunday – the bells of the mission church are ringing. "You hear the white people blowing their horn?" Kar asks. He was up early this morning to pray, but now he washes his hands and face again, takes off his shoes and moistens his feet through his socks. He doesn't say anything, but I suspect these are the preparations for our long-awaited visit to the graveyard.

Barou goes with us. The cemetery isn't far from his house, back behind the new Italian *projet* – a hospital where traditional medicine is practiced. Kar says they have a generator. My thoughts are already focused on our visit to Pierrette's grave, but Kar is still talking about the ice for the water-cooler Barou can fetch from there later on.

It's a cemetery like many in this part of the world. A pile of stones here, a piece of wood sticking in the ground there. Anyone used to churchyards with neatly tended graves, flickering votary candles and black-bordered portraits of the dead would feel out of place here. But Kar and Barou know their way perfectly in this maze, and pull me to one side when I accidentally step on a grave. We pass a concrete headstone, but Kar says that's against Islamic tradition. "When you're dead, it's between you and God."

The spot where Pierrette lies buried is set off by rocks and cactus. Kar removes his shoes, kneels in the sand, bends over and begins to pray. He's reciting verses from the Koran, to bring peace to Pierrette's soul, Barou whispers. As I stand there, a sad melody blows through my mind. *Where is my Kalilou? Where is my Badialo? Where is the woman who bore my children? Pierrette, may the earth be light.* I look past Kar and into the distance, and see the pieces of wood in the cemetery as arms and legs sticking helplessly out of the ground. Pierrette was barely forty when she died – younger than I am now. I feel the defiance coming up again. Couldn't her death have been prevented?

Kar is leaning forward on his knees now, and lays his right hand on Pierrette's grave while he murmurs quietly to himself. Then he gets up, finds a piece of wood and sticks it in the ground, as if to mark his visit.

We follow a different route home. You have to do that on your way back from a cemetery, they say, although neither of them knows why. They learned it from their parents, and they'll pass it along to their children. Kar and I walk along pensively, but Barou is already planning the next side-trip. Didn't he hear me talking about Amadou Hampâté Bâ yesterday? Did I know his widow lived here? Would I like to visit her?

I hesitate, but Kar, who's heard me mention Hampâté Bâ at the most unlikely moments in the last few weeks, says I shouldn't miss the chance. Barou trots along excitedly in front of us. I try to recall Hampâté Bâ's complicated family history. He barely knew his father, because his mother remarried soon after he was born, and he was dragged from one house to the next in his younger days. Most of the last thirty years of his life were spent in the Ivory Coast, where he served as ambassador, UNESCO official and finally as advisor to President Houphouët Boigny. In whose family would his widow have ended up?

We enter a big courtyard where women are pounding sorghum and a young man is sitting cross-legged, reading the Koran. Passing through a whitewashed alleyway we arrive at one of the wings of the house, where a slender Peul woman is sitting on the ground, wrapped in what looks like kilometers of fabric. She must be well over eighty, but she's lost none of her grace. A plastic mat is rolled out for Kar and Barou, and I'm given a stool to sit on. While Barou opens with a series of courtesies in Peul, I sneak a look around. Part of the house has collapsed, as clay walls so readily do. Next to the tea service lies a folded pamphlet from the anti-cholera campaign, obviously serving as a hot-pad. Through the open door I see a bed with a pile of clothes on it. Nothing points to that other, richer life of which Hampâté Bâ was a part.

Mrs Hampâté Bâ stands up: she wants to show us something. She fetches the key to her storeroom and comes back with a biographical folder the Senegalese made about her husband. Is that all there is about him in Bandiagara? She nods. The other books are at her children's house in Bamako, she explains through Barou.

"Something must have happened in that family," Kar says once we're out in the street again. "Otherwise, how can you explain the fact that the children have never fixed the house, and that their mother lives off in one corner of the yard?"

It's one of his hobbyhorses, something we've had heated arguments about before. Children must honor the soil where they were born and care for their parents as long as they live. Why shouldn't they live somewhere else and lead their own lives? I'd objected. "Maybe that's normal in Europe, but not here," he'd contended. "Without his parents' blessings, no African can ever make anything of his life."

When I'd asked him what his elderly mother thought of his departure for France, he blew up. "How can you ask a stupid question like that?! Did you find me here as some poor tenant, with no money for food or cigarettes? You didn't, did you? Without my mother's blessing I would never have earned money in France, I wouldn't have a house of my own!" Had I, even once, bought him a pack of cigarettes? Anyone else would have done that long ago, but those kinds of things never occurred to me. And then I had the gall to insinuate that his mother . . . He ranted on – I was completely baffled. In Bambara, a question like that was unheard of, he said, unless the person you were talking to went around dressed like a tramp. Since then I've stopped trying to defend my empty theories.

"When there's discord in the family, no one has the house repaired and it falls to ruin," Barou says. "There's a Bambara proverb that says family arguments can make even concrete walls collapse."

"She doesn't believe in things like that," Kar says with a smile in my direction. "Shall we show her the house of the former cabinet minister and his brother? Maybe then she'll understand."

They take me to what looks like a vacant lot. Kar points to a little ridge of clay: the remains of what was once a wall. The cabinet minister was a writer and a politician, his brother a religious leader. They fought so bitterly that the family split in two and each went its own way.

I think of the house in Kayes where Kar was born. I see Maciré sitting under the dripping verandah amid plastic tubs, the trails of mud running down the walls. The roof over the sheepfold that crashed to the ground one night, the toilet door that was always falling off its hinges, Kar's grimace when Abdoulaye told him that the rooms where he'd lived with Pierrette had collapsed . . . *Just wait, before long the rest of the house will fall on their heads as well!*

Kar sends Barou out to buy ice from the Italian nuns, then says to me: "Are you thirsty? Shall we go get some ginger juice?" The shop we enter is cool. People are crowded around a high wooden table where a butcher is cutting pieces of meat. In the semi-darkness behind him is a refrigerator with soft drinks. We plop down on a little bench and order ginger juice.

Kar sits with his back against the wall. "Now that I've told you how other people's houses have collapsed, it's time to tell you about my own," he says. "Because anyone who goes to Kayes looking for Kar Kar's birthplace and sees the condition it's in today knows right away that something happened there."

He leans forward, the way he often does when telling a story. "It all started when Maciré fell in love with Mamou." They met at the cement factory in Diamou where he worked at the time; Mamou sometimes went there to visit a girlfriend. Kar's father was worried when he heard that Maciré planned to marry her. Mamou was a Khassonké, a people with different customs from the Bambara. When Maciré insisted, their father said he'd have to wait for approval from Baaba, who was living in the Ivory Coast. Before long, Baaba sent them money for the wedding.

"Mamou brought bad luck right away: my father died shortly after that," Kar says bitterly. When he sees me frowning, he adds: "Of course Allah took my father, but there are always other factors involved."

Pierrette had lived with Kar's family for years since they were married and was loved not only by his parents, but by the whole neighborhood. She never cared whether someone was rich or poor; she treated everyone just as warmly. As the first and only daughter-in-law living in Kayes, she was more or less the mistress of the house.

Mamou came from a troubled home. Her father had four wives who didn't get along at all, and there was a great deal of divisiveness and jealousy in the yard where she grew up.

But everything went well at first. Mamou was friendly and hard-working, and everyone was sorry Kar's father was no longer around to revise his first impressions. But when Maciré left for Abidjan to work in one of Baaba's shops, Kar took Mamou there by bus, while Pierrette and the children went to Bandiagara. Kar remained in Abidjan for three months, and he saw things starting to go wrong with Mamou. Baaba was fairly wealthy at the time, and Mamou got the idea that his money belonged to Maciré and to her as well. It was something her family in Kayes must have suggested before she left, because she was so adamant about it that she got into terrible rows with Baaba's wife. At first Baaba thought his wife was causing the arguments – he even beat her for it – until the upstairs neighbors, who were home all day and heard everything, told him how things really stood.

Discord between the wives of two brothers is more dangerous than that between two wives of the same man, a Bambara proverb says. I've met both wives, and can vividly imagine those two matrons fighting like cats.

Kar went back to Kayes, and it was years before Maciré and Mamou followed. Meanwhile, they made life miserable for everyone in Abidjan, but they acted as though they were the ones who'd been wronged by Baaba and his wife. Maciré was the youngest son; his mother believed him without question, so she had a letter sent to Baaba in which she cursed him. Only years later, when her son Kalilou died and Baaba came to visit her in Kayes, did she forgive him. "But Baaba's money had already *spoiled* by then."

His mother had by now begun to quarrel with Mamou, quarrels that flared up so badly that she made Maciré choose between his mother and his wife. Old friends of the family tried unsuccessfully to mediate between them, and Maciré sent Mamou back to her parents' home. But he kept seeing her, and when Mamou became pregnant again he begged his mother to let her come back. "My mother said they should rent a room somewhere, but I was in favor of taking her back," Kar says. "I didn't want any fighting in the family; when my father was still alive, we were always an example to the neighborhood." In the end his mother let herself be talked into allowing Mamou to return.

"That was when the trouble began between Mamou and Pierrette," Kar sighs. The reasons were often piddling: Pierrette had opened the faucet when Mamou walked by, so she got wet; Sambou had fought with Mamou's children.

It all happened during the day, when Kar and Maciré were at work, and after a while Kar noticed that his mother – who had always been very fond of Pierrette – was taking sides with Mamou. If Mamou deliberately knocked over one of Pierrette's gourds full of rice and Pierrette said something about it, his mother would claim she hadn't seen a thing. If Mamou's children provoked Sambou, he was the one his grandmother would punish.

I try to picture those three women in the courtyard. The beautiful Pierrette, who attended a special school in Bamako for girls of mixed heritage, whose hand was competed for by a number of wealthy men, but who finally followed her heart and chose unconditionally for the stubborn, artistic Kar. Pierrette, who had a cupboard with screen doors in which she kept her crockery and who, contrary to expectations, was hard-working and down to earth. Pierrette, whose children had light skin that made everyone envious.

Mamou must have been overshadowed by her from the start. Not only did she come from a family where everyone tried to edge out everyone else – leaving her better trained for war than for peace – she was also married to the spineless Maciré, the mummy's boy who could barely stand on his own two feet and who, after his aborted stint in the Ivory Coast, found a job in a bank through a friend of the family.

And then there was Kar's mother, the tall, dignified woman I'd seen pictures of. "If my father had still been alive," Kar says, "everything would have been different. My mother had watched Pierrette's children grow up, they'd fallen asleep against her breast, but suddenly it was like she no longer knew them. When Sambou or Shekna would come to say hello, she'd ignore them. One morning, when I went into her room to give her a hug before I went to work – the way I had for years – she asked me what I thought I was doing and threw a shoe at me!" He gives me a look of distress. "Then I knew things were really bad. At first I could hardly believe it, but more and more things indicated that my mother had been *fixed*."

It's out in the open. I'd always suspected the story would take such a turn, but I'm still shaken. In Bamako, Pierrette's brother Mamadou once mentioned in passing that Kar's mother had become a bit 'senile' towards the end, but those aren't the terms in which Kar thinks.

"That something like that had to happen to our family!" Kar hides his face in his hands. One day he suddenly remembered his childhood visit to the marabout and the man's prediction: *There will be fighting in your family someday*. His mother hadn't believed him because she was her husband's only wife, but it turned out the danger came from other quarters.

"But who fixed her?" I ask quietly. "And how?"

"You people don't know about these things," he says sadly, "but I promised to tell you about the wickedness of Africans, so I'll try to explain."

Mamou went to a marabout. He saw to it that she slowly gained control over her mother-in-law. "A marabout who makes things go well is hard to find, but the ones who do evil are there for the taking!"

As in all families with more than one woman, Pierrette and Mamou took turns going to the market and cooking for the whole family. But one day Mamou said that everyone should cook for themselves. "Breaking up the kitchen is the worst thing a family can do. I got down on my knees and begged my mother not to let it happen. But she'd already started refusing food that Pierrette made."

A council of ten wise men were brought in to try to make Mamou change her mind. They gave Maciré money, which he gave to Mamou to do the shopping for the whole family the next morning. She threw it on the ground in a rage. When Baaba came to Kayes to mediate, things went well for a week. But afterwards it started all over again. Baaba has never been back to Kayes since.

"From then on, Pierrette cooked outside. She was no longer allowed in the kitchen, the one I'd built with my own hands!"

"And Maciré just stood back and watched?"

"Maciré!" Kar hisses condescendingly. "He'd never had a say, and then even less."

Fanta, an old confidante of Kar's mother who loved Pierrette very much, saw it all happening and decided to go to a marabout herself. He said things had already gone too far, that something was buried in the house that had to be dug up before he could do anything. "Burying something is the worst thing you can do," Kar says. "Anyone who does that . . . *gris-gris* buried in a house will make your best friends turn against you as soon as they walk into the yard." It must have been done a long time ago, because at first his mother was only angry at Sambou and Shekna when they were in the house; as soon as they went to work on his father's land, she was back to normal.

The marabout said he could find what was buried – if the family agreed – with mirrors. But when Fanta brought him to the house, Kar's mother threw herself on the ground and shouted that no one was going to dig up anything as long as she was there. "Fanta had been my mother's friend for more than fifty years. She did everything she could to change her mind. But nothing worked, and she never set foot in our house again." Kar looks at me. "You met her, remember? She lives on the corner." A skinny old woman, dignified as his mother had been. She held onto Kar when she talked to him, and used a corner of her *pagne* to dry the tears in her eyes. "Oh, Fanta," Kar says, "since Pierrette died, she cries whenever she sees me."

The atmosphere in the house finally became so tense that people no longer came by. They had all stopped talking to one another, and Sambou and Shekna had to play out in the street because Mamou's children always picked on them. Kar couldn't say anything; if he opened his mouth, things would only get worse. He began leaving the house more frequently in the evening to go to a movie or visit friends.

And then things started going badly with his shop. According to Kar, Mamou had a hand in that as well. Sometimes she would get up early, at the same time he did, and build a fire. That must have been what the marabout told her to do, because on those days not a single customer came into his shop. "Not one! That had never happened before."

I think about the way Kar interpreted the indifference of the American impresario in Angoulême, and how he sometimes misinterprets the things I do. Didn't he make similar mistakes in Mamou's case? Someone else is always responsible for his misfortune: Mamou saw to it that his shop went downhill, the Malian *griots* saw to it that his foreign tour fell through. He blames his suspicious nature on what he's been through, but wasn't that suspicion there to start with? The word 'paranoia' flashes through my mind again, but, like 'senility', it's not a term that fits in Kar's world.

"Why did you all stay there? Why didn't you leave?" But even as I ask it, I realize how senseless the question is. Where were they supposed to go? Would they have had enough money to rent another house?

"Leave? No . . . When my father became ill in 1975, I quit my job to be with my parents. I couldn't leave my mother in the lurch after he died, could I?" He kept working on the land and brought home sacks full of peanuts and sorghum each year. When he tried to give his mother her portion, she sent him away, so he'd leave the sacks next to the door of her room. Sometimes he'd sneak up behind her and throw his arms around her. Or he'd buy snuff and leave it lying on her bed. He couldn't be angry with her. He knew she couldn't do anything about it – she'd been fixed.

"And what about Pierrette? Didn't she want to leave?"

"Pierrette?" Kar hesitates. "Yes, she wanted to leave. I don't know how often she asked if we could move . . . it must have been a hundred times! But I couldn't. Renting rooms in the same town as my father's house, the one I'd built with my own hands! Pierrette realized that I couldn't leave my mother, that I'd be cursed. We kept thinking things would get better, that it wouldn't last much longer. No woman but Pierrette would ever have put up with it, any other woman would have asked for a divorce . . ." Softly, he adds: "That's why I can't forget her, because she suffered so much for my sake."

In 1986 he took the deed to the house out of his father's suitcase for safekeeping. If he'd wanted to, he could have sold the house just like that. Amid all the powerlessness and sorrow, that gave him a secret feeling of superiority.

It's hard for me to imagine that the man I've come to know in the last months as a tough fighter could let himself be cowed by a woman like Mamou and her malicious marabout. If I hadn't seen the picture of a skinny Kar in his shop, I probably wouldn't believe it at all. *Like a piece of fruit hollowed out until only the rind is left.* "If anyone had told me I would be going to Europe one day, I would have laughed in his face," he says. "I was tired of living, I was completely downhearted."

But there were more blows in store. In 1987 they lost two children within a week. "Pierrette was totally discouraged . . ."

"Are you trying to say that Mamou . . ."

"No, I'm not saying it was her fault, but when the first child died, she laughed and said another one would die before the end of the week."

A photograph from that time shows Pierrette sitting in the yard, a cloth wrapped around her head, a withdrawn, wavering look in her eyes. Her weak smile is obviously intended only for the camera. She's put on weight and looks exhausted. So many births and dead children later. Is that why she went to Bandiagara when she became pregnant again, to protect her new baby? Is that why she took all her children along?

I'm crying, and I see that Kar notes the fact with a certain satisfaction. I'm not crying so much for what Mamou did to them, but because they believed in it and became caught in it. I'm crying because of the domestic peace Kar tried so desperately to keep, and to which he sacrificed the woman he loved.

At the end of that year he was in Bamako, and Malian television invited him to the studio for the first time. He had to borrow a guitar; his own instrument was in Kayes, leaning in a corner, without strings. One of the songs he sang was *Pierrette*, in which he professed his love for her in front of the whole country. *Pierrette Françoise, you loved me. Family and neighbors said bad things about me, but you loved me. My dearest, I'm thinking of you.* The sensitive melody was a success, as were the lyrics: it was unusual in Mali for a man to sing his love for a woman he'd been living with for twenty years.

But those little moments of glory were reduced to nothing by the drama in Kayes, which was slowly coming to a head.

"One day my mother and Mamou told Pierrette that, if I died, she and her children would be out in the street." Kar shakes his head in despair. "*If I died!*"

Not long afterwards, Pierrette decided to go to Bandiagara. Maybe if she went away Kar's mother would see that she was innocent and start missing her, she thought.

"And what about you, what did you do when she was gone?"

"Nothing. I waited. I only came home to go to bed. Accepting Mamou's food, no . . . I ate with friends."

Five months later his friend Sidi sent a boy to get him. There was a call from Bandiagara. Kar closed his shop and went out to his field. It was harvest time, and his sorghum and peanuts were ready to be brought in. He had to get the crops to safety before he left.

"Couldn't you have waited until you came back?" I ask in surprise.

"You still don't get it," he says bitterly. "They ruined everything I did. They were capable of saying they had done all the work, or of letting everything be eaten by the cattle of some passing Peul!"

He brought part of the harvest to his mother. As usual, she scolded him and said she didn't want anything of his, after which he left the sacks next to her door. The rest he left with Fanta. Then he stood wavering in his room. Pierrette's crockery – he had to take that to Fanta's house as well.

"Couldn't you have locked your room?"

Kar laughs scornfully. "As if they couldn't have broken the lock! They would have taken everything away and said it was thieves who'd done it."

The train to Bamako didn't leave till the next morning, but he didn't want to spend another moment in Kayes. He took the first train that came along. That night he slept on a bench in the station at Mahina, barely a hundred kilometers from Kayes.

In Bamako he called Mamadou, who until then had heard nothing of all this. When Mamadou arrived at the bus station he was covered with dust and badly shaken. On the way down he'd run into an old man and fallen flat on the ground – he had the feeling that Pierrette was in a bad way.

Kar stops talking. "You know the rest," he says when I look at him questioningly.

He stayed in Bandiagara for five days. While he was there, the news of Pierrette's death was broadcast on the radio. People were shocked – hadn't he just sung of his love for her on television? One of Pierrette's brothers-in-law, the chairman of the Malian parliament, sent a jeep to pick him up. Kar traveled to Bamako with a six-week-old baby in his arms, and forty cartons of milk in the back.

A few days later he went to Kayes to receive the condolences of his friends and neighbors.

"And what did Mamou say then?"

Kar laughs harshly. "Mamou, Maciré, my mother – they all laughed! Their problem was solved: this was what they'd been waiting for the whole time!"

I stare at him in disbelief. "No," he says, "you still don't understand. The neighbors came pouring in, weeping. Everyone knew how much I'd loved Pierrette and what she'd been through for my sake, and my own family laughed! I began selling all the things in my shop. I knew I didn't have a home anymore, that I'd have to go looking for a place to live . . . When your own brother does something like that to you, what is there left to believe in?"

We've been sitting here for a good two hours while customers walk in and out, the butcher cuts up meat and the big refrigerator opens and closes. But the people float by as if they inhabit a different, more innocent world.

For the first few months in Bamako, he didn't know which way to turn. Only when Mai Sangaré began talking about France did hope return. He wasn't thinking about music – he wanted to earn money so he could build a house where he and his children could live.

In Paris he gradually came to his senses; he forgot that marabouts and fetishists even existed. He'd just received the contract for his British tour when he heard that his mother had died, but he never considered canceling it. He felt he had her blessing: her death had opened a door.

When the tour was over he flew back to Mali, and took the train to Kayes. "That you could still go there after all they'd done to you," I say. "That you could take me with you!"

"Oh, but that's all over. Now their time has come. Maybe you didn't notice, but Mamou and Maciré didn't say a word to each other the whole time we were in Kayes. Mamou complains that Maciré is lazy, and Maciré keeps saying he wants to send Mamou back to her parents. Last I heard, Maciré was about to lose his job at the bank.

"The marabout Pierrette entrusted Abdoulaye to once said to me: 'There will come a day when you'll have to give Maciré

287

money to buy food.' I didn't believe it, but he laughed and said: 'Wait and see: people are in a hurry, but God takes his time.'

"You'd better believe they're sorry for what they did, but now it's too late. God will punish them for it, and if he doesn't punish them, he'll punish their children. Have you seen Mamou's children? You can't take them anywhere, they fight wherever they go."

Mamou chasing her oldest daughter around with a piece of wood, unhappy little Bintou, first in a party dress, then squatting naked and crying against a tree . . . "But the children can't help it," I object. "They're not responsible for what their parents did, are they?"

"After everything that's happened, that's not my problem anymore. They'll have to figure out how to help themselves. Their game is up! After seven years, the thing they buried has lost its power. It's decayed, like a dead person in the ground. I still have the deed to the house. If I want to, I can sell it tomorrow and they'll be tenants from one day to the next."

He suddenly seems hard. But still, when we were in Kayes he bought sacks of rice and sorghum for Maciré, and he gave Mamou money every day to got to the market. "Maciré and I are brothers," he says, "we drank at the same breast. No one can ever change that. But, like the Bambara proverb says: *The war between two people may come to an end, but the words that have been spoken will not be forgotten.*"

At first he'd hoped to build a new house in Kayes, but later he realized it would be better for his children to stay in Bamako. "Someday the music will end – then I'll go back to Kayes. I've already got my eye on a plot of ground."

He stands up, and a moment later we're outside in the bright afternoon sunlight of Bandiagara. We walk along for a while in silence. "Maybe now you understand why I'm so short-tempered sometimes," Kar says. "For years I had to bottle it all up inside." He sighs. "Pierrette suffered. Her heart was full of sorrow and bitterness. She was dead before she even left for Bandiagara . . ."

After the semi-darkness of the shop, the sun hurts my eyes. I walk along beside him in a daze. I'm relieved that he's finally given me the key to decipher his life, but the wistfulness I was expecting is there as well. Kar seems to feel it too. He speaks in broken sentences, coloring in his story with detail, shifting the emphasis here and there, the way he sometimes does when he's become so caught up in what he's telling that he doesn't want it to come to an end.

"Now I've told you my story," he says when we arrive at Barou's house. He looks at me and laughs mysteriously. "At least . . . part of the story!"

GLOSSARY

beignet: sweet fritter, similar to a donut

boubou: long robe; traditional dress

brousse: bush, wilderness

djinn: spirit

douroudourouni: (literally, little five-five) van with benches in the back; a popular means of transportation in Mali, named after the original price of a ticket, twenty-five francs

Fouta Toro: area along the Senegal River, named after an old Peul kingdom

foyer: short for *foyer d'immigrés,* a boarding-house for immigrants

grin: friends' club

griot, griotte: troubadour belonging to the caste that traditionally sings the history and heroic deeds of noble families

gris-gris: amulet

hawli: long, thin shawl (Mauritania)

korté: poison a fetishist sends to his victim; e.g., in the form of a serpent

marabout: Muslim holy man

medersa: Koran school

melahfa: colorful, transparent veil worn by Moorish women

métisse: female offspring of French and Moorish parents

muezzin: Muslim crier who gives the call to prayer

pagne: strip of colored cloth; traditional dress

talibé: student at a Koran school

taxi-brousse: taxi with approximately eight seats; common means of transport in the African interior

wadi: dry riverbed

wouya-wouya: worthless (Bambara)

LONELY PLANET JOURNEYS

JOURNEYS is a unique collection of travel writing – published by the company that understands travel better than anyone else.

It is a series for anyone who has ever experienced – or dreamed of – the magical moment when they encountered a strange culture or saw a place for the first time. They are tales to read while you're planning a trip, while you're on the road or while you're in an armchair, in front of a fire.

These outstanding titles explore our planet through the eyes of a diverse group of international writers. JOURNEYS books catch the spirit of a place, illuminate a culture, recount an adventure, or introduce a fascinating way of life. They always entertain, and always enrich the experience of travel.

'Lively, intelligent and varied . . . an important contribution to travel literature' – *Age (Melbourne)*

BRIEF ENCOUNTERS
Stories of Love, Sex & Travel
edited by Michelle de Kretser

Love affairs on the road, passionate holiday flings, disastrous pick-ups, erotic encounters . . . In this seductive collection of stories, 22 authors from around the world write about travel romances. A tourist in Peru falls for her handsome guide; a writer explores the ambiguities of his relationship with a Japanese woman; a beautiful young man on a train proposes marriage . . . Combining fiction and reportage, *Brief Encounters* is must-have reading – for everyone who has dreamt of escape with that perfect stranger.

Includes stories by Pico Iyer, Mary Morris, Emily Perkins, Mona Simpson, Lisa St Aubin de Terán, Paul Theroux and Sara Wheeler.

THE GATES OF DAMASCUS
Lieve Joris (translated by Sam Garrett)

This best-selling book is a beautifully drawn portrait of day-to-day life in modern Syria. Through her intimate contact with local people, Lieve Joris draws us into the fascinating world that lies behind the gates of Damascus. Hala's husband is a political prisoner, jailed for his opposition to the Assad regime; through the author's friendship with Hala we see how Syrian politics impacts on the lives of ordinary people.

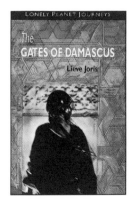

'she has expanded the boundaries of travel writing'
— *Times Literary Supplement*

GREEN DREAMS
Travels in Central America
Stephen Benz

On the Amazon, in Costa Rica, Honduras and on the Mayan trail from Guatemala to Mexico, Stephen Benz describes his encounters with water, mud, insects and other wildlife – and not least with the ecotourists themselves. With witty insights into the phenomenon of modern tourism, *Green Dreams* discusses the paradox at the heart of cultural and 'green' tourism.

Provocative and absorbing reading.

SONGS TO AN AFRICAN SUNSET
A Zimbabwean Story
Sekai Nzenza-Shand

Songs to an African Sunset braids vividly personal stories into an intimate picture of contemporary Zimbabwe. Returning to her family's village after many years in the West, Sekai Nzenza-Shand discovers a world where ancestor worship, polygamy and witchcraft still govern the rhythms of daily life – and where drought, deforestation and AIDS have wrought devastating changes. With insight and affection, she explores a culture torn between respect for the old ways and the irresistible pull of the new.

THE RAINBIRD
A Central African Journey
Jan Brokken
(translated by Sam Garrett)

The Rainbird is a classic travel story. Following in the footsteps of famous Europeans such as Albert Schweitzer and H.M. Stanley, Jan Brokken journeyed to Gabon in central Africa. A kaleidoscope of adventures and anecdotes, The Rainbird brilliantly chronicles the encounter between Africa and Europe as it was acted out on a side-street of history. It is also the compelling, immensely readable account of the author's own travels in one of the most remote and mysterious regions of Africa.

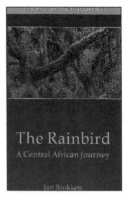

PLANET TALK
Lonely Planet's FREE quarterly newsletter

Every issue of PLANET TALK is packed
with up-to-date travel news and advice
including:

- a letter from Lonely Planet founders
  Tony and Maureen Wheeler

- travel diary from a Lonely Planet
  author

- find out what it's really like out on the
  road

- feature article on an important and
  topical travel issue

- a selection of recent letters from our
  readers

- the latest travel news from all over the
  world

- details on Lonely Planet's new and forthcoming releases

To join our mailing list contact any Lonely Planet office.

LONELY PLANET OFFICES

Australia: PO Box 617, Hawthorn 3122, Victoria
tel: (03) 9819 1877 fax: (03) 9819 6459
e-mail: talk2us@lonelyplanet.com.au

USA: 150 Linden St, Oakland, CA 94607
tel: (510) 893 8555 TOLL FREE: 800 275-8555
fax: (510) 893 8572
e-mail: info@lonelyplanet.com

UK: 10a Spring Place, London NW5 3BH
tel: (0171) 428 4800 fax: (0171) 428 4828
e-mail: go@lonelyplanet.co.uk

France: 71 bis rue du Cardinal Lemoine, 75005 Paris
tel: (01) 44 32 06 20 fax: (01) 46 34 72 55
e-mail: bip@lonelyplanet.fr

www.lonelyplanet.com

THE LONELY PLANET STORY

Lonely Planet published its first book in 1973 in response to the numerous 'How did you do it?' questions Maureen and Tony Wheeler were asked after driving, busing, hitching, sailing and railing their way from England to Australia.

Written at a kitchen table and hand collated, trimmed and stapled, *Across Asia on the Cheap* became an instant local bestseller, inspiring thoughts of another book.

Eighteen months in South-East Asia resulted in their second guide, *South-East Asia on a shoestring*, which they put together in a backstreet Chinese hotel in Singapore in 1975. The 'yellow bible', as it quickly became known to backpackers around the world, soon became *the* guide to the region. It has sold well over half a million copies and is now in its 9th edition, still retaining its familiar yellow cover.

Today there are over 240 titles, including travel guides, walking guides, language kits & phrasebooks, travel atlases and travel literature. The company is the largest independent travel publisher in the world. Although Lonely Planet initially specialised in guides to Asia, today there are few corners of the globe that have not been covered.

The emphasis continues to be on travel for independent travellers. Tony and Maureen still travel for several months of each year and play an active part in the writing, updating and quality control of Lonely Planet's guides.

They have been joined by over 70 authors and 170 staff at our offices in Melbourne (Australia), Oakland (USA), London (UK) and Paris (France). Travellers themselves also make a valuable contribution to the guides through the feedback we receive in thousands of letters each year and on our web site.

The people at Lonely Planet strongly believe that travellers can make a positive contribution to the countries they visit, both through their appreciation of the countries' culture, wildlife and natural features, and through the money they spend. In addition, the company makes a direct contribution to the countries and regions it covers. Since 1986 a percentage of the income from each book has been donated to ventures such as famine relief in Africa; aid projects in India; agricultural projects in Central America; Greenpeace's efforts to halt French nuclear testing in the Pacific; and Amnesty International.

'I hope we send people out with the right attitude about travel. You realise when you travel that there are so many different perspectives about the world, so we hope these books will make people more interested in what they see.'

– Tony Wheeler